# 920 O'FARRELL street

## A JEWISH GIRLHOOD
### — *in* —
## OLD SAN FRANCISCO

*introduction by*
## CHARLENE AKERS

*Heyday Books*
*Berkeley, California*

Original edition copyright © 1937, 1947 by Harriet Lane Levy
Introduction © 1996 by Heyday Books

Interior Design and Production: Wendy Low
Cover Design: Jack Miles, DesignSite, Berkeley
Printing and Binding: McNaughton & Gunn, Saline, MI

Special thanks to Leona Shapiro for her generous contribution toward republishing this book.

Special thanks to Gray Brechin for having brought this work to our attention; to Kim Bancroft for editing assistance; to Albert S. Bennett for his generous loan of family photographs; and to Gladys and Ben Elkus and Helen and Richard Bibbero for sharing memories of the Levy family.

Please address orders, inquiries, and correspondence to
    Heyday Books
    Box 9145
    Berkeley, CA  94709
    (510) 549-3564
    www.heydaybooks.com

ISBN 0-930588-91-6
Printed in the United States of America

10  9  8  7  6  5  4  3  2

Front and back cover photos of Harriet Lane Levy and friends ca. late 1880s courtesy of The Bancroft Library.

# 920 O'FARRELL
## street

*A California Legacy Book*

Santa Clara University and Heyday Books are pleased to publish the California Legacy series, vibrant and relevant writings drawn from California's past and present.

Santa Clara University—founded in 1851 on the site of the eighth of California's original 21 missions—is the oldest institution of higher learning in the state. A Jesuit institution, it is particularly aware of its contribution to California's cultural heritage and its responsibility to preserve and celebrate that heritage.

Heyday Books, founded in 1974, specializes in critically acclaimed books on California literature, history, natural history, and ethnic studies.

Books in the California Legacy series appear as anthologies, single author collections, reprints of important books, and original works. Taken together, these volumes bring readers a new perspective on California's cultural life, a perspective that honors diversity and finds great pleasure in the eloquence of human expression.

*Series editor:* Terry Beers
*Publisher:* Malcolm Margolin
*Advisory committee:* Stephen Becker, William Deverell, Charles Faulhaber, David Fine, Steven Gilbar, Dana Gioia, Ron Hansen, Gerald Haslam, Robert Hass, Jack Hicks, Timothy Hodson, James Houston, Jeanne Wakatsuki Houston, Maxine Hong Kingston, Frank LaPena, Ursula K. Le Guin, Jeff Lustig, Tillie Olsen, Ishmael Reed, Alan Rosenus, Robert Senkewicz, Gary Snyder, Kevin Starr, Richard Walker, Alice Waters, Jennifer Watts, Al Young.

Thanks to the English Department at Santa Clara University and to Regis McKenna for their support of the California Legacy series.

# Contents

*Photo section between 100 and 101*

# Introduction

"A world where variation was perversity" is how Harriet Lane
Levy describes the stifling environment of her upper-middle-
class Jewish family in San Francisco during the 1880s. "A slight
deviation from the norm, which was O'Farrell Street, a collar rolled
back exposing a triangle of throat to the daylight, revealed its wearer
to Mother as an eccentric; a broader step to the left and a girl's
honor fell from her like a loosely buttoned petticoat."

With dry wit and obvious love of language, Levy pokes tender
fun at her starched society, using each room of her childhood home
as a point of departure for intimate descriptions of family and neighbors, the latter furtively spied upon from behind discreetly drawn
curtains. The child's fascination with the half-understood ritual of
Passover, the drama of suitors calling at the front door, the rites of
passage for a young woman seeking a college degree surrounded by
doubting men—all these scenes shimmer with Levy's intelligence
and humor. But the emotional intensity and zest with which she
brings to life her adolescent experiences is not the work of a young
woman. Far from it. When this touching memoir was first published in 1947, Levy was eighty years old, nearing the end of a long
and extraordinary life.

*920 O'Farrell Street* was written almost exactly one century after Harriet Lane Levy's father, Benjamin Levy, fled the anti-Semitism
of his Prussian village in search of wealth and opportunities in the
Far West. In 1850, after an arduous journey by mule train across
the Isthmus of Panama, Benjamin Levy arrived in San Francisco, a
city transformed overnight from a quiet little bayside village of eight
hundred people into a boom town. Canvas tents and hastily con-
structed shanties housed the 40,000 men who had come to get rich,

including Benjamin Levy. Imposed upon the Spanish, Californian, and Native American stock came a new population from all over the world: Fijian sailors, Russians with furs and sables, turbaned Turks, Australian criminals, Chinese, Japanese, Mexicans, and Europeans, as well as, from America, upright, puritan New Englanders, freed Blacks, aristocratic southern gentlemen, and homesteaders from the Midwest. Drawn by a single purpose to this isolated frontier, men from every station—politicians, physicians, dentists, merchants, farmers, criminals, editors—were hewing out a new social order on the banks of the bay.

Working side by side with the rest of the pioneers, Jews like Levy helped forge the modern city of San Francisco. From the beginning, Jews suffered the same hardships and successes, and so were accepted into the mainstream of society, welcomed in politics and social organizations, in a manner unprecedented in Europe and other American cities. Unlike many gold seekers who planned to return home after making their fortune in the Sierra mines, most Jews arrived in San Francisco with the intention of settling in the city and establishing homes and businesses there. Levy prospered as a merchant, outfitting ships that crowded San Francisco's thriving port as well as prospectors heading east in search of gold in the Mother Lode. Other fellow Jewish immigrants succeeded as artisans, tradesmen, bankers, and manufacturers.

In 1858 Benjamin Levy married Henriette ("Yetta") Michelson, who had voyaged around Cape Horn by sailboat to arrive in San Francisco. When the last of their three daughters, baby Harriet, was born in 1867, San Francisco's Jewish population numbered between 20,000 to 30,000. After the Civil War, however, a wave of anti-Semitism swept the country, and with it went the acceptance Jews had enjoyed during the early Gold Rush years. Elite social clubs, like the Bohemian, Olympic, and Pacific Union, which had previously been open to Jews, now closed their doors. Interaction between Jews and Gentiles became less frequent, and, as Harriet relates in *920 O'Farrell Street*, a "pleasant disassociation no one wished to change" characterized the relationship between the two groups.

As the Jewish population expanded, rigid social stratifications developed within the Jewish community itself, and an intense internal rivalry grew between the Polish and German Jews. Young Harriet was acutely aware of the fissure within the Jewish social body. "That the Baiern (Bavarian or German Jews) were superior to us, we knew," Harriet notes in her memoirs. "We took our position as the denominator takes its stand under the horizontal line. On the social counter the price tag 'Polack' confessed second-class."

The history of this conflict had its origin in 1772 when Poland was partitioned, and Prussia acquired provinces containing the majority of Polish Jewry. With the annexation, these newly Prussian Jews became German subjects and often spoke the German language, but they remained Polish in culture, in their identity, and in the eyes of other European Jews and Gentiles who still thought of them as "Polacks." In contrast, the highly assimilated German Jews considered themselves intellectually and culturally superior to the Polish Jews who clung to the traditional Jewish culture of Eastern Europe.

The daughter of Polish parents, Harriet Levy pretended to be of German origin in school to avoid being considered lower class. "Were I asked in the schoolroom the birthplace of my mother or father, in an agony of fear lest the truth be detected, I quickly answered, 'Germany,'" she confesses. The only hope of elevation into the elite clique of German Jews rested on making a good marriage.

One hundred years earlier, Jane Austen had chronicled how the constricted lives of women in 18th-century England narrowly revolved around the business of getting married. With Austenian powers of observation and a similar light, clever style, Harriet Levy describes the anxiety-ridden quest for marriage in San Francisco's wealthy Jewish community, specifically the scramble to find husbands for Harriet's sisters, Addie and Polly. Harriet herself was prepared for another destiny. "I was bright but plain-looking, and must not expect a marriage of any consequence." While the freewheeling, spendthrift, madcap life of San Francisco percolated around them, the daughters of rich orthodox Jews were sealed into their opulent mansions, isolated within the constraints of their Old World culture. It was understood that their every action affected their value as a commodity on the marriage mart and, for most, marriage was the only acceptable disposition.

Harriet Levy had another aspiration: college. Father's friend warned that "education was fine for a boy, but would spoil the chances of a girl. Men did not like smart wives." After weighing the risk of remaining an "old maid," Harriet decided to take the chance. Accompanied by Polly as chaperone, Harriet boarded a ferry boat for Berkeley across the bay. Not yet sixteen years old, still wearing a girl's short dress and hair hanging in a long braid down her back, Harriet took the entrance exams for the University of California. Although in her memoirs she makes sport of her youthful naiveté, pursuing an education was a heroic endeavor.

After graduating from the university in 1886, Harriet opted for the literary life at a propitious moment in San Francisco's literary history. During the last decade of the century, San Francisco witnessed a literary renaissance brought about in part by a lively periodical called *The Wave,* "A weekly for those in the swim." Founded in Monterey in the late 1880s, *The Wave* evolved into a high-quality literary publication, featuring theater and book reviews, fiction, poetry, humor, and news. Relocated to San Francisco and reputedly the most luminous paper in the West, *The Wave* attracted a group of gifted young writers, including Frank Norris, Jack London, and Harriet Lane Levy. John O'Hara Cosgrave, the imaginative and liberal-minded new editor, regarded Harriet as a rising star. When *The Wave* later folded, Harriet continued her journalistic career as a drama critic for *The Call,* a then-popular San Francisco newspaper.

Meanwhile, Harriet confronted the threat of Victorian spinsterhood which hung over all single women, with its prediction of humiliation and lifelong, bitter boredom, a spectre that the writer portrays vividly in *920 O'Farrell Street*. But Harriet belonged to a new generation of independent women who, for the first time, could contemplate the possibility of fulfillment without marriage. Her intimate circle of friends was comprised of young Jewish women who aspired to the creative life, including her neighbor at 922 O'Farrell, Alice B. Toklas. A woman of "strange, austere beauty dressed in monastic livery," Alice quietly served as housekeeper and comfort provider for her grandfather's all-male household. Only Harriet knew of her friend's secret life: for a precious two weeks every spring, Alice fled from O'Farrell Street for a vacation in

Monterey, her "nun's garb . . . disgarded for a brilliant red mandarin coat." Once Harriet accompanied Alice on this retreat.

> The last night of our visit we celebrated with a dinner to each
> other at Louis's French restaurant. A porterhouse steak, a
> double order of French-fried potatoes, a bottle of champagne,
> and we snapped our fingers at grandfathers, uncles, German
> cousins, and all the impedimenta of life, liberty, and the pur-
> suit of happiness.

Fortunately, Alice Toklas was not forever doomed to what Harriet
described as her life of "faultless service to Grandpa Levison and his
tribe of relatives." In fact, Harriet helped arrange Alice's deliverance. The eventual European escapade for both young women was
facilitated by another neighbor from O'Farrell Street, Sarah Samuels,
a woman described as overpowering and opinionated. In 1895 Sarah Samuels had married Michael Stein, director of the Omnibus
Cable Company railway, and financial provider for his brothers and
sisters. In 1903 the couple left for Paris to move in with Michael's
siblings Leo Stein and Gertrude Stein. Following the trend set by
Leo, Sarah began collecting modern art, especially Matisse. Imitat-
ing Gertrude, Sarah held a salon on Saturday afternoons.

When news of the 1906 earthquake reached the Steins in Paris,
they hurried back to San Francisco to investigate the damage to
their property, bringing back with them the first paintings by Matisse
to cross the Atlantic. Harriet took her friend Alice and Alice's cousin
Annette Rosenshine to see the pictures. On this occasion, Sarah
invited Alice and Harriet to travel back to Paris with her.

Harriet and Alice had debated moving to Paris, but neither woman
wanted to travel with someone as domineering as Sarah Stein. However, Harriet and Alice were not altogether ready to give up a journey to Europe. Even sitting behind a window in Paris, argued Alice,
and watching life go by there could be no worse than being im-
mured in San Francisco. However, wont to live beyond her means,
Alice was in arrears for a set of silver fox furs, and felt she could not
leave home without settling her debts. Fortunately, Harriet had a
thousand dollars saved in the bank, which she readily loaned to
Alice. The two arrived in France on September 8, 1907. At age 40,

Harriet had landed in the very center of the most iconoclastic and bohemian group of the early twentieth century.

On their first day in Paris, Harriet took Alice to see the Steins, then living on the Rue Madame in a converted Lutheran church. In her unpublished memoirs of Paris, Harriet wrote, "I never asked if I would be welcome: I never questioned the right to intimacy but came to the Rue Madame as if I were an expected guest." Harriet took it for granted that the Steins would introduce them to their circle of friends, and they did. Having survived the horrors of the 1906 earthquake in San Francisco, Harriet and Alice intrigued Picasso, Braque, Apollinaire, Matisse, and the rest of Gertrude's acquaintances with this accomplishment. For weeks the women lived by telling earthquake stories. However, a day came when Harriet said to Alice, "I fear that we shall have to add something to our earthquake experience if we hope to maintain our position." Alice agreed, replying, "We may even have to be burned with the house."

Harriet later described their growing self-confidence. "Any sense of inadequacy, of being in an intellectual world beyond our background left us." To feel ever more at home in Paris, they took up the study of French. Gertrude arranged for Alice and Harriet to take lessons from Fernande Olivier, Picasso's beautiful but self-absorbed mistress. With no common interests, making conversation proved a challenge for the three women. Fernande spoke of the poodles of Paris, Alice spoke of poodles in San Francisco, and Harriet, who hated poodles, remained silent. Nevertheless, the young foreigners persisted.

After a few weeks the two Californians yearned for a residence more homelike than their hotel. On Harriet's suggestion, Alice found a delightful furnished flat for rent in the home of a French count. Enchanted, Harriet and Alice moved in immediately. The following day when Gertrude arrived for lunch, she declared the accommodations unacceptable and put an end to life in the flat. At Gertrude's insistence Harriet and Alice found a hotel within walking distance of Gertrude's flat.

In fact, Gertrude was falling in love with Alice and casting a net to draw her in. Alice began spending more and more time with Gertrude. Alone and feeling abandoned in a strange city, Harriet suffered an emotional crisis that seemed to manifest in physical and spiritual problems. Both Sarah and Gertrude took it upon themselves to divert Harriet's attention, including having her sit for her portrait. During the daily sessions with David Edstrom, a Swedish sculptor, Harriet became intrigued by his mercurial personality, and fell in love with him. To her chagrin, Harriet discovered he already had a wife.

Harriet developed a more significant diversion in her growing devotion to contemporary art. She accompanied the Steins on weekly visits to art dealers where she acquired the core of her extraordinary collection, now hanging in the San Francisco Museum of Modern Art. The rest of her days she filled with lunches, teas, dinners, theater, opera, and conversation. "Talk. Talk. And more talk," Harriet complained in her Paris memoirs. "Nothing stopped with the fact. No matter how simple the subject, it led to further conversation."

In the summer of 1908, Gertrude asked Alice to live with her and be her wife. Still loyal to Harriet, Alice demurred, but, thereafter, Alice spent even less time with Harriet. Ever more isolated, Harriet finally returned to San Francisco in 1910 with Sarah Stein, who had to attend to her dying father. Harriet instructed Alice from San Francisco to close up their flat and send her paintings. Gertrude had prevailed.

Harriet's European travels had not ended, however. Two years later she chaperoned her niece Sylvia Salinger to Paris. Addie's beautiful daughter had fallen in love with an unsuitable boy and was to remain abroad until the unfortunate affair had been forgotten. Sylvia's brother escorted Sylvia to Seattle where Harriet was spending time on a rendezvous with a man with whom she was passionately in love. Regretfully, the gentleman had neglected to tell Harriet he already had a wife. Harriet was livid. It was not an auspicious beginning for the trip.

In addition, on the crossing the lovely Sylvia attracted attention from every man on board, engendering a lifelong rivalry between Harriet and Sylvia. Harriet later wrote a short story (unpublished) called "An Aunt Is an Aunt" about a young girl who enchants all the men aboard a ship while her aunt lies seasick in the cabin. When the aunt recovers, her wit and intellect draw all the attention away from the beautiful but vapid girl. Brains triumph over beauty in Harriet's fiction, if not in life.

Once again in Paris, Harriet set up housekeeping in an apartment near the Steins and resumed her association with Gertrude,

Alice, and the other famous Bohemians. More formidable than ever, the implacable Gertrude never resisted an opportunity to mock Harriet. One afternoon Harriet reminded Gertrude, "You know I lent Alice $1000 to come here the first time and I never got paid back." Gertrude retorted, "Oh that's all right, Harriet, we won't hold it against you."

Sylvia's letters home, published in 1987 as *Just a Very Pretty Girl from the Country: Sylvia Salinger's Letters From France 1912-1913,* recorded Harriet and Sylvia's daily activities: lunches, teas, theater, visits to dressmakers, and shopping excursions—a saga of the idle rich. When, after a year, Harriet deemed Sylvia sufficiently recovered from the ill-advised romance, the pair returned home to San Francisco.

That a woman could remain single, much less live alone, and yet still appear to flourish had seemed impossible to a younger Harriet. In *920 O'Farrell Street* she describes her sister's unmarried music teacher: "I believed the shrivelling processes attending delayed matrimony to be a visible law of physiology, yet here was Louise Tourney flowering and redundant. Again, she was the only woman I knew who lived alone. Everybody lived with somebody, a mother or an aunt, or even another sister. But all alone! I tried to imagine such a living." Now here was Harriet, once again back in San Francisco, still single at the age of 47 with two great promises of love come to nothing. And yet she flourished.

A new beau appeared on the scene, Aaron Altman, head of the art department for San Francisco's public schools. Altman squired Harriet everywhere. The distinguished widower, known to the Salinger children as "Uncle Dutch," proposed marriage repeatedly, but Harriet declined. Independence suited her better. The responsibilities of home ownership held less appeal than the unencumbered existence of hotel living (first Nob Hill's Huntington Hotel, then the Brockelbank, and finally Carmel's La Playa Hotel). She enjoyed the unfettered life of an independent woman of means.

Heir to her father's fortune (which was unfathomably greater than *920 O'Farrell Street* would lead one to believe), Harriet was able to indulge her refined taste. Not beautiful in her middle years— her small bright eyes and pointed features gave her an appearance described as ferret-like—she nevertheless cut a striking figure, dressed elegantly in thickly textured suits. In the evenings she draped exquisite shawls over heavy, brocade gowns or donned scarlet silk Chinese robes, richly embroidered in gold thread, and she always wore beautiful, heavy, Florentine jewelry.

Harriet traveled abroad extensively, adding to her art collection. A loving aunt, she pampered her nieces and nephews with cautious generosity. After the death of Aaron Altman, a series of companions freed her from mundane tasks. (She never learned to drive, type, cook, or pay bills.) Most important, wealth enabled Harriet to develop her formidable intellect, leaving her free to explore all the latest intellectual and spiritual trends, from Christian Science (which, after attempting to convert the entire family, she ultimately rejected because "it made no sense") to psychology and psychiatry. She read voraciously and wrote endlessly: poetry, short stories, and humor. But after her youthful success as a journalist with *The Wave* and *The Call*, Harriet was unable to find a publisher.

Finally, in 1937 two reminiscences by Harriet Lane Levy, "The Front Bedroom" and "Neighbors," appeared in *The Menorah Journal,* a publication of Temple Sherith Israel's sisterhood. Ten years later Doubleday published *920 O'Farrell Street*. The memoirs succeeded tremendously, especially in San Francisco where guessing the true identity of the characters became a popular dinner-party activity. (Following the advice of her lawyer nephew, Levy changed many of the names.) Critics compared the style to Jane Austen, as well as Clarence Day's *Life With Father*. Nathan Rothman in the *Saturday Review* called the writing "subtle and intelligent," "the atmosphere alive with detail," bearing "just the right evocative word." He described the characters as creations of "a compassionate and intimate understanding." The *New York Times* critic noted her careful choice of details and candid presentation of the distinct world she knew. Further, Mary Parton of the *New York Herald Tribune* wrote, "Miss Levy, now eighty years old, has restored in this personal reminiscence a brief era in the American scene. She has presented the era with gentle amusement, sly thrusts, and with an appreciation for old days and old ways that is distilled from the enriching years."

"If Harriet had handled her time more carefully and her money less astutely," remarked one of her contemporaries, "she would have been a great woman at 40, instead of at 80." Harriet seems to have subscribed to this sentiment herself, as she demonstrated in a little book of poems published in 1947 by Grabhorn Press titled *I Love to Talk About Myself*:

> I could weep for the talent unused,
> I could blush for the challenge refused
> I could die for the shame, and
>     the taunt and the blame
> If I weren't so highly amused.

To make up for lost time, Harriet set to work on her memoirs of the Paris years—a deliciously waspish account of Alice, Gertrude, Sarah, et al. Unfortunately, this narrative lacks the freshness of *920 O'Farrell Street*. Before completing the book, Harriet Lane Levy died in Carmel, California, on September 15, 1950. (The unfinished manuscript has never been published.)

We are fortunate to have *920 O'Farrell Street* as Harriet Levy's legacy. A worldly cosmopolite looking back after a lifetime of acquired sophistication, Levy captures her childhood in picturesque detail. She writes graciously and humorously, with an enormous affection and a generosity of spirit that keep the satire always gentle, the irony tender and forgiving.

Many years after death and marriage had dispersed the Levy family, Harriet returned to the site that had been her home, but by this time O'Farrell Street had been irrevocably altered. "One automobile company after another bought ground along the length of the avenue and erected their showrooms upon it. And today motorcars drive into the repair department of the Cadillac Motor Company over the invisible, spotless, velvet parlor carpet of my 920 O'Farrell Street." Through her zestful artistry, Levy made fresh and immediate for her readers a way of life that had disappeared fifty years earlier. Now, another half a century later, Harriet Lane Levy continues to delight.

# 1

# *The Bay Window*

Father sat at his ease in the bedroom bay window, looking down upon the street as from the balcony of a theater, approving the panorama like an old subscriber to the opera. Friends, walking along the sidewalk, looked up to wave a hand to him, or to make words with their lips. Along the block each bay window framed a face. Near the corner, at opposite sides of the bay window of their bedroom, old Grandpa Davis and old Grandma Davis stared into space, motionless, timeless, looking as though they had been recovered from the excavation of an ancient city. At her bedroom window, in the house next door to us toward the avenue, Mrs. Levison's fiddling fingers tapped the pane close to her thick dark face. Father's glance toward the avenue made an arc excluding her.

Father approved of O'Farrell Street, which to him was not the full stretch of its length, but the two blocks from Larkin Street to Van Ness Avenue on which friends and acquaintances had built their homes. He saw prestige and commercial value in the closeness of the 900 block to Van Ness Avenue, a block with a future. When San Francisco grew larger, someone would tear down the row of houses on the corner and build a handsome home, which would require our lot to increase its depth. O'Farrell Street represented a high peak in Father's life, the accumulation of savings sufficient for the building of a home for his wife "Yetta," his eldest daughter Addie, Polly, and me, in a new residence district of San Francisco. In like manner his business associates had saved and invested their

1

capital, in a short time forgetting their old homes on the other side of Market Street. As "south of Market" lost in fashionable repute, their children denied them altogether.

O'Farrell Street was a dream come true, a dream which, if it never reached to the grandeur of Van Ness Avenue with mansions of the wealthy retired behind deep lawn and gilded iron fence, yet embodied a vision held and realized. O'Farrell Street proper was but one of the many parallel streets which moved out of Market Street, reclaiming unto themselves wastes of sand until they reached the avenue. Father spoke of our location as O'Farrell and Van Ness, and envisaged it as a corner, although the home of the Levisons and the fenced yard of the Toplitzes separated us from the corner of the avenue by sixty feet.

The 900 block had risen almost as a unit, one building going up after another in quick succession, a lot of sand transformed into residence and garden. The sand dunes at the corner on the farther side of the avenue, which abruptly halted the march of O'Farrell Street westward and which, upon windy afternoons, sent fine sand into our hair and eyes, did not diminish Father's appreciation. In a city where sand dunes rolled from Van Ness to the ocean, our sand dune was a plausible termination.

The houses on the north side of O'Farrell acquired variation by the swell of a bay window, or the color of a painted surface. All buildings gave out a fine assurance of permanence. Father approved of the block not only for its location, but for the honesty of its construction to which he had been witness. It was a solid street; the sidewalks were without dip or break. The planked street, held together by thirty penny spikes, resisted the iron shoes of the heavy dray horses. Houses, sidewalks, street were of the best wood provided by the most reliable contractors, guaranteed perfect; and Father knew our house to be the most substantial. O'Farrell Street, to the senses, was solid as a cube. When I turned the corner, my heart quickened at the sight of our white house springing forth from the drabness of its neighbors. To me its white paint was as marble.

Permanent as the house was the small street garden. If the bloom was pinched, and if the fence offered superfluous defense to plants that never yielded a bouquet, we felt no lack. In the shadowed strip of ground, running along the side of the house beside the row of nipped primroses, chives grew for Father. On Sunday mornings he came down the backway with plate and knife, and cut off a handful for his breakfast. He stopped a moment in the garden to look up and down the street, or to crumble a leaf of lemon verbena or myrtle and inhale its odor. How pleasant to own a garden with an iron fence, and to walk upon the graveled walk around the center plot. Ours was the only garden with a graveled walk. Occasionally a hummingbird flew into the garden, stabbed its single blossom, and was off almost too quickly to register.

The south side of 900 broke away from the ordered arrangement of the north side. Small groups of narrow bay-windowed houses served as rented homes to small families. Near the corner of Polk Street stood the cow barn of old man Waller, to which the anemic children of the neighborhood, glass in hand, hurried in the early morning hours to receive "warm milk fresh from the cow." At night small boys rang the doorbell of the wild-eyed old man and scattered before he answered. The block ended with the store at the corner, where household wants were supplied by Hink, the ashen-haired grocer with bleached eyelashes, who never smiled, but gave honest weight.

The occupants of the south side of O'Farrell were negligible to us. We identified them vaguely as "the people across the street." When they walked down their steps on Sunday morning, our minds registered only "going to church." Their entrance into their homes through the street door, which their keys unlocked, awoke no curiosity regarding their identity or occupation within their homes. Our eyes swept over them, across Polk Street, recovering sight only with the handsome Fuller house, at the corner, which led the succession of aristocratic residences on the block below.

Between the private life of 920 O'Farrell and the street a bay window offered unbroken communication. From the darker rooms we made frequent visits to the window to catch a breath of sunlight, or pick up a bit of news to carry back to the family. If the bell rang, we leaned out of the window to discover who was at the door below, and darted back again within the minute, ready to act upon our discovery. Mother paused a moment in the bay between forays

3

upon dust and disorder. If she sighted a threatening visitor, she calculated the likelihood of having been observed and gave quick instructions to Maggie Doyle, the maid of all work.

Mother warned us to keep an eye out and report if we saw two men approaching with portfolios. They might come any day. Days passed with no sign of them. Then one morning when I was standing at the window I saw two men, each with a large black book in his hand, climb the steps of the Lessings; not the Joseph Lessings, our neighbors, but the S.S. Lessings, farther down the block. I flew to the back of the house, down the backstairs, into the kitchen.

"They're coming!" I gasped.

"Who is coming?" Mother asked, irritated at my excitement.

"The assessors."

What the Assyrians had been to the Babylonians, and the Persians to the Assyrians, what the Huns had been to Rome, and the Indians to the American colonists, the assessors were to us. The assessors were the deputies of the city administration who appraised the value of household and personal effects for purposes of taxation. From house to house they went, extracting data after battles with the tenants. Sometimes they were fine men; that meant that they were easygoing, and susceptible to blandishment. But they were more likely to be mean fellows, unyielding to persuasion. Uncertainty invested their coming with excitement and fear. To me the mission of the assessor was to uncover, to seize, to consume. I felt that no secret was secure from his eagle eye. He could see through mattresses and closet doors. When he appeared, standards were reversed; pride of ownership shrank into fear of detection. He poised a pencil and fate hung trembling upon admission. All codes of polite convention were abrogated; the questions he asked about purchases and prices were those gentlemen never asked. His coming was catastrophic.

"The assessors!" I cried to Mother again.

Even as I spoke the word, fires kindled on the hilltops—signals that flamed alarm from tribe to tribe. Sister Polly at the piano, sister Addie in her bedroom, Maggie Doyle in the basement washroom, caught the warning and hurried to join the defense. Furs, velvet coats, feather neckpieces were gathered from closets and rushed into old canvas-covered trunks. Silver soup ladle, sugar bowl, and napkin rings were thrust behind red braided pillow shams. The diamond rings vanished from Mother's fingers to hallowed places beneath her bodice.

"The table cover," Mother commanded, and Maggie Doyle swept from the dining-room table the richly appliquéd garnet plush cover.

We dismantled as the locust eats. In a few minutes everything that made for opulence had been removed, and the rooms were reduced, as far as possible, to a semblance of shabbiness and poverty. The bell rang, and Mother answered.

"We are the assessors," one of the deputies announced.

Mother's face lit with interest. "Come right in," she said and, quickly walking past the parlor doors, led them with embracing hospitality into the chill of the darkened dining room.

"Be seated, gentlemen," she said, and sat down herself as if in anticipation of a pleasant disclosure.

Then the drama began, a contest between the not too clever political agents, conscientious but not overzealous, and little Mother, determined to admit only where denial was useless, and to fight to the death when there was a chance for escape. The assessors spread their opened books upon the bare table. One rose and opened the folding doors leading into the music room. Mother followed.

"Square piano? Ah, a Steinway."

"Brought from the old house," Mother agreed helpfully.

The assessor's searching eye dropped to the Axminster carpet.

"We are hoping to get a new one as soon as we can afford it," Mother said, as if in answer to a criticism of its shabbiness.

"Any jewelry, diamonds?" he asked as they returned to the dining room.

"Diamonds?" Mother laughed heartily. "One is lucky to have shoes this year."

The assessors chuckled. They would have been helpless before the miracle had she confessed her brooch and earrings. And so they moved on from room to room, Mother growing younger and gayer, parrying questions with lightness and humor. So might Lady Macbeth have beguiled the gentle Duncan.

She tried to avoid entrance into the parlor, but the assessor turned the knob and entered. The shutters were tightly closed, the shades drawn, the tables devoid of ornament. The tall mirrors, dismantled of terra-cotta and bisque figures, wore a strange austerity. But more than removal of decoration would have been needed to make the assessors visualize the dilapidation and decay that Mother sought to project.

"That's a handsome set of furniture," said the assessor.

"Is?" asked Mother archly. "Was, fifteen years ago."

Altogether it was a gay encounter, made up of question and retort, short pauses, and hearty laughter. It ended in the tinkle of glasses.

"You will have a little something?"

They would; and returned to the dining room. The day was hot and many flights of steps lay before them. From the locked cupboard Mother brought forth the stately decanter, realizing with a pang, as she told Father that night, that the decanter was of embossed silver, and the bottles of Bohemian glass. But the eyes of the men were upon the contents and they were no longer officials of the government.

"To your health, madam," they said, rising.

"To yours, gentlemen," Mother responded and, having won at every point, she drank in hearty friendliness.

There was more laughter as they stood talking on the front steps. Then the door closed.

I ran out to Mother. "What happened, what happened?"

"Call Maggie Doyle. Those steps were never washed this morning," Mother said.

I returned to the window in time to see the assessors disappear into the Lessing house, to the accompaniment of small boys of the neighborhood, standing at the foot of the steps, their lips glued to their harmonicas.

There was no activity of the street unheralded and unaccompanied by melody. Every instrument—violin, trombone, even bagpipes—importuned the tender heart or, lacking instrument, the unassisted voice sent forth its plea on a curve of song. A youthful yodel unexpectedly roughened into, "Rags, bottles, and sacks" and, above the seat of a disheveled, lumpy buckboard, eager black eyes smiled up at us insinuatingly from a gaunt bearded face. Twice a week two stalwart beggars, hatless, coatless, one offering a wooden peg, the other an empty sleeve, took their stand on the sidewalk opposite our house, and together discharged at our window the lusty chords of "Die Wacht am Rhein." If we delayed our response, "Lieb Vaterland, magst ruhig sein" was suggested softly, like a secret confidence, and we accepted it as a valid argument for a contribution.

Every Monday morning a hale old Frenchman zigzagged up the street, leisurely swinging from sidewalk to sidewalk, an old broadbrimmed felt hat hanging from his hand. Sometimes he walked in silence, smiling reminiscently, as if his path lay among open fields; then he stopped unpredictably, and addressed to the sky the full content of the "Marseillaise." Like a call for volunteers, "Le jour de gloire est arrivé" displaced the air. He picked up a coin as if it were a bouquet, and bowed acknowledgment of our tribute to France.

A low circling monotone of song, "Any old knives to grind, any old knives to grind," approached and passed before we caught sight of the long, bony back of the grinder, deeply arched under his wheel, as he plodded toward the avenue, ringing a bell softly.

But beyond all the music of the street the melodies of the hand organ made appeal, stirring obscure founts of feeling. Every Sunday for twenty years the organ-grinder lifted the straps from his shoulders, folded his legs at the edge of the sidewalk between 920 and 922, raised his large brown eyes, emptied of recognition or petition, and turning the crank of his organ in the same slow circle, released his changeless repertoire. No matter where I was, in the back bedroom or kitchen, no matter what I was doing, the melodies of *Il Trovatore* penetrated the walls, arresting my thoughts and my hands. The music rippled over the mind to an ancient shore, reminding me of some unremembered, unfulfilled promise, haunting me with the questions, "Don't you know? Can't you remember?" until disquiet impelled my feet to the front window to seek reassurance from the familiar figure below. We never spoke to him, but before the hammer had hit the anvil a dozen strokes, Mother sent Maggie Doyle down to the street with a dime which sentiment never enlarged to fifteen cents nor surfeit ever reduced to five. Father grew into the portliness of the prosperous merchant, and the beard of the organ-grinder grizzled with age, but every Sunday Father opened his window, even when it rained, so as not to miss the "Anvil Chorus." Twenty years were too short to exhaust Father's love for *Il Trovatore*. Sung on the grand opera stage by Kellogg and Carey, clanged by the band in Golden Gate Park, or tinned from a street organ, it stirred Father's tenderness and retouched some dream.

These solicitations of the heart were all in the history of the day, as spontaneous as the crowds moving up to the cathedral at the corner of the avenue for mass, the butcher boy leaping from his cart with a blood-soaked brown-paper parcel, or the baker drawing out from his wagon cupboard trays of twistbread, or round, plump loaves of rye.

But a doctor's buggy, stopping at a house, was another matter. Illness spread excitement like a social celebration. "He is there again!" Polly called, and Addie and I hurried to the window in time to catch sight of the coattails of Dr. Hartman hurrying up the steps of the Simons'. A single call piqued curiosity, a second awoke concern; but a protracted visit disrupted our meal, and fed conjecture for a day. Dr. Hartman's carriage, waiting an hour each morning at the door of the handsome Mrs. Simon, weeks after her recovery from typhoid, was a subject not to be exhausted in one household, but to be settled in conference. If a young graduate drove a carriage and pair, or was driven in a coupé like Dr. Levi Lane, Mother mocked the artifice.

The best of the offerings of the street was the unheralded presence during the night of a two-storied wooden house beneath my window moving slowly toward the avenue. Beheld in the dim light, it moved with a fabled unreality. An old house, lifted from its native foundations, adventuring toward a new location, wore a half-tipsy, dislocated look not unnatural to so fantastic an experience. Through its uncurtained windows it appealed self-consciously, disclaiming responsibility for the unbecoming situation in which it found itself.

"See what they persuaded me to do at my age," it seemed to say. I felt embarrassed for the old house, compelled to leave familiar ground for some more fashionable neighborhood, where, in spite of its fresh coat of paint, it would not be permitted to forget its history.

A windlass accomplished the transit; a single horse circling in continuous motion wound the rope, stepping over it at each turn until roughly called to a halt. If the creaking of old wood and the harsh command of men awoke me, I drew a deep breath to help the poor tired horse pull the house over the ever-shifting rollers before I fell asleep again.

At nine o'clock every morning the men of O'Farrell Street left their homes for their places of business downtown; dressed in brushed broadcloth and polished high hats, they departed soberly as to a funeral. The door of each house opened and let out the owner who took the steps firmly, and, arriving at the sidewalk, turned slowly eastward toward town. A man had not walked many yards before he was overtaken by a friend coming from the avenue. Together they walked with matched steps down the street.

All the men were united by the place and circumstance of their birth. They had come to America from villages in Germany, and had worked themselves up from small stores in the interior of California to businesses in San Francisco.

From the bedroom window we watched them, foreseeing the interruptions to their march. The initial heat of a political argument halted their first advance. Another six yards and they stopped again to face each other and twist a protesting hand. The full stop came at the corner of Polk Street, where gestures were fully unsheathed and fingers touched the chest and swung out into the air. If Father was walking with Mr. Levison, our neighbor, we could measure by the dislocation of his stovepipe the degree of his failure to convince the stubborn Republican that Grover Cleveland was the greatest President in American history.

Compared to the unabashed enjoyment of the private affairs of a whole block, the experience of a single family within its own walls was astringent living. Puffing up the steps of 916 with the package-laden, fat Mrs. Lessing; stepping delicately from the hired victoria with the pretty daughter of the Nathans; or arriving from Frankfort with the new German cousin of the Davises and her basket trunk, we lived spaciously. One glimpse was all we needed. We knew how to spread it over areas of participation.

One morning I looked out of the window and saw three women

in black crossing the street and making for our house. The black extended beyond their bodies, down their sides, flapping brokenly like mortuary wings. They came as one, borne upon us not by the wind, but by the current of an inner purpose. I was afraid of them, although I knew the mission of three Jewish women, coming together on a morning visit, to be a merciful one. I knew that they were our itinerant associated charities outward bound to relieve a private need.

I called Mother. She quickly exchanged her purple wrapper for a dress, sought her purse, and went down the stairs to receive them.

The Eureka Benevolent Society ministered to avowed poverty; but no public channel existed to the concealed distress, which must be discovered by a friend, whispered to another and another, creating a trio of benevolence which would move upon the land, knocking upon the door with a stern compulsion to charity.

When Mother entered the dining room they had just alighted, three large, black shapes austere and imposing. They unfolded their tale in orderly procedure. One introduced the grievous story, a second elaborated upon it, the third drew it to a conclusion, deepened in value by threefold affirmation. The tale was told under the breath, with lids lowered against the knowledge which they were obliged to divulge. Occasionally eyes sought eyes for corroboration, in reproach of life. Then they sat in silence, resting the case, having asked for nothing. Mother left the room, returning with the purse already in her pocket, and offered her contribution which was appropriated, though apparently unperceived.

"A nice day," Mother said as she opened the street door, letting in the sunshine.

But the trio refused the message of the sun. In sustained, sullen gloom they descended our steps, and ascended those of our neighbor.

The south side of the 800 block held a story. I walked along it with delight, my interest concentrated upon the large double residence in the middle of the block which gave balanced grandeur to the whole neighborhood. It was the home of John Mackay, king of Consolidated Virginia, the mine that, at the turn of a shovel; had converted a poor miner into a multimillionaire. Daily I passed

10

Jewish homes before which my spirit automatically drew back; the Friedenthals sat upon my heart heavily; the proud obscured the sun. Not so the home of John Mackay. The Mackay house swept away all small barriers; it trailed clouds of glory from the mining centers of Nevada; it broke life into claims and stakes and tips and noble gamblers and inexhaustible outpourings of gold. It brought to our doors the Comstock Lode and Virginia City.

The broad staircase, leading to the entrance, was high and the time required to climb and descend it provided moments for satisfying observation. What matter that the street door closed upon the curious; the outside offered enough. The steps democratically descended to the sidewalk, and young girls ran up and down them, swinging into the street with easy stride. Could a prophetic eye have seen in them a future Italian princess and a Vanderbilt of New York, it would have remained permanently glued to the entrance door. The occupants of the house and their friends filled their roles like characters in a novel; carriages stood constantly before the door, barouche, coupé, and high stanhope. Wooden coachmen sat in aristocratic immobility, footmen sprang like acrobats from their seats to hand out the ladies of the house. The solid silver-mounted harnesses clinked with the very tinkle I had read about in novels of the titled. The horses *were* bays, their flanks *did* shine. On the night of a ball the elite of the city stepped, if they were women, or sprang, if they were men, from their carriages to a crimson velvet carpet, which glowed from the street to the entrance door. However, better than all this confirmation of imagined pageantry, more enlarging to experience, extending horizons to the limitless unknown, was the daily arrival of the milkman and the delivery into the house of huge cans of milk for the Mackays' daily bath. Beside such witness to fabled treasure, diamonds were pebbles, golden dinner service, plate.

I told myself that it was not the flourish of wealth but the romance of the triumphal passage from mining cabin to a city mansion that commanded my obeisance, and I made an effort to resist the argument for importance offered by the display of private parade. Before a victoria with a single driver it was easy to retain my assurance; but coachman and footman, clad in colored livery, rigid above a closed coupé, scattered my identity. At the approach of a plum-colored livery, the forehead of my spirit brushed the sidewalk.

Between the Jews on the north side of the street and the Gentiles on the south a pleasant dissociation existed which no one wished to change. The great wealth of the Mackays, and of their successors, automatically created its own barrier, but the privileged intimacy of observation provided all the enjoyment that anyone could hold. A new carriage and pair, a daring imported novelty from Paris, a bizarre visitor from abroad, and along some grapevine route the news was communicated to the street, providing deeper flavor to already happy lives. The seclusion of the Gentiles across the street was not distorted into intentional distinction or racial prejudice. No one desired to break through the natural barriers established by difference of race or background. The north side was satisfied that their enjoyment should be heightened by high-toned neighbors who so fortuitously embellished their view, gave distinction to their neighborhood, and provided exciting entertainment by the glamorous variations of their lives.

# 2

# *Neighbors*

We were intimate with neither of our next-door neighbors, the Levisons nor the Lessings. Although the "L's" of our houses touched, we were separated from the Levisons by the abyss of a superior culture. Mr. Levison enjoyed only a vicarious prestige. The business of the Levison Brothers, a general merchandise business in Stockton, was in no way above the level of such enterprises; nor were the three brothers, who made up the firm, distinguishable from the mass of merchants of the interior. The Levison Brothers shone by the light of the sisters who were their wives—solemn-faced, swarthy women, so short that, sitting, their feet hardly reached the floor. They were educated, and the knowledge of the fact fed them unremittingly, like the spirit of the Holy Ghost. The younger sisters bore the honor easily, but to our neighbor, Mrs. Louis Levison, it was a moral principle to be upheld, or a precious state of consciousness to be safeguarded.

Her heavy features, high cheekbones, and fleshy nose intensified the soberness of dry lips, unsmiling under the exigencies of her exclusiveness. She did not unbend in social intercourse, but brought to each encounter an awareness that the uneducated was the negligible. She spoke little, but overpowered us by accomplishment. She referred to her knowledge of foreign languages but we had no means of verifying it. That the adornments were not displayed, we attributed to our unworthiness. To one accomplishment we were occasionally permitted to bear witness: she played the piano, a unique attainment in the world of our parents.

All three sisters played the piano. They played alone or in twos or threes. Mrs. Louis played as a solo the "Polish Dance" by Scharwenka. Mrs. Adolph and Mrs. Isaac played "Poet and Peasant" in duet. The two city wives of the firm of Levison Brothers earnestly sat on two low stools, side by side. Four little hands hit the keys smartly and bounded back into the air; four little boots felt down and around and around in search of a pedal, while the sad-faced visiting sister from the country stood at the piano, peering shortsightedly, turning the pages with an emphatic accuracy which made of the duet a trio.

One day I brought a letter to Mrs. Levison for translation. I wrote to the great for autographs and they responded with a name, sometimes with a line. Everybody answered. Once when I wrote, asking for the origin of the magic carpet referred to in *Keramos*— the subject of our high school study—Longfellow answered with a long letter, which I framed between glass and swung on a slender bronze crane from the mantel in my bedroom. I wrote as to a friend, occasionally permitting humor to enter into my note of request. To Samuel Clemens in Hartford I told of my appreciation of *Tom Sawyer,* reminding him that its author was also a resident of Hartford, and asking that Mr. Clemens use his persuasion to induce Mark Twain to send me his autograph. When the reply came I sailed the air, for he wrote, "I hunted him up, Miss Hattie, and got it without difficulty," and signed two names: Samuel Clemens and Mark Twain.

Nobody failed to answer. "And here it is," came like a handclasp from John Greenleaf Whittier. "It is better to know less than so much that ain't so," Josh Billings advised. President and poet replied so inevitably that refusal did not suggest itself and I extended my reach to Europe, confident of answer from statesmen and crowned heads. The successive failure of Gambetta and Gladstone to respond to the irresistible solicitation of an enclosed stamped envelope dimmed my faith, which the silence of Queen Victoria extinguished. But before the shock of the royal rebuff had halted my pursuit, a letter written in Italian arrived from Rossi, the Italian tragedian second only to Salvini in the role of Othello. For translation I could look to no one but Mrs. Levison, whose vaunted accomplishments included familiarity with Italian. Here was an opportunity to test it.

I called upon her and asked for a translation of my letter. To the name of Rossi she nodded soberly, as if consenting to his existence. Then she slowly adjusted her spectacles and read the letter. *"Amore,"* she said, as if that were the only word on the page, "means love. *Mio"*—she pointed to the word—"means my." With that she returned the letter in dismissal and resumed her position at the bay window at which she sat for hours each day, from time to time tapping the pane. Disappointment did not shadow my retreat, as my visit had not been conceived entirely without malice.

When she came to pay us a visit (we could see duty prodding her to our doors), Mrs. Louis preserved the proud detachment of one who, though seemingly among us, was still at her own fireside. She gave little heed to the conversation of my parents, but maintained the flow of her own thinking, her fingers fiddling the arm of her chair. At unpredictable intervals her forehead loosened and rose. My eyes never left her face for fear of missing the phenomenon.

*"Viel' Besuch, viel' Besuch* [much company]," she boasted under her breath, in protest against the strain of a social urgency which, from the vantage point of our upper bay window, we knew to be mythical.

"More letters from Hamburg. Must answer them. And she wrapped herself closer in the greatness of the city of her birth. "Foffie out again tonight with the Brandensteins; won't go anywhere without her." Her brow rose and fell in agitation.

Foffie, diminutive of Flora, was the large, slow-moving, wide-mouthed daughter who wore her flesh like floating drapery. I saw her rarely and knew her as the voice that came through the wall of our music room. Her song never varied in tempo or color; no matter what the theme, once passed through her spirit, it issued forth a stream of woe. She had but to strike the first chord of "When the Tide Comes In," and the beach was strewn with the dead. On calm nights in summer I would be puzzled by the moaning of the winter's wind until I recognized the voice of Flora wailing the tipsy drinking song from *Girofle Girofla.*

15

To my mind the Levisons were also distinguished from their neighbors by the frequency of their funerals. From no other house did funeral processions proceed so often. Without a word of preface somebody was dead; not a member of the family proper, but a relative from the country. Countless nephews and nieces never lived for the city family, or for us, until they died, when the patriarchal instinct of Mr. Levison demanded that they should be interred in the family plot. It was an ordinary experience to look out the window and see, all unheralded, little clusters of men on the sidewalk, and a coffin being borne down the Levison steps; to see Mrs. Levison sitting woodenly in her usual seat at the bedroom window, tapping the pane with three fingers, and the young granddaughter, Alice Toklas, escaping furtively through the side basement door between narrow strips of garden to the street.

Every man had foreign relatives grafted upon his family tree. They were an ever-present menace. No man might say, "We are five," confident that his family would be regulated by natural processes. If he believed himself secure, a letter might already be on the way from a village in Germany announcing the departure of a daughter or son with his home as a destination. "My son is a fine fellow, willing, strong, ambitious, too. He will be of a great help in your business," Uncle Michael wrote. Or, "You will love our little Huldah who is coming to you, a sweet, amiable girl, but with no suitable prospect for marriage in our town," Aunt Mathilda explained. One was helpless. The ambitious boy and the amiable girl were already on the ocean, or, worse, on the train, and protest would profit nothing. When they arrived, it was unconscious and expectant, as if in answer to urgent invitation. So came Cousin Max, the dandy, touchy and fastidious; so came Cousin Huldah, indolent and haughty; so came Cousin Gustav, stolid and boorish. Nobody dreamed of sending a poor relative back to his village; each in his heart agreed to his obligation to provide for him.

Some families, like the Levisons, had better fortunes than others. Sometimes the nephew proved capable of assistance to the business. In that event a younger brother was sent for and he, in turn, was followed by a still younger one, until a whole family of children had been transplanted successfully.

16

"Other people have luck," Father complained, glowering at Cousin Gustav, humped up like a stableboy at our family table.

Every evening a brother of Grandfather Levison, or a cousin or two, or a few nephews returned with him from town to dinner. The household was set alike for marriage or funeral, ready for any human ceremony except birth. In the dining room, after dinner, problems of the young men were discussed under the tutelage of the old. Of the younger men, Cousin Eugene alone had authority. Every week the newspapers announced that: "Eugene Levison, the distinguished attorney from Stockton, is at the Palace Hotel." The older men of 922 leaned upon his advice as did his clients in the San Joaquin Valley. When Uncle David spoke of him to Uncle Martin, or Uncle Martin to Uncle Louis, it was to reiterate their conviction that Eugene was "a crackerjack." From his decision on a political or economical situation there was no appeal.

Alice Toklas, the granddaughter of Mr. Levison, was a strange note on the Levison canvas. When her mother died at an early age, her father brought twenty-year-old Alice to the grandfather's home at 922 O'Farrell Street, and dropped her and his responsibility for her among the aggregation of family relatives.

Among the ever-present, shifting group, Alice remained the only woman there. In spite of her youth she existed to them only as a housekeeper, provider of food and of general comfort. Any opinion that she might venture at table was ignored or sponged out by a laugh from the distinguished attorney from the interior. Each night she sat at the long table, unnoticed among the repetition of relatives. Her strange, austere beauty passed over them unsuspected. Alice was odd, they said, and forgot her. Unnoticed she fled the after-dinner, cigar-laden talk of local politics, and recovered her identity among congenial circles within the pages of Henry James. When she fled the house, a streak of gray, friends of Mr. and Mrs. Levison who met her corroborated the appraisal of 922. When she acknowledged their greeting on the street only to hurry past, escaping conversation, they told one another how, for her mother's sake, they had offered hospitality to Alice only to meet with rebuff or evasion. An odd girl!

To Alice was given an allowance to cover current expenses. Within its fixed limit she met the unpredictable invasion of dinner guests. If a sudden inroad upon her treasury, following a fresh wave of immigration from Germany, left her without money for a needed hat or dress, she did without it, her renunciation expressed in monastic livery. At a period when street dress was bright and decorative, Alice wore only gray. A severe tailored suit, the long coat buttoned from collar to hem, a cloth turban of the same color, gave to her slender figure the appearance of a furtive nun. The super-clean gloves and smart shoes which she wore were expected, she said, to arrest the eye and persuade approval not warranted by the remainder of the costume.

In return for her services she asked nothing of 922. At no time did she invite me to her house. A knock at my window and a bouquet of flowers quickly passed from her hand into mine and she was gone.

Every spring Alice prepared for her annual flight from 922. From the year's accumulation of discarded wearing apparel and hardware in the cellar she made a selection calculated to catch the eye of the secondhand man. One overcoat, three pairs of woolen underwear, and a cracked kitchen stove secured a week's holiday. Once in Monterey, she established herself in the lovely old adobe home known as Sherman's Rose.

Sherman's Rose (a sign above the gate announced the place to the tourist) was the home of Señorita Bonifacio, reputed to be at one time the beautiful young fiancée of General Sherman who, according to the legend, when a young lieutenant, planted a rosebush in her garden, promising to return to marry her when it bloomed. The rosebush grew, covering a broad trellis with heavy Maréchal Niel blossoms; other rosebushes grew and bloomed beside it, but the general did not return. Thirty years passed. Tourists, attracted by the story, visited the garden. They bought a bouquet of the heavy golden roses while their eyes searched the delicate features of the señorita for signs of desolation. The twinkle in her eye disconcerted their curiosity. She delivered her roses with gracious detachment and retired into the house to exchange lively gossip with Spanish women friends, or to take her seat behind the shutters of her bedroom window, from which for hours she regarded the happenings of the street.

It was to Sherman's Rose that Alice came each spring as a paying

18

guest. The nun's garb was discarded for a brilliant red mandarin coat, and Alice read in the romantic old garden and held conversation in a sign language all her own with Señorita Bonifacio. She relished the reserve so successfully maintained by the Spanish woman for more than thirty years. Sometimes she speculated upon her lack of understanding of English. In rare moments she entertained the possibility, which was almost a hope, that the general had never planted the rosebush at all. If an artist were a second guest, a romance budded but did not blossom, for Alice fled before the pressure of a wooing.

Altogether Señorita Bonifacio remained a delight to Alice, who found full satisfaction in conversation made up of nods and smiles of mutual liking. To sit beside the old fountain and look out through golden light upon fragrant rosebush and tiled adobe house, reflecting upon the legend of the general's infidelity, was congenial reverie for an afternoon in spring.

On the third day of her vacation Alice went to the fashionable hotel at Del Monte, lunched alone, and engaged a four-wheeled stanhope for an afternoon drive. Perched high above the ground behind a "spanking bay," confident in white gloves and smart boots, she drove the seventeen miles which skirt the rocky ocean shore through a forest of pine and beaten cypress. At the door of the Del Monte hotel she dropped an extravagant tip into the hand of the groom, descended from the carriage, and made her way back to Sherman's Rose on foot.

One spring we went to Monterey together and lived for a week at Sherman's Rose. The last night of our visit we celebrated with a dinner to each other at Louis's French restaurant. A porterhouse steak, a double order of French-fried potatoes, a bottle of champagne, and we snapped our fingers at grandfathers, uncles, German cousins, and all the impedimenta of life, liberty, and the pursuit of happiness. I begged for a toast.

Enravished by emancipation, Alice swung herself upon the table and raised her glass toward the ceiling. "To the eternal damnation of the Crackerjack of San Joaquin Valley," she cried, and we drank the toast choking with laughter. The single act of release restored her soul. The next day she returned to San Francisco, re-entered her

19

monastic livery, and gave faultless service to Grandpa Levison and his tribe of relatives for another year.

To the left of us lived the Lessings—an odor and a vision to me. When my nostrils were assaulted by the smell of frying oil I called out to Mother, "The Lessings are having a poker party tonight." Mr. Lessing's lack of interest in cards did not discourage Mrs. Lessing's love for poker parties. Mr. Lessing, a mild, light-bearded man, followed his bristling wife upstairs and downstairs, or in a walk around the back garden. Punch and Judy, their old and bleary-eyed English pugs, waddled after them. I felt sure that, out of sight, he held her hand. Once a week flounders fried in oil provided the main dish of their late supper.

On the morning of the party the kitchen window was raised to let out smoke and the odor of frying oil. A round, jovial, creamy, spectacled face appeared for a minute through the steam, a voice, excited and bustling, called across to Mother, "poker fight tonight," and the window closed again. To these parties came scuttling or waddling, according to their bulk, women with their husbands, or, as often, unaccompanied. We could hear the murmur of conversation during the game, and hear the clatter of dishes when the hour came for supper. My parents did not play poker, so there was no permanent basis for social contact with the Lessings.

Olga Lessing, the oldest daughter, opened a door to romance. She was as tall as a tall man, slender, and as beautiful and exotic as the wax figures in the window of Strozynski, the fashionable hairdresser. Her eyes opened twice as wide as any eyes I knew, and the pupils were large and fixed. Her eyelashes were separated, spreading like a fan. Her hair was a dull, beautiful red, parted in the middle and waved over the ears. She was of another species and not alone. Three women friends, equally tall, equally pearly-cheeked and wide-eyed, used to visit her, and tall men walked with them in the garden. Their great height and staring eyes separated them from the young girls who came to our house, and vaguely resembled the "fancy women" who colored and enlivened the crowds of Market Street on Saturday afternoons. They were too statuesque and authoritative for belittlement, and the impression of their beauty was

20

not to be relinquished to whispers of "bella donna" or the damning word "paint."

Olga Lessing and her friends were not only extraordinary in looks, but in what they did. Many a moonlight night the crack of a whip brought me running to the window to behold a kindling sight. An open three-seated carriage on high wheels stood before the Lessings' door. Pat Finnegan, the millionaire turfman, sat in the front seat, in one hand holding the reins of the horses, in the other a tall whip. The Lessing door opened and four tall figures, hidden beneath long black capes, ran down the steps. Rich-voiced men helped them into the carriage; the doors clicked, the whip snapped, and away they drove. On other nights the carriage was replaced by a deep wagon filled with hay. The crowd was larger, the voices higher and merrier. Four horses, two abreast, pranced up O'Farrell Street to the broad avenue; beautiful star-eyed statues laughing deep in the hay, all galloping away into the moonlight. A thrilling spectacle! Where were they going? What could they be doing? I could not know. Our lives provided no measure for delight so mysterious and supreme.

One day I realized that the tall girl, who was walking down the steps of the Lessings, no longer matched my romantic image of Olga Lessing. When the change had taken place, whether it had been gradual or pinned to an event, I could not know; but there she was at twenty-five, another person. The fan of her eyelashes was folded, the sunset hue of her hair dimmed to a sobered brown, the bravura gone from her dress and carriage. The glory of Olga Lessing had melted into the light of common day.

From the circumstances of her life the luster also had faded. What had happened, when or if it had happened, I did not know. The transformation was complete. The only answer to my astonished mind was this tall figure with unpowdered face, her hair drawn into a tight knot, her body compressed into a tailored suit, and her feet into stern English boots. For all time to come the beautiful Olga Lessing, so like an entrancing Strozynski manikin, had become an old maid.

Every morning at nine o'clock Mrs. John Boas, our German neighbor, who lived next door to the Lessings, stood on the porch of her house surveying the street. Gold-rimmed spectacles caught and reflected the light as her head swung sharply from side to side as on a pivot. Her body was as stiff as her black pompadour, smooth and tight over a heavy "rat." The genial smile of her broad face, her high-colored cheeks and friendly squint, offered hospitality; but woe to the ignorant who accepted it too confidently, unsuspecting the imperial claims of its wearer.

A little gnome of a man, the "John" of the name upon her visiting cards, followed her always with goggled eyes and hopped at her feet awaiting instructions.

Bianca, the stunted young German niece of John, who had come to San Francisco when a little girl to be part of the household, was a thorn her aunt's flesh. Her features and build announced her relationship to John, and her aunt, after the first sight of her, never forgave her the physical unattractiveness that defied ornament. No degree of willingness could compensate for her lack of charm, and Bianca's days were spent trying to earn the approval which she could never hope to win.

Of the circle of German ladies who gathered at Frau Boas's on Friday afternoons, not one questioned the imperialism of their hostess. With no distinguished background to justify her claims, Frau Boas received the respect she exacted, generating the royal atmosphere in which she moved and out of which she never emerged. The group of friends offered gossip for her approval, opinions for her confirmation. "And what do you think, Frau Boas?" and "What would you have said, Frau Boas?" hanging upon her smile, while she replenished their garlanded plates with twist bread, and filled coffee cakes, and enameled cookies. German was the language of their intercourse, but sometimes Frau Boas would lapse into English and relate how she had taken Bianca to the Concordia Ball "in her custody"; and how, "concealed in ambush," she had overheard the words of a trusted friend that revealed her unworthy of Frau Boas's friendship.

Frau Boas's birthday was the high mark of the year, observed by the usual weekly kaffeeklatsch, heightened by special entertainment. Verses, written by the hostess in honor of the day, printed on hand-painted cards, were found beside each plate;

verses recapturing tickling experiences in the life of the group. They were sung to the music of *Boccaccio,* the popular operetta. Frau Boas sang a verse by herself, then signaled the table of friends for the chorus. If the volume of their voices diminished, Frau Boas prompted them: "With goosto," she urged, and their voices swelled until, restraint released, they ended the refrain with a "tra-la-la" and a "tra-la-la-la" which halted on its rollicking curve for her approval.

It was a happy hour for everybody but Bianca who, throughout the merrymaking, had been nerving herself to present the mantel drape she had crocheted as her gift. The drape was of heavy corded macramé lace; she had worked upon it in secret for months, giving to it an extra width that it might fall over the mantelshelf and cover the top of the iron grate. She knew that, in spite of the hours stolen at night and in the early morning, the lambrequin lacked four inches of its accomplishment. She hoped that, in the good fellowship of the celebration, her aunt would overlook the incompletion.

Frau Boas accepted the gift, opened it, and regarded it approvingly until she came to the unfinished edge, when she lifted her menacing brow in the direction of Bianca.

"Not finished?"

Bianca faltered an explanation. The force of indignation, which lifted the forehead of Frau Boas into habitual furrows, now raised her body from the chair. Never, never, in a lifetime of birthday observances, had such an indignity been offered her.

"For me, for me! I am speechless," she cried. "An unfinished gift for me!" She gathered the heavy drape from the table to which it had dropped from her disdaining hand, and returned it to Bianca who, shaking with sobs, ran from the room.

Frau Boas returned to her guests.

*"Noch ein mal* [Once again]!"

She refitted her genial smile and raised a playful finger. Once more her spectacles sparkled upon the guests. *"Noch ein mal,"* she cried, "and this time with goosto."

Whereupon Frau Shirk and Frau Lewis and Frau Greenberg and Frau Mashke, their eyes upon the hostess, obliterated from their minds the insult of the unfinished lambrequin, and sang a "tra-la-la" and a "tra-la-la" with "goosto."

From the opening front door of 912 O'Farrell Street the Hirshes poured out at any hour of the day—Blooma, Gertie, Deborah, Eva, Minna, Albert, and Samuel. They did not come singly but in a rush as if in escape from an immigrant ship, exultant to explore a promised land. Sometimes Minna and Gertie, caught in a collision of wills, checked the descent. One awaited a bounce from their impact upon the sidewalk. There were many of them but they seemed even more, because they were noisy and scattered wide. As if their native fires did not burn hotly enough, their eyes sought the length of the street, sweeping unorganized material into the orbit of their experience; or they looked up to a bay window on a chance of adding a nod of recognition to the full flame of their excitement. Often we pretended not to see them, using astronomical observation as excuse for so wide an exclusion.

The block disapproved of the Hirshes, resenting their violent splash upon the refinement of the street. Their coming to San Francisco was an accident. Remembering the intellectual solidity and personal elegance of our old Dr. Sigmund Hirsh, the board of the synagogue invited a younger brother to his vacant pulpit without investigating his endowment, a serious omission. Once elected, he could not be asked to withdraw. One glance at his bulk and his black-bearded face prepared them for the thick speech that quenched forever the hope of enjoying again that caressing diction and literary style that had distinguished the sermons of the original rabbi. Nor was the content of his sermons any more to the taste of the congregation, which Sabbath after Sabbath turned its head to avoid the assault of his crude eloquence.

The weekly sermon was introduced by an inevitable parable. My lips mockingly repeated with him the introductory sentence: "In order to understand the full significance of the text, ma friends, I shall relate the following parable." If he says "ma friends" once again, I thought, or relates another parable, I won't be able to endure it, and I set about mentally seeking ways and means of discovering the source from which he drew his endless supply, that I might

24

possess myself of it. I would destroy it, I told myself, and derived malicious comfort from my mental picture of a distracted rabbi in black silk gown and velvet cap floundering among troubled waters in search of a lost parable.

We accorded to the Hirshes a reluctant social recognition, feeling that their invasion lowered the tone of the block. We stopped at their step occasionally for a word of conversation with Blooma or Eva, then hurried away on an errand. Deborah, the third daughter, kept within doors, practicing scales. Through an open window her rich contralto boomed. She was fresh and free and I should have liked to know her.

Eva, the second daughter, was less truculent than her older sister; Eva dreamed. Even at the foot of the steps, where she stood, full blown, roses coloring her creamy skin, she dreamed. Her hazel eyes moved from the avenue to 916 O'Farrell and back again in pleasing remembrance. Oscar Lessing, eldest son of the fat Mrs. Lessing, coming down the steps of 916, flushed at sight of her and lost a step in his flight toward town. Eva confided to Polly that she did not know what to do about Oscar Lessing.

"He seems to like you," Polly said.

"He's drunk with love of me," said Eva.

"Do you like him?" Polly asked her.

"No," Eva said sorrowfully, "I cannot reciprocate."

Blooma, the oldest daughter, shared none of the intoxicating charm of Eva.

"You're lucky," she said to Polly reproachfully at one of their encounters at Hink's, the grocer at the corner. "You've got money and can marry anyone you want. What chance have I got?"

The chance presented itself sooner than she hoped and in a fashion so dramatic that it shook the street. Out of the nowhere in material time and space, like the visitation of a fairy queen, an unknown woman and her son appeared in our city. She was tall, still youthful looking in spite of great corpulence and, above all, genial. She displayed every outward sign of wealth: carriage, coachman, footman. Even on the street she glittered in satin and precious stone. I thought that the slender young son, not yet thirty, had the ease and reserve which, to my mind, told of Gentile contacts of a high order.

Mrs. Frances Goldberg speedily gained a reputation for generosity. The president of Sherith Israel to whom she brought letters of introduction melted before her contributions to the activities of the synagogue. Donations, so generous as to be miraculous, followed, each unheralded and spontaneous, each presented with shy coquetry, a gesture extracted from a child's game of good fairy. Unpredictably the gifts fell upon members of the synagogue. Soon the Hirshes were marked as objects for that lavish giving. Mrs. Goldberg became a frequent guest of the Hirshes, who strained the salary of the rabbi in lavish entertainment. It was a good risk, Mother said, for Theodore Goldberg, the young man, showed a visible tenderness for Blooma, until the street glowed with romantic anticipation.

Now I wished that we had been more intimate with the Hirshes. We regretted our aloofness, and questioned our exclusiveness as excessive. They must have something we had overlooked to attract these widely traveled visitors. The swing of carriages to and from 912, the arrival of huge bouquets from the florist, and boxes of candy held fast beneath the arm of the young suitor reduced Mother's earlier convictions. Mother was obviously disturbed.

"You're sorry now, aren't you," I asked her, "that we did not invite them to our house?"

"Mind your own business," Mother said.

Mrs. Goldberg and her son no longer came alone. Conrad Sweitzer, the handsome bachelor, accompanied them on her visits. He accompanied her everywhere. Her approval of him was open for everyone to see. Her black eyes waved curly lashes at him, encouraging him to greater intimacy. He helped her carefully up the steps.

"You'd think she wasn't able to walk alone," Mother said. People said that it would be a fine thing for Sweitzer, whose haberdashery needed expansion.

Then, just as we were feeling justified in expecting the announcement of two betrothals, romantic hopes and prophecies were brought to a sudden end.

One early morning the San Francisco *Chronicle* published photographs of Frances Goldberg and Theodore. They had been arrested for trying to swindle Joseph Magnus out of $5,000. Investigation disclosed that Mrs. Goldberg was none other than "Big

Bertha," nationally known "confidence queen," and that Theodore was her lover and accomplice. Why they had come to San Francisco, what they had hoped for among the modest members of Sherith Israel (neither was Jewish), we never learned. They had come out of the unknown to which, after a short trial, they returned.

"You never get into trouble," Blooma Hirsh said in harsh reproach to Polly, and gave a bitter laugh. "You Levys are always lucky."

Polly did not answer. She was not interested. What had the Levys in common with the Hirshes?

Deborah, the third daughter of the rabbi, traveled alone. By some mental twist she detached herself from her family. Step by step she improved her social position. About the house she moved disheveled, as if newly risen from bed, as if she found neither person nor circumstance worth the effort of adornment. In spite of a neglected appearance, however, she gave an impression of personality in abeyance ready to blossom. Blue-green eyes framed in black lashes leaped from the dark skin of her face. When she shook her heavy, tousled, short black hair and walked away without a backward glance, I wanted to follow her. What friendships she made she fostered on the outside and brought no one home. She sang. Every morning her deep contralto rolled out like smoke through the open parlor window. No one told us that a wealthy woman was providing singing lessons for Deborah, nor that her interest was great enough to send her to New York later. When we heard of her again she was in Paris, still cultivating her voice. Then came news of her marriage to a Frenchman. Later still, she was living in London married to an Englishman of affluence, a Mr. Orton. When the rabbi's tenure of office expired, he secured a post in an eastern city. The Hirshes drifted from O'Farrell Street like a dark cloud. They moved eastward, and returned no more.

"Everybody's stuck up in this place," Blooma charged the city in parting. "I'll be glad to shake the dust of this place from my feet." She scowled at the next block toward the inaccessible solidity of Browns and Friedenthals.

Years later I was present at a dinner of the Round Table, a group of local women interested in letters. All had written books or contributed to literary magazines. We met once a month at the St. Francis Hotel, dined, and discussed a recent book or play. This evening was to be given to a new novel by Mrs. Humphry Ward. Mrs. Duncan, beautiful wife of the editor and publisher of our evening paper, was chairman of the discussion. I was late for dinner and hurried to the dressing room to leave my wrap. I thought the room empty, but as I sat at the dressing table I saw reflected in the mirror a tall, dark woman. She wore a beautiful low, square-necked gown of black velvet and a toque and muff of chinchilla. Swift recognition lifted me from my chair.

"Deborah Hirsh!" I exclaimed. "It can't be true."

"Harriet Levy!" came the answer with equal surprise and pleasure. Breathlessly she poured out her history since she had left O'Farrell Street, punctuating the story with the old contagious laugh. What was she doing here tonight? She had come with our chairman whose house guest she was. We would see each other again after dinner. I must tell her everything.

At the table she retained her toque and muff, withdrawing a white-gloved hand to manipulate a knife or fork, or to straighten the string of pearls around her neck. She was a stunning worldly looking figure in contrast to the simply gowned members of the club. Her reddened lips and rouged cheeks dulled the complexion of the other women just as the richness and smart cut of her clothes reduced their style. During the dinner she took no part in the conversation, remaining a silent, handsome spectator. From time to time Mrs. Duncan sent her a reassuring smile across the table.

With the dessert Mrs. Duncan took up for discussion Mrs. Humphry Ward's novel, *Lady Rose's Daughter*. In the story, Julie, illegitimate daughter of Lady Rose and Lord Chantrey, has established a strong social position for herself as companion of Lady Henry. Julie's cleverness and talent for diplomacy win her a power exceeding that of her employer. She furthers the ambition of a handsome young officer, with whom she passionately falls in love. He returns her love, but is already plighted to a young English girl whose delicate health makes a severance of his pledge impossible. An important service calls him to Africa; that completed, he will go to India to marry. Three days remain before his final departure. He

28

entreats Julie to spend these days with him in France. She agrees to meet him outside of Paris.

"An impossible situation," declared Mrs. Duncan with the cold finality of her habitual impassivity. "No spinster could possibly entertain such passionate feelings, or consent to such a proposal. A preposterous situation."

Either hesitation to confess a contrary personal conviction, or reluctance to question the authority of the chairman restrained the audience from voicing an opposing opinion. Only from the direction of the dinner guest came a low gulp quickly appeased by a swallow of ice water.

Mrs. Duncan continued at length to develop her theme which, in some way, led to Bernard Shaw and to *Mrs. Warren's Profession*.

"You know *Mrs. Warren's Profession*," said Mrs. Duncan.

It was not so long ago that the play had dislocated our conventional thinking. Now we turned our faces to express a sober, impersonal interest in a case history.

"Do we know *Mrs. Warren's Profession?*" Like a challenge the voice of Mrs. Orton of London rang out, calling the whole table to bear witness. "Do we know *Mrs. Warren's Profession?*" she called, separating each word from its neighbor, savoring the content. She laughed richly, happily taking all the women into her intimacy. Now she was at ease. Literary or not literary, here was something that they all knew together. She laughed contagiously and a white-gloved hand slapped the air repeatedly, indicating a knowledge too deliciously indiscreet for words. *"Mrs. Warren's Profession!* Oh la-la-la!"

A silence followed upon her joyful release and sober eyes under shadowing lids, moving toward Mrs. Duncan, disclaimed the torrid sophistication of her guest. After a little the customary quiet of good breeding descended upon the Round Table and continued until the end of the evening.

Once again in the dressing room I met and spoke to my old neighbor. Once again we chanced to be alone. She would be in San Francisco many weeks, and we agreed to meet soon. I would have to tell her about everything and everybody.

"To think of seeing Harriet Levy in this unexpected place," she said.

"To think of seeing Deborah Hirsh again after all these years," I answered.

She laughed gaily. "Once Deborah Hirsh, now Mrs. Orton of London, in the literary set."

If her gown had not touched the floor, I would have sworn that I had seen a satin-slippered foot lift itself and flick back in a kick of delight.

A few nights later Mrs. Duncan stopped me at a reception.

"Something has been puzzling me," she said. "The other night at the Round Table I thought that Mrs. Orton was not a complete stranger to you, that you had met her before."

I waited.

"I asked her if she had known you and she said that, often on her travels, people mistook her for people whom they had known."

"Mistakes do happen," I said.

"I was mistaken then?"

"Surely."

It was a close call for Deborah Hirsh, but I couldn't betray her to this woman whose guest she was. Perhaps the magnitude of her audacity paralyzed me. Perhaps I was ashamed for her. Later I wondered why she had not had more confidence in me, why she had not said to me, "Don't give me away, Harriet darling. Don't tell them that I was a nobody on O'Farrell Street," trusting to my generosity. After the Round Table dinner I saw her name in the social columns of the papers, a guest at the great houses of the city and peninsula. I followed her history through successive marriages, but I never met her again.

I did not regret my forbearance, but I did believe that I merited some requital. When the Spreckles and the Crockers drove her about, showing her the sights of San Francisco, Golden Gate Park, and the Cliff House, I should have liked to have been one of them. When they stood on the shore of the ocean, waving toward the Seal Rocks for her surprised appreciation, it would have given me pleasure to have exchanged a wink with somebody, even a seal.

The death of Hannah, her oldest daughter, was a double sorrow to the *dicke* (fat) Mrs. Lessing. Parties were the passion of Mrs. Lessing. She loved to give a party as much as her friends loved to come to one of them. Whatever the variation in food, she loved to watch them eat. Roularda, that roll of smoked beef with its outer layer of fat, was a certainty. Mrs. Lessing, standing with the huge loaf of rye bread held close against her heavy bosom, cut thick slices toward her body as fast as her guests possessed themselves of slices of smoked meat. They might hope, too, for boobas, little buttered rolls of sweet dough filled with raisins and almonds, baked to a shiny brown crust. There was always dancing.

Now, four Sundays had gone by since the death of Hannah, and there had been no party at 916. No capacity for self-denial had been cultivated by the *dicke* Mrs. Lessing, and she could not endure the quiet living. One month after the burial of poor Hannah, she invited everybody to a party at her home.

We did not know what to do about it. We were shocked. We spoke to friends. They were shocked, too. There was no question of their going. But how decline the invitation without betraying our indignation? Custom had provided no standard of behavior for such a situation.

"It would be different had she waited two months," Mother said.

"Even six weeks," said Father.

It was only to a gathering in the neighborhood to which a whole family was invited that I could hope to be asked. I wished that the *dicke* Mrs. Lessing had not been in so great a hurry. It would have been fun to go. It would have been doubly interesting, I continued, stretching out the possibilities of the subject, it would have been particularly interesting because this party would be different. It would be a little like the anniversary of a funeral. One would be feeling different things at the same time. One would be feeling happy and sad at once. It was because everybody thought of the party in terms of the funeral that they knew they could not go. Only yesterday, as it were, we had sent floral pieces to the grave of Hannah.

In a wave of maternal sympathy Mother had purchased the expensive "Gates Ajar," made of white stock, that had risen so imposingly at the head of the coffin. The "Rest in Peace" scroll of white carnations, lettered with purple immortelles, was as fresh to our minds as it had been the day it accompanied Hannah to the cemetery. No, no one with respect for himself could go to that party.

31

Could Hannah, I asked myself, lying out there dead, alone, rest in peace with her friends forgetting her so soon? It was unthinkable, and mentally I wrote to Mrs. Lessing, courteously explaining that a previous engagement prevented our family from accepting her very kind invitation, almost adding "to the party for your departed daughter."

Later in the day I wondered if, after all, it would not be possible to go to the party, preserving a proper separate feeling for the dead and for the living. For example, could one not go, only partially surrendering oneself to pleasure, while maintaining sadness or a wistfulness that would communicate to others the understanding that, although one seemed to be completely present at the party, a section of one's thoughts was really far away in the cemetery (The Hills of Eternity) with Hannah. I could even envisage the facial expression appropriate for so complex a feeling. Opening the door even further to possibilities, the suggestion quickly followed that we need not wear bright colors, not red or yellow or pink, but subdued hues suggestive of a tempered gaiety. No one shared my urge to joy. A conviction, strengthened by unanimity, established itself that it would be clearly unseemly—"indecent" said Mrs. Bowman— to lend our presence to the Lessing party. The subject was dismissed, ended for good.

Early next day, in a fierce swing back from that decision, as if afraid of being taken too hastily at his word, everyone accepted the invitation to the party.

Everyone went—the neighbors and everyone else who had been invited. It was a fine party, waltzes and games, roularda and boobas. No one had ever had a better time at the Lessings'. Never once did I remember to think of poor Hannah. I forgot her completely. Not only that but, after that evening, people forgot to speak of her. The party had extinguished her for good. Perhaps so much discussion had exhausted her claim to further consideration; at any rate, there she was, deposited into eternity, much deader than she had been after her burial.

Only Mrs. Lessing remembered her. At rare moments, hesitating between the persuasion of a raisin ring and a filled coffee cake, she would sigh softly and confide to a visitor, "My poor Hannah loved filled coffee cake."

Mabel, the second daughter of the *dicke* Mrs. Lessing, married young. Unlike Hannah, who had been pale in spirit as in complexion, Mabel reflected the richness and ample friendliness of her mother. She had the same inviting smile for everyone, tradesmen as well as guests. One felt neither aggression nor resistance in her; rather an imperceptible giving to friendly advance, a good-natured, lovable girl. Mabel was without accomplishment in parlor or kitchen. She could sing a little and play the piano a little, but had not received the serious musical instruction which later enticed her younger sister to offer herself as a teacher of piano.

Before Mabel was thirty her husband died, and Mabel left without means of support, returned to her old home.

"What will Mabel do?" Mother asked Father.

"What does a woman do who can do nothing?" Father answered. They talked often of Mabel in terms of her lack of income, and decided that she must be drawing from a life insurance. Then Father learned from Mr. Lessing that there had been no life insurance. This again opened the subject of the source of her living, for Mabel dressed well and maintained a good standard of well-being.

One day a woman called at our door and asked to see Mme. Sybilla. We explained that no one of that name lived at 920. She apologized for her mistake, she thought that our number was 916. But even at 916 there is nobody of that name, we told her.

"But there is," the woman protested and showed us a card on which was printed:

MME. SYBILLA
CLAIRVOYANT
916 O'FARRELL STREET

On the instant, by some clairvoyance of our own, a shaft of understanding pierced old conjecturing and we knew that Mme. Sybilla was Mabel Lessing, that it must be Mabel. That it could not be true altered nothing; we knew it was true.

"What does that word mean?" Mother asked, and we understood she was mentally pointing to the word "clairvoyant" on the card.

Polly explained.

"You mean a fortuneteller?" Mother demanded, looking from one daughter to another, while she mentally bound a red bandanna around Mabel's head and hung necklaces of brass and bone around her neck.

"Not exactly," Polly said.

"A *schöne Geschichte* [a fine story]!" Mother said but, thinking of the *dicke* Mrs. Lessing relieved of the support of a widowed daughter, she spoke without full conviction.

Our minds were scattered; protest, condemnation lost themselves in astonishment and the accusation "impostor" died upon our lips, dissolved even before it was framed into admiration for this ingenuity that had burst the limits of explored, familiar employment, and pioneered a profession in the transcendental.

We did not really think in those terms, having never heard of the transcendental. What silenced criticism was wonder that anyone we knew, least of all the placid Mabel (the *"dumme* Mabel" Mother called her), should have discovered this completely fresh way of earning a living.

Later, astonishment cooled before accomplished fact and, as strange Gentile customers continued to mount the steps of 916, we grew to respect the woman who had met the exigencies of widowhood in so original a fashion and had established herself independent of her parents.

No stigma attached itself to Mabel, that kindly soul, nor to a profession which, once assumed by her, took on the dignity of her sweetness and sincerity. The name itself, "Mme. Sybilla," inspired respect from being printed on a card. It was a reassuring name, awaking confidence. No stigma attached itself to the name or to the profession as it held none for the seeress herself, who doubtless, in all sincerity, based her predictions upon a textbook which, to her thinking, invested them with authority.

In the beginning we threatened to call at 916 and ask for Mme. Sybilla and a reading of our future destiny, but we could not do it, reluctant to embarrass so gentle a woman. As time went on she acquired a validity. When I met her on the street, well-gowned and smartly booted, a figured veil descending from her broad-brimmed sailor hat, a piquancy added itself to her personality by the realization that, once in her home, she became Mme. Sybilla whom people consulted for advice and for whose wisdom they paid money.

We felt confident that her divination would carry no hurt to the seekers of light, that her native softness of heart would palliate destiny and substitute for catastrophe a gentler prediction, leaving fulfillment to a co-operating Providence.

As she walked down O'Farrell Street, her gentle rhythmic sway reproducing the deep nautical waddle of her mother, hearts went out to her, wishing her well.

"Business good?" Father asked not altogether in irony.

"Very good," Mabel answered, smiling up at him warmly.

What ended her pleasant calling we never learned; we knew only that, shortly before the S.S. Lessings left San Francisco to take up their lives in southern California around the opening real estate business of their son Oscar, the mystical sign was removed from the door of 916. Customers were turned away.

Some people said Mabel had made enough money to retire, others darkly spoke of licenses and investigations. Whatever the truth, the Lessings moved away and we were left to experience how dull a street can be without its personal clairvoyant.

# 3

# *Bins and Babies*

In the home of a good housekeeper every object had its place by classification almost divine. Similar order governed the arrangement of the mind. Bins, black and white, received and designated the foreign idea; discrimination was ability to recognize the bin in which it properly belonged. Once in the bin an idea, and he who held it, remained classified forever, unless ejected by social revolution. A black bin and a white bin housed all normal types. The unclassifiable, representing any deviation from the norm, which was O'Farrell Street, was a "nut." Between nut and nut neither curiosity nor justice paused to differentiate. A new sensation and the stimulus to it were tossed into the basket reserved for the unfamiliar. Judgment was simple!

Jacob Blum married Theresa, his second wife, six months after poor Sophie passed away. Was he wrong, was he right? Every intelligent person must have a conviction. Which bin for Jacob Blum? Decision presented no difficulty. Each man only had to ask himself, "What would I have done in Jacob's place?" and he had the answer.

"Perfectly right," said Jonas Frank. "In Jacob's place I would want my daughters to have a mother. Theresa is a good daughter, and a good daughter makes a good wife and a good mother."

Into the white bin went Jacob.

Opposition failed to confuse. "Jacob Blum ought to be ashamed of himself," declared Ernestine Hart, sister of the departed wife. "Poor Sophie not yet cold in her grave and he must go a-courting." The added insinuation that Jacob had been awaiting his chance disturbed no one. The black bin was there to receive mean tongues. You were right or you were wrong, you were good or you were bad; a good woman or a "fancy lady," a truth-teller or a liar. Each wore the insigne of his moral status. You read, you knew, and there he was, and there you were.

Mrs. Ostroski told Mother that she had paid $20 for her winter bonnet. Mother saw the same hat in Coughlin's window, went in and priced it, to learn that it cost only $15. Mrs. Ostroski was catalogued. No further analysis was necessary. Ostroski—liar; that was finished. Judgment was simple!

To a resident of O'Farrell Street three choices of expression offered themselves to communicate the pregnancy of legal motherhood. The young woman was "expecting," or she was "expecting an addition," or she was "in an interesting condition." The unwed had no choice but to be "in trouble."

Illegitimacy, as a word, was reserved for royal pedigree. O'Farrell Street did not know it. The bastard in the house of royalty might find his way cozily among rightful heirs, even striking out boldly to possess a throne. On O'Farrell Street the illegitimate child lodged upon no family tree. Mothered by a girl "in trouble," he created a hole into which he vanished.

When Trouble came to a family among our relatives or friends (I saw it descend with black wings outstretched like a raven), I sought enlightenment in a novel, my only reference library for illicit love. From a story of Ouida I might learn that, just as the married daughter divulged her expectation to an applauding parent, so the unwedded girl concealed her condition until detected by her mother; then it became her plight. A plight was hidden from father and brother. Discovered, the father and brother of a girl "in trouble" pursued one of two courses: they forced the scoundrel to marry the girl at the point of a pistol, or shot him down like a dog.

Among our acquaintances the scoundrel always must have accepted marriage as the more agreeable alternative, for no man we knew had ever been shot down like a dog. If he found safety in flight, or was a married man, the male relative of the girl glowered in futile rage, while the mother whisked the daughter away to some secret seclusion.

37

I knew of only one woman, a Gentile, who had experienced a shot-gun marriage; she also had undergone a subsequent divorce. I thought that I read in her eyes the desolation of her double tragedy until, suddenly, she carried the little minister of her church away from his pulpit and secured him, unfrocked as he was, in lawful wedlock.

To a vacation in the country, taken alone by a daughter of a family during any but the summer months, the brow lifted incredu-lously. Attention would surely have been directed upon the sudden departure of the handsome married Austrian boarder from the par-lor bedroom of the Heinemans' had anyone realized significance in its coincidence with the vacation of the pretty sixteen-year-old daughter of the house. My suspicion of something dubious in that sudden leaving was founded upon a sharp cessation of conversa-tion between my parents upon my entrance into Mother's bedroom. The Heinemans had sent for Mother, I gathered. They were in trouble. Secret trouble in their home I translated into a shadowed tangle to the unraveling of which Mother had been beckoned as into a darkened alcove, a black curtain falling behind her. Conjec-ture was useless. Mother would carry the secret beyond the grave. Olga Heineman was going to Stockton on a vacation, Mother told me, her negating profile forbidding further questioning.

My imagination stirred. Set deep within a walled garden, in a thinly peopled countryside, I pictured a large double house, painted gray, screened behind a growth of eucalyptus trees; doors flung sud-denly open to receive a trembling girl, rushed there behind fast-flying horses. I knew that Olga's vacation would be mentioned by no one; that the silence which would follow her return would be as a huge blot, obliterating a page of her history; that, within six months of her homecoming, my parents would be invited to the marriage cer-emony of Olga to some older man from the north or the south, at present a stranger.

My sister Addie told me, years later, how she had learned of the unhallowed birth from a cousin of the girl. A friend, who had dis-credited the idea of a vacation in the middle of winter, had told the cousin, who had told Addie of the sheltered hospital in the city where the girl had been taken for her confinement, her parents pay-ing her daily visits under cover of night.

"How did she happen to tell?" I asked.

"To get even," Addie said. "You see, one of her own daughters . . ." Addie began, and stopped.

"Not really!" I cried, as shocked as if the characters of the two stories had not been dead for ten years. "Which one? Surely not Minnie?"

But Addie would tell no more; one did not speak evil of the dead.

The procedure for one girl "in trouble" was satisfactorily explained for me by contemporary fiction; but situations arose for which a novel supplied no guide. What happened, for example, when two sisters got into trouble? What about the Friedman girls? What was their relation to each other? Years separated them and their circles of friends. Did they talk frankly to each other of their experiences, or did they retire behind separate silences? Did Mathilda, the matronly older sister, who had been in trouble only once, exchange confidences with Cecelia, who roamed the sidewalks during the late afternoon, a free-lance, hurrying to a rendezvous. People said of Cecelia that she might as well have been included in one of the groups of girls who walked Market Street at that hour, sedately conspicuous, under the eye of the keeper of their house.

The Friedmans constituted a family of tall, frizzled-haired, swarthy-skinned girls, small-waisted, deep-bosomed, all "fine figures of women." The two older girls were lively, buoyant, irresistibly impelled to seek experience. Only the third girl stood anchored within the home. The mother, unequipped for defense, was helpless before the force of the current that swept the two girls from the house out upon the highways. She expostulated to my mother; she had to bear her burden alone, afraid to tell her husband, a man of violence. She lisped her complaint with a deep sigh, ending with the fatalistic, "now I have told you. What is the truth, is the truth, and nothing but the truth" (she called it "troot"), easing her present pain in the cooling abstraction. She knew no peace and was always afraid of some unpredictable scandal. She avoided the town, unable to risk an encounter with the audacious coatless figure of her daughter, hastening along Market Street in open pursuit.

"Both the girls are headed for trouble," she said. "What shall I do when it comes?" she repeatedly asked Mother, and finally answered the question herself. After a short illness she died.

Friends told themselves that, now that the last obstacle was removed, the end of the girls was certain. Resigned to witness the punishment of wickedness deaf to counsel, they awaited, with prophetic sorrow, the descent of the two Friedman girls upon that decline known as "going to the dogs." Sometimes they broke their vigil to tell one another that "the girls had made their beds and must lie upon them." When all heads were bowed in acceptance of the anticipated catastrophe, Mathilda announced her engagement to Sol Paulson of Portland, Oregon, a shoe merchant of excellent standing, whom she had met romantically on an Oakland ferryboat. The small boy bringing the glad tidings added that Mathilda and the prospective groom would be "at home" to their friends on Sunday afternoon of that week.

The feelings of the friends were best expressed by our cousin Flora. "I was nailed, Yetta," said Cousin Flora.

Everybody was nailed. This requital to indiscretion was so lacking in propriety, so disrupting to moral convention, that friends were left inarticulate. When, instead of getting her just deserts, a girl, who was no better than she should be, secured a prosperous husband, how could the disconcerted mind find simple expression?

Again Cousin Flora voiced the collective protest: "Don't say nothing!" said Cousin Flora.

The reception in no way helped to calm the agitation. Far from being a bride-to-be, chastened by a miracle of grace, Mathilda, in a new dress of rose-colored brocaded satin, greeted her guests with infectious laughter, gathering them into the embrace of her happiness until they, too, reflected rejoicing. She extended a handsome diamond ring on her finger, and indicated a pearl brooch on her steel-repressed bosom, while she laughed in comradeship with everybody as one who had enjoyed their uninterrupted confidence over the years.

Everyone was relieved and happy; they wished that poor Mrs. Friedman had lived to see the day. Their bewilderment at the strange trick of Providence was exchanged for satisfaction in the reclamation of Mathilda, whom, they told themselves, they had always liked.

After all, marriage was its own justification. Reflecting the glow of the betrothed, they even surrendered a limp handshake to Cecelia who, gleaming darkly above her dress of sky-blue velvet, moved among them easily in good fellowship. Beside the glowing delinquents the pale composure of the virtuous sister appeared drab, anemic of spirit. Mathilda married and went to live in Portland and was forgotten by her home acquaintances. The agitation, the jar to judgment, subsided, and the divine law of reward and punishment recovered its ancient authority, stabilizing itself as the fresh audacities of Cecelia invited divine attention.

Then Cecelia married.

This time no house-to-house announcement, no Sunday reception, tempered the impact. As the wife of Joe Mulligan, the well-known mining man from Gold Hill, Nevada, Cecelia occupied a suite in the Baldwin Hotel in front of which she had been wont to lope so buoyantly before the "mashers" stationed at the Baldwin Cigar Store. Her manners changed little; as she walked through the lobby of the hotel, from long practice, her eyes still roamed, but her restlessness was purged by affluence into a twinkling benevolence.

Try as she would, no friend of her mother was able to rejoice in the good fortune and rehabilitation of Cecelia. From the window of her plum-colored coupé she bowed to old acquaintances with the cordiality of a prima donna acknowledging the last curtain call before retirement into private life. Fragments of shattered judgment bordered the sidewalks of Van Ness Avenue when Cecelia Mulligan drove by.

At the close of the Yom Kippur service, as we shoved our way step by step up the central aisle toward the exit door, I saw the Harris family coming up the side aisle. They were a group of short, blond boys and girls over whom towered the broad-shouldered figure of the oldest brother, a black-bearded giant, shepherding them as under an enchantment to some distant cave.

"How did he get into that family?" I whispered to Mother.

"Hush," she said. And when I asked her on the street why I shouldn't have inquired about Leopold Harris, she gave no response beyond a frown of annoyance.

Leopold Harris, even by himself, was a strange bird, I thought. But among the family of small-featured, dainty-limbed brothers and sisters, his great height and breadth, his clumsy movements and lumbering gait exaggerated his strangeness into the legendary. He had but to appear in a room for inquiry to form itself in my mind, needing explanation more satisfying than the citing of the Harris family as but another example of the surprising variations among children of the same parents. Surely it was strange, people said, but didn't one see similar differences in other families; wasn't Joe Coleman a musical composer, and his brother a haberdasher?

I was not at ease with Leopold Harris, and retreated before his bulk. If he stood in our parlor he looked like a huge sideboard of unpolished oak, incongruous amid the elegance of our furnishings; but his thick shoulders and great hands and feet intimidated me less than the crude address which snapped our social niceties and kicked aside the fragments. One night he sat beside me in our home. I told him of my longing to go to Alaska. Did I like the sea, he asked, and without waiting for my answer he cried, so loud it was a shout: "I love the sea. I love it more than anything in the world. Every time I see a ship I wish to God that I was on it." I was shaken by his violence, and I told Polly of it.

"He *should* love the sea," she cried. "His father was captain of the ship that brought his mother to San Francisco from the old country."

Polly tossed me the story of the little German girl who came all alone in the early fifties from Hamburg to marry Joe Harris, her German cousin, an earlier immigrant. He had written for her, and paid her passage to San Francisco. Six months after her marriage she bore him a son, Leopold Harris.

"What did Mr. Harris say?" I asked.

Polly was ready with her answer. "He said that he was surprised that a six months' baby could be so strong."

After I knew his story I lost my fear of Leopold Harris. On the bridge of the sailing vessel to which I transplanted him, steering his ship through a wild southern gale, his rough speech became eloquent, his huge bulk commanding.

Of the strangest drama of our circle, the melodramatic story of the girl we had known so intimately over the years, I had no certain knowledge. A suspicion that faintly shadowed an episode of her life, at the time of its occurrence, had been quickly allayed when Mother refused to give ear to it.

Years after the death of our friend the truth was brought to me. It came by accident from someone who believed that I must have known it always. The little girl, whom we had believed to be the younger sister of our friend, was her own child. As I listened and reassembled the events of our friend's life, in the light of this new understanding, I was moved to pity by the realization of the pain she must have carried alone.

How I longed to call her from the dead, to tell her of my sympathy! How I longed to execute judgment upon her child, who had treated her so lovelessly in her loneliness. I would go to her, I told myself. I would shake her ignorance with my knowledge of the truth. I would fling the fact in her face, and find satisfaction in the self-reproach that would never again leave her.

So realistic was the scene of my accusation, as I painted it to myself, that I retreated before my own violence. I knew that this woman would be forever safe. I knew that as she had lived, encased in selfishness in the past, so would her present illness safeguard her against the knowledge which I held, with which I hoped to wound her. I rebelled against the protection which a weak heart gives to its possessor. I never told her. After a while I ceased to want to avenge.

The story concerns people of a distant past. Perhaps a secret, safeguarded for years, ought to be forgotten. Perhaps sanctity binds to secrecy the history of one ghost above another.

Nevertheless, even today I would like to tell her. I would like to call her back to earth from wherever she is and bare the secret to her, on the chance that no one has yet done so.

# 4

# *Mother*

As if the general laws of conduct of the period were not enough to shadow the day, Mother added to them the five books of the Law and all the more recent prohibitions, evolved by the Jewish merchant class to which we belonged. "Thou shalt not" burst from her lips like an anthem and, when her native habit of denial was re-enforced by an equally strong urge to thrift, refusal closed on every enterprise outward bound.

"Can I?" I began.

"No," said Mother. "Now what do you want?" No pleasure was too slight to warrant a refusal.

"Let us pop corn tonight."

"Yes? And get the coal dust over the whole room."

"Then can we make candy?"

"And dirty up the pans?"

"Please let us. Please. We'll clean up everything." Mother's lips pursed, her head turned away, isolating our proposal.

"Let them, Yetta," said Father. "Let the children have a little pleasure." Mother was silent.

"She's not saying 'No,' are you, Mama? We can? Yes." And we ran into the kitchen, for the consent was a pallid one, a "No" in abeyance. We pulled the candy, and it grew cleaner and lighter; we laughed, and called to one another.

"Try a piece, it's fine. Try a piece, Mama."

"Look," said Mother, and pointed to the beads of molasses on my dress; but Father chewed vigorously and declared that he had never eaten better candy in all his life.

When we went into the kitchen to wash the dishes, Mother was already there and had washed them herself. We heard Father as we went upstairs to our bedroom, "Can't you let them have a little innocent pleasure? Why must you always . . ." We did not listen further; we knew the sequence.

What made Mother not want to enjoy anything? What made her not want to be pleased with anything we did? Why wouldn't she give herself a chance to find out if she liked something new? Never the acceptance of a new plan; always, if not a "don't," at least a "why must you?" or "why should you want to?" or "why must my children always . . . ?" We asked one another these questions, not expecting an answer. This was the pattern of our lives which never changed. Parents were as they were. Children did not judge them. They respected and loved them. I did not suspect that Polly was hating, that she was telling herself that Mother was mean, mean, that she was wishing Mother would die.

We saved our birthday money and bought a handsomely draped couch for Father, with an adjustable headboard that could be pulled up as straight as the back of a chair or let down to the level of a couch, a beautiful lounge, draped with dull flowered chenille of terra-cotta plush. Mother was furious when it appeared, because of the price we must have paid for it. She knew it would not wear. She would have returned it then and there, but Father refused to part with it, and rested upon it after lunch for thirty years.

On Mother's birthday she upbraided us because she had not been remembered. Her children had forgotten her, so little consideration did they have for her. Even as she spoke, Maggie Doyle entered behind a huge package and unrolled a white bear rug at Mother's feet. "How's that for a present?" we cried, and we regarded the rug and Mother triumphantly. As Mother looked upon the rug her face softened and her eyes looked pleased. "Save the cord," she said, and we understood the rug was to be returned. We protested that it was not costly, that Father was to share the expense with us. "Don't you like it, isn't it all right?" "Very nice," Mother said. "Save the paper, too." Her hands slipped into her pocket from which came the jingle of keys.

45

Like a jailer, locking, unlocking, Mother habitually moved to a faint click. Ours was a locked house: storm doors, street doors, closets, bureau drawers, all locked. At the end of the dining room, below the glass-enclosed sideboard, were two paneled cupboards; one concealed a crusted silver decanter holding tall slender bottles filled with sherry and port; the other held secrets closer to our hearts' desire, perhaps a cluster of raisins, perhaps a square of coffee cake. To rifle them I had only to remove the top drawer and use the tools of my craft, a long, thin arm arched deep into the cupboard and long, thin fingers tactile for a cake of chocolate or a yellow glazed cookie. Behind the door of the dining-room closet, fastened to safeguard a bowl of nuts or a dish of fresh fruit, lingered always the odor of mice. I hesitated to open it for fear of precipitating the dart of a shadow or of beholding a puff of dark fur, frantic-eyed, seeking escape from a wire trap.

Behind the barred door to her emotions Mother sat, severe, detached, ready with judgment to wing the errant impulse.

"Everything can't be wrong about me. There must be something that is right. Can't you find anything, Yetta?" Father asked, teasing her, but Mother would not answer; nothing had ever been right, or ever would be—least of all Father. That her early background, in the German village of her birth, had been as lowly as that of Father did not appease her reproach of him. She felt herself an aristocrat and she assumed the dignity of the highborn, wearing her double pompadour as a coronet. She did not suspect that Father had married her because he was touched by her unhappiness, her dependence in the home of her married sister, that he had expected to see her bitterness dissolve into grateful tenderness under his kindness, her slender body round into the pleasing plumpness that he so much admired. To his disappointment Mother had remained thin and her bitterness had deepened; for Father, to whom the coronet remained invisible, felt no spur to provide a ducal setting for his bride, but continued to enjoy lively friendships with policemen and streetcar conductors, to acclaim the Democratic party ("Bricklayers," Mother protested), and to alienate men of social importance by his unfailing forthrightness. After every visit together to friends, Mother found fault with Father. Why had he said this? Why had he done that? He never changed. If she pressed his foot beneath the table, he asked—and anyone might hear—"What's wrong now? Why are you stepping on my foot?"

Mother might have created a social environment befitting her tastes had she been willing to spend the money for entertainment, but she could not spend money. *"Mach dich gar nicht wissen* [Make believe you don't know]," she advised us when the birthday of a friend suggested the propriety of a gift, and she was surprised and indignant that we received no invitation to the birthday party. In later years we might have explained to our satisfaction that Mother's denial to us was a staying hand to the onward flow of life at some point where she herself had ceased to live; that her refusals were her revenge upon the destiny that had dethroned her before she had been crowned; but we possessed no psychological yardstick and, if we had, we would not have applied it to our own mother, profaning her. One did not analyze parents, nor make deductions from their actions to throw light upon their characters, not even to point a virtue. We accepted, without analysis, Mother's devotion to German nieces whom she bedecked and unerringly piloted to the marriage canopy, and to nephews whom she housed and educated, whether they came from the valleys or distant mining towns. Albert Michelson, the son of her oldest brother, lived in our house during his high school years. Later, Mother remembered the world-renowned scientist only as the bright, good-looking boy whose boots left marks on her Brussels carpet.

To the call of illness Mother answered like an ambulance and, if the hand that felt my forehead did not linger on my cheek, I was not sensible of a deprivation. I did not wish that I might have had a different mother. I asked only that she should let me have my pleasure without having to work so hard to obtain it. Behind her lips, drawn to conceal the early humiliation of teeth not her own, waited for obstruction an infinite succession of "Nos."

Before her refusals, which came like reports, Addie, too gentle for opposition, ebbed noiselessly. Polly retreated, spitting accusation. She resented being called back for admonition, being scolded upon her return from a party. She protested that there had never been a time when she had not been unhappy at home, from the days when, anticipating her growth, she had been made to wear muslin underdrawers two sizes too large for her, to the age when every swift impulse to pleasure was held up by Mother's opposition.

"Leo asked me to go to the New Year's party," Polly opened coquettishly in the hope that God had rearranged the order of the stars.

"No girl goes to a party alone with a man," Mother said. "She goes with her brother, you know that."

"But suppose she hasn't a brother?"

"Then she is unfortunate," Mother said, and the stars continued in their eternal pattern.

"Julia Arthur opens at the Baldwin Theater Monday night," Polly tried again another day. "Robert asked me to go."

"Since when does a girl go to the theater with a man, like a servant? Let her go with some girl friend and her brother."

"But no girl with a brother has asked me."

"Don't bother me," closed the argument.

When Polly went to a party with a group, Mother called after her, "Be sure to stay with the others." To which Polly answered with lowered lids, promising nothing.

"It's very queer," Polly would say. "I can't go to a party with a man, yet I am supposed to have an escort to take me home."

"That's entirely different."

"Why is it different?"

"*Man muss manches Menschenwegen thun* [One has to do much for the sake of people]." Against the pronouncement of "*Menschenwegen*" there was no appeal.

Summer vacations aggravated the friction. Every summer we were taken to the mountains to drink the waters of some medicinal spring. An hour ahead of schedule Father, in gray alpaca duster and broad-brimmed, rolled Panama, gathered the family at the ferry gate. We wore our shabbiest clothes as correct for travel. We were all possessed of unimpaired digestion, but Father relished the easy sociability of the springs and, once there, felt it would be wasteful not to profit by medication offered free to guests. Water, potent to cure the disordered stomach, must surely be able to prevent trouble, he reasoned, and he forthwith established a rigorous regime for himself and his family, drank deeply and often, and returned home enthusiastic and sunburned, declaring that he had never felt better, forgetting that he had never felt worse. The following year we would seek new waters and lay the family kidneys upon the altar of his radiant faith.

We, too, however, enjoyed the life at the springs. Neither intense heat nor poor housing (sometimes a cow; sometimes a pig walked through our cottage) could affect the romantic opportunities of a summer resort where stranger guests were closed in for a month; where the spring itself offered excuse for those frequent meetings, which provided a stimulus equally strong, if not identical, to mother and daughter. Every disappearance beyond the field of vision of the veranda of our cottage was an occasion for irritation, and Polly, drawing all men to her and habitually lost to view, precipitated daily collisions.

"I suppose you would like me to sit on the veranda all day and crochet?"

"It wouldn't do you any harm if you did."

Every night there was a fresh engagement. Mother could not understand her daughter; Polly was a wayward girl with strange impulses. Every night she must go out for a walk over the trail or along the creek and always with a young man. Sometimes she would have the young man ask permission of Mother, knowing that she would not refuse a stranger. Then Mother kept her resentment warm for Polly's return.

"*Schöne Geschichte* [A fine business]." "Going out into the woods at night! You are spoiling my summer."

"But it's moonlight. Would you expect me to go to bed on a night like this?"

"Haven't you a father to take you out walking if you have to go out walking?"

"You know it's not the same."

"Why isn't it?"

"Oh well," said Polly, "What's the use?"

"What do you think that young man thinks of you?" began Mother anew. "Staying out with him until ten o'clock at night?"

Polly did not answer. The young man had just told her. She was tired of trying to please Mother who did not want to be pleased, whose eyes looked their disapproval. From the way Polly looked at him any man could tell she liked him, Mother said.

"A girl has feelings," Polly objected.

"Feelings! A girl has self-respect, she controls her feelings. Does Addie want to fly about the mountains at night with strange men? All girls can have the quiet dignity of Addie. *Man muss manches Menschenwegen thun!*" Mother added, and Polly, flicked by the phrase, retorted that her reputation would have to take care of itself.

In a world where variation was perversity, nothing short of immolation could maintain reputation intact. A slight deviation from the norm, which was O'Farrell Street, a collar rolled back exposing a triangle of throat to the daylight, revealed its wearer to Mother as an eccentric; a broader step to the left and a girl's honor fell from her like a loosely buttoned petticoat.

So had Etta Kahn forfeited her good name, though I could detect no outer sign of loss. Her costume continued to possess the same incomparable smartness, and some legerdemain made a provocation of the tiny handkerchief twisted into the slit of a pocket on her basque. When her brown eyes rolled drolly and her laughter ran a scale, she continued to be irresistible. That the color of her cheeks was not natural had been unsuspected until the early morning when fat Mrs. Lessing waddled into our house with the disclosure that Etta had emerged from the pool, over in the Alameda baths, with cheeks that were not alone colorless, but yellow. "*Gelb,* Mrs. Levy."

"Paint! *Das auch noch* [That, too]!" cried Mother.

Early rumors rushed forward to strengthen dark suspicions, and Polly was forcibly withdrawn from the peril of that companionship.

And was not the fat Mrs. Lessing right? Did not the years prove her wisdom? Did not Etta Kahn go on the stage and become an actress? And what was an actress but a "fancy woman"? Mother, remembering Polly's irrepressible spirits, even madder than the gaiety of Etta, her moving contralto and rollicking mimicry, recalling Polly's pleading to become a comic-opera singer, thanked God for the escape.

When Mother spoke of it, reputation acquired substance. No girl with self-respect, said Mother, would enter a restaurant with a man. She could not do so without losing her reputation. I saw reputation like a coat left hanging behind in a restaurant corridor. If the restaurant were French, it was irrecoverable. By their opaque curtains "French restaurants" could be distinguished from other dining places. You could not see into them as you passed, however hard you tried to find a slit in the curtained windows; but if the street door chanced to open as you went by and you looked sharply, you might catch sight of a waiter with a tray held high above his head, stopping to knock at one of a sequence of doors along the aisle. Private rooms! The heart thumped at the name. Mother never made mention of French restaurants without excitement, speaking of them in the same high voice that she used when she spoke of "houses."

"My husband saw her at the Poodle Dog," a woman said of a girl we knew.

"At night?" Mother asked sharply.

"No, at lunch."

"Not with . . . ?"

"With!"

"In a private room?"

"In the main dining room."

"Bad enough." She had compromised herself, become shady, was no longer fit for association with Addie and Polly, and other pure girls of spotless reputation.

Under the menace of *"Menschenwegen"* we were shepherded into a social security. But our safety was precarious. Even conversation offered its peril. We tiptoed among the authors we had read: Dickens, Scott, Thackeray, George Eliot; we might discuss without hazard, even with pride, and confess lighter literature with smiling apology, entreating indulgence for a reader who fed normally on the classics. Thus we drew a novel of the Duchess from behind our back, laughingly admitting our audacity; but *Camille* was savored only behind the locked toilet door.

Illness was a misdemeanor, a stigma to be defended as we screened a false tooth. To a few temporary disorders Mother raised the bar; a sore throat, a headache, an upset stomach, even mumps we might divulge without diminution of matrimonial asset; but the ear listened stethoscopically to the protracted cough—consumption! And anemia, like an unsanctioned pregnancy, was whisked away to a country farm. A dormant instinct, ancient as the race, stirred to warn the debutante against disclosure of the demented second cousin or the great-uncle's suicide. A man wanted a sound wife, Mother said, and it was well that health should announce itself in a high color and a full figure.

Curious stories were sometimes told. When Frieda Lowenthal married Rothschild, the wealthy shoe merchant, people said, in commenting upon the short engagement, that Mrs. Lowenthal had never left Frieda, her daughter, alone with her betrothed, but had remained in the room alert for conversation, so that it was not until after the wedding that Rothschild discovered his wife's deafness. The story strained credulity without destroying it.

Conversation skirted many sections of the body denied recognition by a sparse vocabulary.

"When you have cramps," I asked Mother, "where do you say that you have them?"

"Why do you have to tell that you have got them?"

"But suppose you did? You can never tell."

"Say stomach," Mother said.

"But stomach isn't where I get them. I never get pains in my stomach. I have cramps."

"Say stomach anyway," Mother commanded, and the area of the stomach broadened to distant circumferences. But when the vegetable man, arriving an hour late, his hand upon his abdomen, referred his delay to an awful bellyache, Mother put up no restraining hand, condoning the localization as seemly for the working class.

By the withdrawal of her sanction, other areas of the body were excluded from reality. Neither the form nor the fullness of the bosom counted in my estimate of beauty, though I knew in a hidden way that they entered into the fine figure of a woman that was Mother's praise of Polly. There were screened references and, when the details of an evening party were relived, I observed how Mother drew in her breath, or bit her lower lip, or closed her eyes to the rapid shake of her head, and I caught the murmur, "Much too low." The swell of the bosom overflowing the restrictions of the corsage— once only did I behold that.

52

On the opening night of the opera a tall, dark, foreign-looking woman entered a stage box accompanied by two men. The murmur of her name spread as she appeared, reviving rumors of dishes of gold and a day couch of white velvet. She rested a moment, leaning back in her chair, and my opera glasses and those of the audience fastened upon her. Then she unclasped the chinchilla collar of her cape and slowly motioned back the drapery of the flame-colored velvet. My glasses and my eyes swerved from the sight. Never, not even upon the stage, had I looked upon anything so staggering, so undisguised, so deep, so sudden, heaped up and rolling over the balcony of a corsage. I awaited the repercussion, fearing that the audience might hiss its consternation and that I should have to suffer the picture of a closely wrapped figure with bowed head moving against the wall out of the theater into the street. My sensitive ears, self-shielded for the shock, relaxed only when the curtain rose and *L'Africaine* unfolded before a composed audience that made no betrayal of a shattering experience.

"What do you expect?" Mother said next morning. "A French-woman!"

After the revealment of that night, the bosom again subsided from consciousness until the night, years later, when I attended my first formal dance—for days a heart-stirring experience because of my dress, the apple-green-and-white brocaded satin that had been Mother's wedding dress. A polonaise opened in front over a heavy ribbed, white satin skirt and swept behind from the bouffant below the waist over a long train, accentuated in weight and flair by a pleated ruching of crinoline. The pointed bodice, buttoned down the front with glass buttons, was high at the neck with a small V in front; close-fitting sleeves ended at the elbow with a frill of real duchess lace.

So grand a costume, I felt, must be unique at any ball. The high neck and elbow sleeves I accepted as I did the meagerness which they covered. Plump arms, no sleeves; thin arms, long sleeves; a simple rule no more important than the high neck appropriate to the thin shoulder blades ("hatchets," Mother called them) which it covered. As my long arms disappeared beneath my cape, Mother expressed the wish that she might lend me her arms. "Pipestems," she called mine. I laughed in agreement and hastened to my first ball with untroubled heart.

In a room where a maid received me I removed my warm wrap and waited. A tall, large girl entered and seemed to me to fill the room. She may have been two or three years older than I, but years alone did not explain my sudden disquieting sense of her completeness. A wrap of many layers of thin material added to her amplitude. Her head, topped by blond waves and curls, was carried on a full, long throat, and when she lifted the floating mantle I looked upon a breadth of flushed flesh, large arms, and a bosom so white, so round; pink, soft, beautiful flesh, a magnificent area of body. Suddenly I knew that this was beauty; this robust nakedness was not only health into which Mother had translated it, but beauty. Why had no one told me? Free of Mother, I was seeing with my own eyes. I was frightened and exhilarated.

The girl left the room, the strength of her loveliness drawing me after her. She walked down the steps like an empress. I followed, shaken, shaken now by something besides the shock of the discovery. A new uneasiness crept into my consciousness; a concern which clung to me during the party and lingered with me when I returned home. Mother was up to receive me. I tried to tell her of the beautiful girl, but under her eyes my confidence left me. Alone in bed, nothing of the glory was left to me, only the deepening suspicion of my own inadequacy. The sharp shoulder blades, "hatchets," had cut their way into consciousness.

Years and experience did not help to overcome the early feeling of inadequacy, and deep into middle age I continued to meet men with a barrier of conversation meant to divert, so that they might not approach closely and become aware of the thin arms and the hollows in my neck, long since covered with redundant flesh.

Mother's store of criticism never exhausted itself. We all feared her, for we knew that she was not feeling with us. She did not laugh with us, and her barbed humor was not our humor. I never placed my hand in hers nor sought encouragement in her eyes. If, at dinner, I recounted some jolly happening, my ardor passed from Father to Addie over the sober face that gave no echo to my enjoyment. If we were gay, by ourselves, laughing at improvised nonsense, she had only to enter the room and remark, *"Tanz allein, spiel allein* [Dance alone, play alone]," and a full-blown fancy collapsed; we should have been laughing with friends of the best social circles.

In the evening, when we were gathered cozily in the music room, listening to Addie singing, Mother sat alert on the edge of her chair, as if alighting between occupations, as if slices of salmon were waiting on the kitchen table to be salted for the morrow. Age did not lower Mother's resistance which, with the years, acquired a surface tranquility more and more impervious to the penetration of a new proposal. Before a distasteful invasion her face spread to vagueness and her eyes glazed into retirement.

When Mother saw Addie lured into the enclosure of Christian Science, she met the new challenge without visible animosity. Addie, whose faith exceeded her works, was eager to convert the family. She explained Christian Science to Mother as the modern dress of Mother's own familiar faith. Tactfully she kept to the Old Testament, gradually approaching the New through familiar promise from psalmist and prophet.

"Hex," Mother said to the name of Mary Baker Eddy, and Addie retreated to Isaiah. "Then the eyes of the blind shall be opened, and the ears of the deaf shall be unstopped. Then shall the lame man leap as an hart, and the tongue of the dumb sing," Addie reminded Mother with smiling insinuation, and she recounted testimonies of miraculous cures given on Wednesday-night meetings in Mother's own city.

*"Bei andern kälbern die Ochsen, bei mir nicht die Kühe* [Other people's oxen calve, but not even my cows]," Mother commented to herself.

On Yom Kippur, the Day of Atonement, Addie accompanied Mother to the synagogue. Mother would not ride upon the sacred day, although the distance was long; nor would she rest on a doorstep and jeopardize the spotlessness of her black silk Sabbath dress. She moved laboriously down the block, puffing evenly.

"That's fine," Addie glowed, encouraging her up the steps of the synagogue. "All this distance and here you are not at all tired."

"According to your religion I may not be tired," said Mother. "According to mine, I am very tired."

After that day Addie more gradually introduced Mother to the new doctrine, to the Allness of God and the illusion of evil. Mother regarded her gravely as Addie made tentative excursions into the gospels, ran back for safety to David and Hosea, and identified the books of the New Testament with the miracles of the Old, artfully avoiding the name of Jesus.

"You remember Daniel in the lions' den?" she asked, ready to point a happy analogy.

"That *Geschichte* [fairy tale]," Mother said.

"But surely, Mother, you must believe in the miracles of the Bible. Wasn't Elijah fed by the ravens?"

"I never saw a raven," Mother said.

But Addie refused to see Mother other than as a child of God whom no error could deprive of her right to the Truth. Warily she introduced the name of Jesus into Mother's mezuzah-guarded bedroom, offering the astonishing news that He was not a Gentile, but a Jew.

"Think of that!" Addie exclaimed as one who brought glad tidings. "He was a Jew. We never used to know that, did we?"

"No," Mother said.

"And He was good. He taught that we should love one another. 'Do unto others as you would have them do unto you,'" Addie quoted, corroborating herself. "Nothing so bad about that."

"No," said Mother.

"He loved everybody, the sick and the old, and above all little children and sinners. He loved Mary Magdalene."

"*Who?*"

"Never mind now. I'll tell you about her later. Jesus divided the loaves and the fishes so that all the people might be fed. Everybody! Would you like me to read you a little about that?"

"No," said Mother.

"That's quite all right. For today just know that Jesus was a good man, a fine man, and that He loved—Jews," she improvised as she closed the flexible black book in her hand. She was pallid from the restrained urge to read to Mother from its healing pages. As she arose to leave she turned with a lingering hope, but Mother, with her lips pursed, was looking beyond her.

"If I wanted to, I could tell you something about Him not to His credit," Mother said.

The Allness of God and the illusion of evil should have been plausible to Mother whose life was one of unbroken harmony. When she came to live with Addie, after Father's death, Addie gave her days to her. The time that should have been given to her husband and family she devoted to Mother, sitting in her room, keeping her company for hours in the teeth of Mother's accusation that she was a *"Herumlauferin"* (a gadabout).

At all hours Addie's sister-in-law darted in and out of Mother's room, entertained her with gossip, smiled upon her, bringing to her love and sunny laughter. "Pottawatomie," Mother called her in disdain of the small Kansas town of her birth. No devotion could offset the obscurity of her origin. Neither did Mother restrain her disapproval of her son-in-law, whose handsome gifts to her she resented. *"Macht sich gross mit mein Geld* [Makes himself grand with my money]," she said, remembering her daughter's marriage portion.

Miss Moliere, Mother's companion, grateful for the shelter of Addie's home after bruising conflict with New York theater producers, focused upon Mother the richness of a creative talent. She admired Mother's directness and honesty and relished her sharp humor. Her love and entertainment and immense devotion received no praise from Mother, who believed devotion to be canceled by salary. Following Addie's leadership, children, sons-in-law, grandchildren, companions, nurses, maids surrendered affectionate service to the impervious force that accepted it with the unquestioning authority of a Romanoff, in full faith that her acceptance of it was sufficient recognition.

Over the decades the family expanded, but always fell into pattern around the changeless fact of Mother; and while her children, hypnotized by years of negation, unable to fall into the step of swift and complicated living, pursued health and serenity on metaphysical levels, Mother, unsuspecting their dilemma, continued to draw vitality from deep reservoirs of wrath that sustained her for ninety years in unbroken health and power.

# 5

# *Father*

No other room warmed the eye and chilled the spine like our
dining room. Even as we shivered, our eyes responded to its
glow. Every detail radiated richness and comfort. The paneled wain-
scoting contrasted brown and golden yellows; the couch and walnut armchairs offered areas of wine-colored leather; through the
glass of the sideboard, inserted in the wall at the end of the room,
gleamed red glass and gold-and-blue scrolled porcelain. At night,
when the shaded lamp descended from the convoluted bronze chandelier amid a rustling tinkle of chains, the tan carpet and the garnet
plush table cover flushed, and the smooth leather sofa invited relaxation. The room was icy. The couch that preserved the roll at its
head, as undented as if it were stretched afresh each morning over a
mold, sent along the length of one's body a continuous chill, as if
self-generated. Father must have suffered from its deceptive hospitality, for he imported into the room one of the high-backed plush
chairs from the music room, which ever after became Father's chair,
as the corner in which it stood became Father's corner.

Wrapped in his woolen *Schlafrock* (dressing gown), Father sat in
his armchair, close to the glass paneled doors opening into the music room. In a half circle before him sat his friends, drinking cognac
from small red glasses of our Bohemian set: Manassah, the
lantern-jawed jewel merchant, imposing in height, rigid of bearing,
who wore the hair mole on his chin like a decoration; Wilzynski,
the explosive wit; and B. Joseph, soft-spoken and soft-stepping, a
silent, sober man, his white face clamped between extensions of

jet-black beard. These were city friends from Father's birthplace. J. Meyer had come down from Virginia City, and H. Lippman up from Santa Barbara to replenish their stocks of dry goods. Lippman's chair, drawn far away from Father, his head declined upon his chest and his upper lip stretched tight over his lower jaw, were entrenchment against Father's advice and supervision of his purchasing.

It was a needless precaution, for Father had been sitting there many minutes before their coming, engrossed in ancient problems that led him now, as always, into perplexity and confusion. Today the deception of Jacob had again invaded his serenity; Jacob, the son of Isaac, the son of Abraham. How could a righteous God reward a son who had pressed advantage over his fainting brother to possess himself of his birthright and defraud him of his rightful blessing? With his predilection for sadness, Father identified himself with the aged Isaac and was moved to pity and bitterness as he contemplated himself, an old man, helpless and blind, deceived by his own child. Eve, fashioned from the rib of Adam; Jonah, swallowed and ejected from the belly of the whale; the extravagance of these stories encouraged jocular evasion, but the deception of Isaac by his own son was a matter of different complexion. What about it, Father asked himself with varying hues of passion. And the answer failing, he passed on the burden to his friends.

"What about Jacob cheating his father?" he asked them.

Meyer wagged his narrow, rectangular beard from Father to the others and back to Father, mocking him.

"*Er fängt schon wieder an* [He's starting all over again]," Meyer cried. His agile eyes darted about, seeking confirmation, but Lippman crumpled in his chair and twisted a shoulder, disclaiming responsibility, and Wilzynski continued the telling of a story to Manassah: "And when he brought his bill to me, I said to him, 'What is that?' and he said, 'It's your bill, Wilzynski, your bill is due.' And I said, '*Aber es ist nicht du* [But the money isn't here].'" Wilzynski spluttered his play on words over three rolls of chin and pounded the floor with his heavy, gold-topped cane.

"His old father," Father said, pursuing his separate way. "He lied to his old, blind father, swindled him, and God made him the founder of a nation."

"After all it didn't happen yesterday, Benish, or the day before," Meyer protested.

"It didn't happen yesterday, Benish, it happened a little after the Flood. Very shortly after the Flood!" Wilzynski choked in his cognac. His silver snuffbox fell to the floor.

Father smiled a half-bitter, secret smile. Their unconcern was incredible. Could they not see that the conduct of Jacob must be explained if God was to be justified? His eyes sought Manassah, the authority of the group, but Manassah gave no answer beyond upturned palms that said without irreverence, "You know the Lord." He replenished his glass carefully from the decanter on the table and turned the talk to conditions of the wholesale trade. When his friends left the house, Father would again take up the trail, again get lost in the contradictions of the Bible; his faith would chant the goodness of the Lord, and wince at the vision of Hagar and her child driven by God's command into the wilderness.

Why could nobody resolve his perplexity, Father asked himself. He could accept with a natural faith the revelation of the Ten Commandments amid the lightnings of Mount Sinai, the cleavage of the waters of the Red Sea for the passage of the chosen people, the fall of the walls of Jericho, as phenomena appropriate to omnipotence. The contemplation of them lifted his imagination to a height commanding emotional acquiescence; but the consent of God to the violation of the ordinary, homely laws of human relationship shadowed Father's faith and tangled simple impulses to confidence. He needed to approve God in all His ways, to love Him with all his mind, with all his heart, with all his might; to discover in Him judgments transcending the judgments of men, and here he was questioning God, obliged to doubt Him, if he was to be honest with himself. To bridge the discrepancy between God enthroned and God operative in the affairs of men exhausted Father's leisure, so that doubt was delayed in its progress to unbelief. He was so occupied, weighing the justice of God, that he never reached the point of questioning His existence. The problems of the Bible remained forever unsolved. To the end of his days Father observed the precepts, doubt running like a shadow beside him.

However, obedience to the commandments of the Lord, that he

might abide in His House forever, was an injunction congenial to Father's disposition. He abridged no service in honor of his Maker; he challenged every reform that threatened to alter a tittle of the Law, and triumphantly preserved to the members of the congregation, frequently against their will, the tradition of the temple from the covered head in the synagogue to the observance of the first two days of Passover.

On Friday afternoons he hurried away his late customer that he might attend the service in the synagogue and hasten home to usher in the Sabbath with prayer and thanksgiving. As the Passover found his house cleansed of leaven, so the Day of Atonement found his heart purified of sin.

Mother must have known of the fowl in the sack on the washroom table in the basement, left there by the delivery boy of Miller, the chicken man. Maggie Doyle surely knew; but Addie, Polly, and I suspected nothing until Father appeared at the kitchen cellar door, the day before Yom Kippur, hat on his head, and the live duck and drake pendent from his hand. On the eve of each new Yom Kippur we agreed to run away from the house the following year, and every new year we forgot until it was too late for escape.

"Come," said Father, leading the way. Addie, Polly, and I slowly followed him up the stairs to the back bedroom where Mother sat waiting. Father laid the ducks upon the carpet, left the room, and returned with two brown hens which he dropped at Mother's feet. From a shelf of the open mahogany bookcase he took the worn black cloth-bound prayerbook and sought a page.

Addie, Polly, and I sat close together at the foot of the couch, looking sideways, now at the white duck and drake, limp on the carpet, their legs tied together with strands of yellow rope, now at the hens that lifted their captive bodies and thudded them against the floor. When Father stooped to pick up the hens, we huddled closer and lowered our heads. He read aloud and suddenly swung the birds over us. They awoke to terror. Three times the clattering wheel rotated over us, dropping feathers into our hair and eyes. Once an outstretched wing smote my cheek. It was over, but we continued to sit with lowered heads while Father dropped the hens, lifted the white duck and, reading again from the book, circled it three times over Mother. Above his own head, in wider circles, he swung the gray drake that quacked wildly, thrusting out its long neck and yellow bill. Then he dropped the disheveled birds to the floor and left the room.

We had assisted at a practice, common to the whole human race, an offering to the Great Spirit in propitiation for our sins. Alas, vicarious sacrifice had no meaning for the three of us. We knew only that, without asking our leave, panic-stricken birds, squawking with terror, had been whirled over us, shedding feathers into our eyes. Far from experiencing sanctification of ourselves and cleansing of the house in which we lived, we only suffered humiliation. To no one would we have betrayed our feeling of indignity to ourselves, the violence to the birds, and our participation in so unseemly a racial ceremony.

"I don't see how we will ever be able to eat them," Polly shuddered. But next day, quiescent upon the big hand-painted platter of our formal poultry set, the duck presented so changed a personality that, by covering memory with sufficient gravy, we were able to eat it. Some virtue, however, may have been wanting in us, or our brothers, the birds. Perhaps it is the contrite heart, or the acquiescent spirit, which makes sacrifice acceptable in the sight of the Lord for, despite the correctness of the ritual, no special grace descended upon the atmosphere of the house, which continued to heave under the repeated impact of emotion accenting its history.

No one gave himself to the service of the Lord more joyfully than Father. If only he could have approved His judgments!

"If you are always questioning the Bible," Polly demanded, "why must we be so strict?"

Father smiled whimsically. *"Tomme ya* [It may be true]."

The reformed synagogue observed only one night of the Passover.

"You don't really believe that God expects us to celebrate two Sedars," said Mother, protesting against the double labor. But upon this point no doubt divided Father. He could not be forced to yield a Sedar. His tenacity may have had its origin in other sources besides his desire to honor the Lord. The Sedar was pre-eminently Father's night, the night upon which he was head of the family as well as Levite of the temple. Seated at the head of the table, behind the ceremonial matzoth, he sat relaxed, prepared to read the service in its complete beauty, slurring no note or phrase of praise. It was he who led the singing of the Hebrew chants, we who followed, rolling sacred melody into rich, swelling choruses. At times we grew daring in the exhilaration of the repetition of a refrain as we gave the response for the tenth time. We played a game with our favorite melodies, dropping our voices to a whisper, or lifting them to a sudden volume, accelerating the time to an indecorous speed which ended with a prodigious click.

Father's eyes, shadowed by the brim of his tall hat, looked at us over his spectacles in an effort toward reproof, but the sight of his family, his wife and children, and the few Christian friends welcomed into intimacy, softened his protest into tender approval. Our gaiety penetrated the service and, when Father voiced the ancient hope of the nation that the next Passover would find us back in Jerusalem, Father, smiling sheepishly at us, substituted for the Holy City, San Francisco, separating the syllables and drawing out the last *"co,"* letting God know by this exaggeration the jocular nature of the substitution.

Addie and I left our seats at the table now and then to sit beside Father and read in his book the English translation of the Hebrew text, returning to our places faintly stirred by reminder of the ancient story: the enslavement of our ancestors under the yoke of Egyptian bondage; the separation of the Red Sea; the forty years in the wilderness and the salvation of the Lord, whose mercy endureth forever. The reading animated the symbols on the plate in front of Father: the bitter herb, the horseradish, the bone of the paschal lamb—all witnesses to the pain of the captivity. The filled goblet, beside the triple layer of matzoth before Father, awaited the coming of Elijah, the Prophet. Every year it stood in the same place, while the door leading to the front hall stood open for his entrance.

Suppose, I thought, suppose he should come, come on this Passover? I tingled to the hope of beholding a Prophet, but I was relieved when the door was closed and I knew he was not coming. When Father dipped his little finger into his glass and withdrew it quickly, as if shedding water, we knew that he was dispersing the plagues of Egypt. We counted to be sure that he missed none of the ten and, for some unknown reason, felt cheered by the remembrance of them.

We were a happy family party. Melodies, food, raisin wine, all were new, peculiar to the festival, not staled by familiarity; never savored upon any other occasion, they reappeared like half-forgotten friends, the delight of whose charm we had only half-remembered.

*Addir Hu, Addir Hu, Yiuneh beso b'Korov*
*Bim bero, bim beroh, b'yomenu b'Korov*
*El b'nei, El b'nei, b'nei bes-cho b'Korov!*

We boomed at each other across the table as we emptied our glasses of raisin wine. Understanding little of the Hebrew text, we toasted, with equal enthusiasm, the deliverance of the children of Israel from the bondage of Pharaoh and the ten plagues of Egypt.

Father's passionate obedience to religious observance was only one aspect of his ardor for righteousness. He wanted to be good, he wanted to do right; he wanted profoundly, above all things, to be a good man, a good father, a good citizen. This seemed so simple a wish that he was perplexed that events did not reward his honest intention. He trusted his customers, even giving them goods when their credit was wavering, because he sympathized with their dilemma, and could not resist their appeal. He believed in giving the unfortunate another chance. They failed in business, and he lost his money. He turned a questioning eye upon the Lord, but there was no reproach in his inquiry.

When his German nephew dropped like a changeling at our door, Father addressed himself to old business friends and secured a good position for him. The nephews of other men, imported from Germany, adopted American ways and climbed to high position. If Cousin Gustav succeeded, it must have been in the northern city to which he fled a few weeks after his arrival, clad in the new suit of clothes bought by Father to impress his employers. Again Father questioned the Lord, and again the Lord hid His face.

He saved his money so that Yetta, his wife, would wear pretty dresses for him to enjoy in his home. She preferred the purple wrapper. To return home, after a day of business, to a smiling wife, fresh in organdy, seated at a generous table, defined Father's vision of

64

domestic happiness. Mother was sparing of charm, as she was of all expenditure. She greeted him daily in the purple wrapper, which was odious to him. Her genius for thrift found even fuller expression in provision for the table, and she served Father dishes which were distasteful to his eye and aggravating to his palate.

What did it mean? How had he failed? What had he done to make the Law of Good inoperative?

He accepted Mother's irritability with whimsical resignation until the repression of his grievances became unbearable, and then we witnessed an outburst of violence so unusual that we were frightened. After a succession of dull, meager meals Father's anger began to bubble. We recognized premonitory signs and grew uneasy.

"Can't you have all the money you want? Do I ever complain? Do I stint you? If you need more, ask for it, but at least let me have something to eat."

The blood mounted dangerously to his face and head.

The familiar pastry closed the meal.

"Apple pie, *schon wieder* [all over again]."

Then it burst forth, the great oath which made us tremble.

"God damn—hellfire!" Father shouted, and left the room.

Mother was abashed and, early next morning, hurried to market to purchase a duck or a goose as offering of propitiation.

Hardly less exasperating was the purple woolen wrapper which Mother refused to relinquish. Father published his dislike of it the day of its purchase. Age and shabbiness augmented his aversion, and the purple wrapper grew to be a symbol of ugliness in the world, and of his frustrated craving for charm. Mother clung to it; Father hid it today only to behold her within its furtive folds tomorrow. That was leaven for silent irritation, but when the purple wrapper came into conjunction with an apple pie, the great oath tore the sky.

Then there were the affairs of the synagogue. What was wrong with the cantor that the rabbi and members of the church wanted to rid themselves of him? No other cantor had ever sung with greater feeling.

"He sobs," they said.

"Sobs! He sings with feeling," protested Father, to whom the note of desolation was profoundly sympathetic. What was wrong with a cantor who sang chants as they were sung in the time of David? The poor cantor, already middle-aged, who had a wife and four children; and whose congested face foreshadowed an early apoplexy. Would they like him to sing the "Ave Maria"?

"He bellows," the rabbi repeated.

"Did you expect him to whisper?" Father retorted.

But here at least the hand of God was visible, and Father, who helped to re-elect the cantor over the opposition of his persecutors, found reward in the new wail of anguish that rocked the lamentations.

Father's passionate urge to help, to correct wrong ways, to show relatives how their small family affairs should be managed, their businesses run, met with the same baffling lack of gratitude. He marveled that people should lack zeal for knowledge of their shortcomings, that they should not be eager to profit by his counsel, so free from self-interest. Unwittingly he pressed a painful subject; he possessed a genuine flair for tender places; money lost in foolish speculation, a misplaced confidence, a brother secreted in an asylum—Father uncovered them like a divining rod.

"And how much are you worth now?" he asked a young friend, instinctively selecting the hour when a speculation of her husband had reduced their capital. When, taken aback, she named the exact amount of her fortune, embarrassment clouded Father's day, for his curiosity was without malice.

"He's a good man," Father told Cousin Bertha of her fiancé, feeling it right to prepare her for the marriage which he himself had arranged. "He's a good man, but the biggest liar in the state."

And Bertha had shown no gratitude. Why was that?

Curiously enough, whenever he tried to help (seeing so clearly the needs of other people), whenever he thought to see his friends approach bearing myrrh and frankincense, as it were, he beheld their heels fleeing the pursuit of his solicitude. As the years went by, this forthright kindness reduced the ranks of his associates, leaving him increasingly discouraged. The right way, which he sought so whole-heartedly, mysteriously turned out to be the wrong way, and he could not discover why it was so. Truth was the banner under which Father walked most confidently; no graduated scale of truth for Father, no acquiescence in deception for admirable ends. Honesty and deceit clearly defined themselves to every man. What excuse was there for a lie?

On the day of Addie's confirmation, the rabbi learned that Father did not fail to make known his contempt for the false witness, though he walked in high places, even upon the altar of the synagogue. It was customary for the confirmation class to present a gift to the rabbi at the conclusion of the exercises in recognition of his instruction. This year the speech of presentation had been awarded to a close friend of Addie's, Norma Samuels. We knew it by heart. For weeks Norma, curled up on our dining-room sofa, practiced inflections of fervor. "And to you, our kind and loving teacher, who have spared no pains toward our spiritual education, inculcating the true significance of the precepts of our beloved religion, we offer a slight token in remembrance of happy hours passed under your untiring guidance and loving ministration."

From his corner Father listened, savoring the cadence, respectful of the words of many syllables—"inculcating," "ministration"— and approving the sentiment of gratitude, echoing in his own blood the beat of youth, its aspiration and easy accomplishment.

Addie walked the halls committing her own address to memory. I did not approve of her interpretation, but felt constrained to accept the reading of Norma, because of our knowledge that the rabbi, leaving nothing to chance, had graciously written it.

The confirmation was achieved without misadventure. Boys and girls together discharged the Ten Commandments at the rabbi like a salvo, or came forward singly to declaim a prayer or protest a creed. Addie, in her turn, approached the altar rail; the tremolo of tears, always close to the surface when she was frightened, charged her voice with religious fervor, and she disclosed, as if it were a recent personal revelation, that "Truly the light is sweet and a pleasant thing it is for the eyes to behold the sun. Ecclesiastes, Chapter 2, Verse 7."

As she continued Father's eyes were moist, and he drew a deep sigh of satisfaction, but not for long. At the close of the exercises Norma Samuels, garlands of daisies binding her auburn hair, rose and made her presentation. "And to you, our beloved teacher," she began, and Polly's lips and my own prompted her as she continued her measured way to a successful end.

"You have taken me by surprise, my dear Norma," the rabbi began, and Father needed to hear no more. To the remainder of the congregation, the words of the rabbi were the customary, gracious words of response to the customary speech of presentation. To Father's zealous ear, the rabbi had branded himself. "Liar! Taken by surprise!"

Never again did Father sit beneath the altar rail, sanctioning the word of that rabbi by his presence. Every Saturday morning, to the accompaniment of the solo which preceded the sermon, Father noisily replaced his book of prayer within the box beneath his pew and walked the full length of the synagogue to the exit, so that the world might witness his contempt for falsehood. Mother suffered under the public display but, up to the day the rabbi left the synagogue, no sermon of his reached the ear of Father.

I was not tempted to circumvent Father. Under his counsel and direction I felt equipped to support not only a specific truth, but a moral universe. On the first day of each month I flourished my high school report before his eyes. I pretended that the marks were low, and Father, troubled, fitted his glasses. When he read for himself the unbroken line of "A's," we laughed together at my deception, because I was still number one in my class. He was happy in giving me the education which, to him, was an incantation commanding the powers of light and darkness. My scholarship dazzled him. Not a week passed but I brought to Father a trophy of championship. I could enumerate the presidents of the United States forward and backward. I could recite pages of history from Sumter to Gettysburg without dislodging an "and" or dropping a "the." The states of the Union and their capitals rolled from my tongue as from a scroll. Before my spelling-match performance Father's lids lowered, that the pride in his eyes might not jeopardize my modesty. Warm shades of companionship he gave me.

Only socially did he fail to contribute to my self enhancement. I wished that he were smart-looking, not so heavy and slow-moving. His broadcloth suit and silk hat, worn even in the morning, brought to the college campus the alien atmosphere of the synagogue. He did not carry his head high and walk the earth with authority, as I should have liked; I wanted to present him to the members of the faculty with pride. "Professor Richardson, my father." Instead his responses were late, and he regarded new friends, to whom I introduced him, with searching curiosity, and asked awkward questions which embarrassed me.

After Father's passionate defense of the South, where he spent his early years in America, the Civil War was never to concern itself for me with the freeing of the slaves, but only with injustice and devastation. Over long years I could not hear of Sherman's march without distress, nor could I read American history without feeling Father looking over my shoulder, blurring the text with murmurs of "damn lies." Decades later, Drinkwater's play, *Abraham Lincoln*, addressed itself to an unresponsive heart and, when Grant appeared upon the stage, had the audience not been absorbed in the drama, it must have heard my whole nervous system shout "Ruffian!"

Though Father never overcame his bitter hatred of Grant, he consented to the humanity of Lincoln. I liked to find a resemblance to Lincoln in Father's heavily furrowed face, but could not strain the likeness beyond the parentheses that encircled his gravely cynical mouth. The hair of his head and short black beard was soft, black, and wavy. His eyes held humor and sadness. The long aquiline nose, tilted to what seemed to me an enormous distance from his face, imposed upon it an unexpected Celtic cast. In spite of strength of feature, the face spoke of wistful inquiry and of unrooted being. He might have found satisfaction in a society which discussed social problems, had he known that there were such groups. He might have found ease for his concern in philosophical theory, had he known of philosophy. Had he read books, at least he would have been comforted by the knowledge that others, besides himself, were questioning institutions, but he read only newspapers. Alive to insincerity in all the organizations to which he belonged, he fought against the pretense he was not equipped to probe. He resigned from boards of directors who refused his leadership, and was wounded that they should accept his resignation. He always remained on the unpopular side, combative, but cherishing no vision of a better order.

"Why do you always have to be different? Why can't you be like other men?" Mother protested. "Agitator," was her comment upon Father's passion to reform and convert. "A regular Dennis Kearney," she exclaimed, referring to the first exponent of the rights of labor in the state, encourager of strikes and violence.

But she was wrong. Father's "redness" did not extend beyond his flannel underwear.

His political conviction was vindicated when, after the long obscuration of its light, the Democratic party returned to power with Grover Cleveland. A spontaneous demonstration in the streets of the city celebrated the election, and Father took me to town where we waited hours for the procession. When the tumult swung before us, I felt a painful pressure of the big hand that held mine and, looking up, I saw tears falling from Father's eyes. I begged him to tell me what was wrong. "This is the happiest moment of my life," he said.

To spare me the pain of future disappointment, Father prepared me for my destiny. I was bright but plain-looking, and must not expect a marriage of any consequence. *"Hässliche Näslein* [Ugly little nose]," he said, and tapped my nose tenderly. In a moment it overshadowed my face like a fortress, and in every glance directed toward me I read amazement at its grotesque proportions. I learned the angles which exposed the profile, and avoided them. As I grew to womanhood the habit of maintaining my eye-to-eye pose, which had been formed only in defense, developed into a character of frankness and full-faced directness quite unrelated to native feeling.

In the theater alone Father found the richness of the living denied him at home. The stage had been Father's first English school. Had instinct been his guide, he would have walked from the gangplank of the ship, which brought him to America, straight into the nearest theater.

Long before the blur of strange sounds broke into meaning for him, he was climbing to the gallery nightly, absorbing the new tongue in rolling phrases saturated with feeling. The stage became book, club, and society to him. Over a lifetime if a famous actor came to the city, Father disappeared each night after dinner as to a rendezvous. Without a word of explanation, forestalling Mother's mock-

70

ing inquiry, he stole sideways across the end of the dining room and vanished into the hallway. Sometimes he took Addie with him; more often he went alone.

I cannot say how many plays I saw and how many of my memories are only records of Father's ardor. The elongated form of the Prince of Denmark, prone upon the carpet, his eyes shifting from the players to the king and back to the players—did I breathe to the heartbeat behind that wary watching, the fanatical gleam in the eye, and the twitching of the long fingers? Was it I who saw Edwin Booth play Hamlet? Was it I who followed the fevered gesture of Janushek? Or did Father picture for me the ghostly drag of palm on palm as Lady Macbeth strove to rub into oblivion the blood of King Duncan?

If no actor of renown was playing in San Francisco, there was always the Tivoli Opera House. The Tivoli was the most beloved theater in the United States. At first a public garden, it developed into a concert hall for light opera and musical comedy. The price of the two thousand seats, which sold for fifty and twenty-five cents, included refreshments served by the ushers between acts—beer for the gentlemen, Queen Charlottes (ice-cold raspberry soda pop) for the ladies and children.

The Tivoli was democratic; members of the stock company and the audience were as one family. Patrons clamored their desires and their desires were rewarded. Ferris Hartman, beloved comedian, remained on the Tivoli stage for years, improvising as he sang, loving himself, permitting himself fresh extravagances, secure in our affection.

Collamarini was made for a Tivoli audience, for families who came night after night, whose boast it was that they had not missed one opera of the long season, not one, from *Cavalleria Rusticana*, when Mascagni himself had conducted, to *The Chimes of Normandy* and *La Fille de Madame Angot*.

Collamarini sang Carmen to one heart. No other Carmen for Father. It was not that he had not heard greater. He remembered the superb singing of Calvé, the greatest of all Carmens, but Collamarini was life itself pulsating among us, an everyday living and loving. Her notes melted into our hearts, and our bodies answered with delight. She was not an actress on a distant stage, but one of us, seductive, endearing. Her audaciousness leaped the orchestral space; she was so near that her listeners gasped at the closeness of the flame.

With Collamarini came Russo, the slender young tenor who offered grace, style, and an engaging voice. Our eyes and ears moved from one to the other, fearful of missing a glance. Russo sang Don José to the Carmen of Collamarini, and Father took me to hear them again and again.

While the school taught me to parse Hamlet's soliloquy and to paraphrase Macbeth's fantasy, Father fed me his enthusiasm for beautiful phrase and great acting. Barry Sullivan played *Richard III* for a week with Father as faithful at his post as the prompter. Edwin Booth varied his role: tonight, *Othello;* tomorrow, *Iago,* and Father sat gravely before him under a self-imposed responsibility to measure and compare, and decide which impersonation best suited the actor's temperament.

Father's interest never palled. He laughed at the same retort every night over a long engagement, and wept as often with the same anguish, protesting the slightest departure from an initial inflection. He sat close to the stage, arriving with the opening of the door, that he might nod to the members of the orchestra, to whom he was a familiar figure, and fully enjoy the orchestral prelude. *Rigoletto, Lucia, Aïda* were dependable expectations, but the answer to his highest hope remained in *Il Trovatore.* No happier preparation for *King Lear* or *Macbeth,* thought Father, than the Anvil Chorus. The prompter's box upon the stage would have been more to his liking, but he contented himself with the first row in the orchestra. He would have felt the loss had he missed the crooking of a finger. Of all the tragedies Father liked *King Richard III* best. The story was too harsh to engage my sympathy, and I did not want to go to the theater with him, but when I protested the seduction of Lady Anne, Father smiled as a soldier of Napoleon might have smiled at a doubt of his leader's divinity.

"Wait until you see him. Barry Sullivan could make any woman marry the murderer of her husband," Father said proudly.

Together Father and I went to see Clara Morris, the great emotional actress, play the New Magdalen. Word of her increasing illness and the terrible remedies she employed (hot irons on her spine) heralded her coming every season. In spite of her suffering, she held her audience under her power and moved them to anguish. Years later the muscles of my stomach contracted at the mention of her name, and I could still hear Father gulp, and feel him slip his extra handkerchief into my hand beside the wet pellet which had been my own.

Throughout the long recital of the Magdalen's tragic life story whispers of physical suffering reached me from the stage, though too low to be heard by the weeping audience behind me.

"I am so tired, so tired, I can't stand this another minute," the woman moaned to herself, while the audience sobbed aloud, and the actress made her passionate plea to her lover.

"Was the older Booth as great as Edwin?" I would often ask Father.

"Yes and no," Father answered thoughtfully, and there followed comparison and discrimination, and finally the story of the great night, which I could have told without loss of a syllable, so often had I heard it. The play was *Richard III*. Booth came upon the stage unsteady from liquor. When he fumbled for his lines and forgot his cues, the audience grew noisy.

Booth stepped to the footlights and regarded them: "Do I go on, boys, or have you had enough?"

"Go on, go on, Booth," they cried back to him.

"Then," said Father (and I had begun to cry in anticipation of the end I loved so well), "Booth pulled himself together, and never in all his life did he play Richard like that."

Because I had read that Edwin Forrest was not great, measured by the standards of our day, that he ranted, I hesitated before I asked Father about him. I was afraid to hurt Father, but I was eager to know.

"Do you think that you would still like Forrest?"

"Still? Listen, my child," his voice lowered to tenderness, "Forrest was a great actor. He felt every word, and he made you feel it. Didn't I see him so lost in his part that he forgot he was on the stage?"

"Where?" (As if I didn't know!)

"In Boston. He was playing Richard. In the duel he completely forgot that it wasn't real and fought Richmond off the stage out into the street."

"Not to the street?"

"To the street. Forrest couldn't act?" Father smiled pensively, as if savoring other evidence too precious to be offered to a mocking generation.

Father delivered to me his measure of the great as a legacy.

To safeguard my future judgment of the heroes of the nation against the authority of textbook and university instruction, he gave me the truth of history as he knew it, and entreated me not to let anyone confuse me in years to come.

"Let nobody influence your convictions, think for yourself."

One day he called me to him. "Sit down," he said, and I drew a low stool before him.

"There are two things that I want you to remember after I am gone. People will contradict you, and histories will support them, but you are never to forget what I am about to tell you."

I waited, my eyes upon his earnest face.

"Grant was not a great general. Never forget that. And Grover Cleveland was the greatest President we ever had."

I promised to remember. I felt that, sustained by these two principles, I was equipped to meet life in its most threatening attitudes.

After Father retired from business at fifty-seven, he was left with neither occupation nor recreation. The theater alone remained to him as a source of entertainment. Other men found social contact and recreation in a private club or lodge. Father belonged to neither club nor lodge. Every afternoon he went to Golden Gate Park to read his newspaper and exchange opinion on current events with other well-to-do men, retired from business because of diminishing returns or ill-health. Not one man was old enough, however, to warrant retirement, but there was no work to do nor a place for them to go. Gradually they ceased to fret at their idleness and took the day as it came.

As if by appointment, they met in the narrow lane protected from the cold ocean wind by tall, close foliage. A facetious young man, seeing the company in the lane, called the place Matzoth

Alley, and the name acquired official validity. It was a kind of open-air club, where the niceties of behavior were respected, priority giving sanction to possession.

"Your chair is waiting for you," Mullahy, the mounted policeman, called when he saw Father approach his destination. All the park policemen knew and liked Father, who called them by name and joked with them. As in a sun-warmed, cozy drawing room, the aging men sat at ease, a San Francisco *Chronicle* flapping in disorder, all sheets open, or an *Evening Bulletin* folded and refolded to the width of the editorial column, according to the habit of the man. Each sat in the respected proprietorship of his favorite bench.

Stretches of silence indicated preoccupation, a knitted brow or contorted posture proclaimed acute interest commanding privacy. Each man respected the absorption of the other until sudden indignation, or shocked surprise, too great to be borne alone, broke the silence and summoned everybody to hear. Caught by a word, or by a heightened inflection, one after another detached himself from his private interest, his voice rolling gutturally into the heart of an argument, or shrilly cutting a channel for itself through a wall of conviction. Newspapers fell from loosened fingers unnoticed, and everybody talked at one time. Supervisor, governor, United States senator—all were tried at the bar of the moral judgment of Matzoth Alley, the feebleness of a Republican matched against the dishonesty of a Democrat until, argument depleted, each man gathered up the scattered sheets of his paper and retired into his special privacy, awaiting another sharp exclamation which would arouse him to discussion anew.

As the sun descended, a man rotated a shoulder and buttoned the collar of his coat. "Isn't it turning chilly?" he asked, and looked behind him, as if expecting to behold Cold approaching through the tall trees.

"I believe it is," another said, and began to fold his paper carefully. One by one the men arose, slowly acquiring elasticity as they moved toward the highway.

As Father walked toward the streetcar that would take him home, a light buggy drawn by a sorrel horse sometimes drove up and stopped at the curb. It was Father Coyle. Of all the priests whom

Father knew (Father met them all on his summer vacations at Hot Springs), he liked Father Coyle best, liked his ruddy face, and shrewd wit, his lips pressed tightly, biting an invisible cigar.

"Jump lively," the priest called, and out of kindly, narrow eye-slits he watched Father clumsily climb into the high, narrow-seated buggy. They looked funny up there, the two stout men pressed together, Father's stovepipe rising above the roof of the priest's flat crown like a chimney.

"It's Father Coyle," announced Maggie Doyle, when the two men came into the house. "It's Father Coyle," she called upstairs. She smiled.

"Why do you always smile when Father Coyle comes home with Father?" I asked.

"I don't smile when Father Coyle comes home with your father," she said. "I smile when your father comes home with Father Coyle. See?"

I didn't see, so I said, "Sure I see."

# 6

# *Education*

I started to school in the morning provided with a lunch box and a quotation from the poets. At night I thumbed through Bartlett's volume of familiar quotations, or I tormented members of the family for a choice sentiment. By indirection, rather than expressed command, selection fell upon verses veined with moral treasure; each pupil entered the schoolhouse sheltering an uplifting thought. Scarcely were we seated when the teacher arose and crisply tapped the bell; time was short and speed essential. "Ready?" she asked, and a girl arose from her seat in the front row, discharged a couplet, and slid back again, making way for the girl behind her, already on her feet. Down one row and up another exploded the wisdom of the sages and the fancy of the poets. Drawn shades would have made visible a ribbon of light serpentining the large classroom:

> *"Those friends thou hast, and their adoption tried,*
> *Grapple them to thy soul with hooks of steel.*
> *William Shakespeare."*

I exhaled breathlessly, and regained my seat not a second too soon, for behind me came in pursuit:

> *"Count that day lost whose low descending sun*
> *Views from thy hand no worthy action done.*
> *Author unknown."*

This was saved by a hair from collision with:

> *"How often, oh how often*
> *Have I wished that the ebbing tide*
> *Would bear me away on its bosom*
> *To the ocean wild and wide.*
> *Henry Wadsworth Longfellow."*

Sometimes the specific need of the individual halted the smooth flow of the exercise.

> *"Oh bloodiest picture in the book of time,*
> *Sarmatia fell, unwept, without a crime;*
> *Found not a generous friend, a pitying foe,*
> *Strength in her arms, nor mercy in her woe.*
> *Hope for a season bade the world farewell,*
> *And Freedom shrieked as Kosciusko fell.*
> *Thomas Campbell."*

It was Elsa Schmidt, the pale, thin blonde, whose daily need for passionate expression arrested the swift, immortal current. A look in the teacher's eye kept Elsa on her feet. "Isn't it right?" she inquired.

"It is very nice," the teacher said, "only it is well to keep to subjects," she hesitated for a word, "closer to our present living."

"I've got another one," the girl urged eagerly.

> *"Sustained and soothed by an unfaltering trust,*
> *Approach thy grave like one who wraps the drapery*
> *of his couch about him,*
> *And lies down to pleasant dreams.*
> *William Cullen Bryant."*

"That's better, isn't it?"

"Much," said the teacher.

"'Don't be proud and turn up your nose,'" admonished Daisy Duffle.

> *"At poorer people in plainer clothes;*
> *But learn, for the sake of your soul's repose,*

> *That all proud flesh where'er it grows*
> *Is liable to irritation."*

Here was a surprise. Not one of us had ever heard that poem, except perhaps the teacher, who supposedly knew all quotations. She
nodded to them, as if returning them to the empty spaces from
which we had abstracted them. I watched her face, hopeful for a
betrayal of ignorance.

"Didn't you forget the author, Daisy?" she admonished archly.

"John Saxe," Daisy replied proudly, "John Godfrey Saxe." And
the teacher relaxed, her authority intact.

I regretted the practice that encouraged short selections. I should
have liked to recite a book from *The Lady of the Lake,* or prefer-
ably a canto from *Marmion.* However, I found hospitality at home
where my recital never failed to arrest conversation. At almost any
moment, even when the family engaged in a game of casino, I had
but to announce on a casual note that "not far advanced was
morning's day when Marmion did his troops array to Surrey's camp
to ride" (as if to observe that the Lessings had just left their house
and were walking down the street), to secure attention. Once started,
nothing could arrest my advance.

> *"And, first, I tell thee, haughty peer,*
> *He, who does England's message here,*
> *Although the meanest in her state,*
> *May well, proud Angus, be thy mate,"*

I cried menacingly to the group, and hurried on with accelerating
speed and passion, skidding with a shout to the great challenge:

> *"And if thou saidst, I am not peer*
> *To any lord in Scotland here,*
> *Lowland or Highland, far or near,*
> *Lord Angus, thou hast lied!"*

The threat was addressed to the whole family, but an outstretched
finger pointed especial accusation at Father who regarded his
*Wunderkind* (wonder child) tenderly, incredulous of his paternity.
So acute was the pleasure of the repercussion of my defiance that

I could not relinquish it. For an hour or more the lines silently re-echoed along my nervous tracts until they had yielded the last glint of satisfaction.

"*Schrei nicht so* [Don't scream so]," Mother expostulated. But deafened by my own thunder, I did not heed her.

To one challenged to feats of memory, the school program offered hourly refreshment. From my babyhood Father had whipped up my faculties by tests. Sitting on the floor with me, he increased the space between jackstones to enormous distances, and laughed joyfully as I swung out an arm and gathered them into my small palm—one, two, even four. Later he made tests of my memory and, when hardly taking a breath, I released pages of history, emitting, at a mouthful, "Peter the Hermit, emaciated by self-inflicted austerities and wayfaring toil," his eyes and those of the family filled with tears of laughter. Still laughing, Father placed me with my back to the closet door and, with his pencil, marked the latest measure of my height, as if to encourage a stature appropriate to my vocabulary.

To a mind that could sponge, with equal casualness, a canto of *Marmion* or a Peloponnesian war, the demands of history were light. For what was history but a library of dates to be memorized? On dates kings and queens were born and died, emperors succeeded one another, battles were fought, and continents discovered. William the Conqueror sailed with his troops from France, and starred A.D. 1066, for all time. Columbus discovered America for the glory of 1492. The trails to learning were clearly marked for teacher and pupil. Important events were indicated by heavy print and greater space in the textbook. Historical truth, exact, permanent, once memorized, became a lasting possession. No invasion of new knowledge distracted the teacher, appointed to enforce the text and police the class into observance of the printed fact.

"Caesar crossed the Rubicon," the teacher read. "He was slain by Brutus."

"*Veni, vidi, vici,*" fifty pupils shouted back in silent reflex. And for us the history of Caesar was exhausted.

As easy to appropriate as facts of history were features of geography. The largest city, the longest river, the highest mountain, alone received attention. A state, or a city, existed if among the ten largest states or cities of the union; like families of the social world, it was either in the first set or negligible. Rolling them off the tongue, in the order of their population, I discovered in the flow of New York, Philadelphia, Brooklyn, St. Louis, Chicago, the same gratification I experienced when I heard the Southern Pacific conductor directing us to our holiday destination, shouting: "Napa, Calistoga, Benicia, Suisun, Davisville, Sacramento trains *this* way." Chicago removed from the sequence would have forfeited its validity.

Our mathematics teacher ceremoniously led us from the simple to the complex. For the introduction to a new topic she wore her black rep silk dress and remained standing behind her desk with especial erectness until blank books had been thrust into desks, pens dropped into their grooves, and we sat, heads high, at attention. She stood motionless, a fresh piece of chalk between her fingers, an artist, demanding from her auditors the heart of silence before she turned and wrote upon the blackboard:

$$(a+b)^3$$

Then she turned to us to confide, step by step, the potentialities of the symbol, which, solitary upon the wide stretch of blackboard, woke to animation as she explained, opened, and expanded beyond the confines of its parenthesis. My mind leaped to the demonstration. I was eager to possess myself of the formula, to manipulate it for myself, to hold it packed like a thin volume $(a+b)^3$, and then draw it out like an accordion:

$$a^3+3a^2b+3ab^2+b^3$$

No less exciting an operation was the extraction of a root, the reduction of the compound, the shrinking of the row of complicated figures back within their narrow limits.

To the invitation of a mathematical problem my sister Polly turned a closed mind. She might be driven through a year of algebra, but she stood obstinate at the threshold of geometry. From the first she regarded a geometric theorem with hostility. Those who enjoyed proving them might have their pleasure. She was satisfied to accept them unproved. "From a point without a straight line one perpendicular and one only can be drawn to this line."

"What of it?" Polly asked.

She disliked her teacher, Miss Sherman, the smooth texture of her parted blond hair, the flawless oval of her cheeks, even more the tyranny of her reserve. Polly would not make an effort toward understanding a problem. Rather would she learn the whole page, diagram and all, by heart. Every night we heard her, committing to memory the theorem for the next day as she undressed for bed. "If one straight line intersects another straight line, the vertical angles are equal. Let line OP touch line AB at C," Polly recited as she plastered circles of hair upon her scalp with dabs of bandoline, circles that were the matrix of the high, fluffy bang of the morrow.

"It wouldn't take you a quarter of the time to understand it," Addie expostulated. "Let me explain."

Polly frowned away the interruption: *"Therefore:* angle OCA plus angle OCB equals angle OCA plus angle ACP. Take away from each of these the common angle OCA . . ."

"You're foolish, you're foolish," Addie persisted. For answer Polly turned out the light and jumped into bed. *"Therefore* angle OCB equals angle ACP," she finished in the dark and added, "Q.E.D." as a tongue stuck out at the universe.

When, thanks to an excellent memory, Polly survived the term to the final examinations, only to have Miss Sherman alter the lettering of the old diagrams and refuse Polly's entreaty to restore the letters of the text, Polly called her "pig" to the schoolyard, a prejudiced judgment in no way faithful to the lineaments of a disposition cloistral rather than porcine.

However, teachers were not like people; they were without body or silhouettes; the whole of one could be reduced to an adjective. If a bit of fun escaped from one of them, it was quickly dusted off like an indiscretion. Miss Anderson had at hand the handkerchief which came into the room with her each morning, a flat white square upon the mustard-colored textbook. At intervals she touched it to the red tip of her small, pinched nose, or covered her lips to erase a smile. Did they fear that we might outstrip any liveliness with excess? Had they always been so tight, so dry, so unbending?

I tried to reconstruct Miss Sherman as she might have been before she had been packed down into what they called "the department." When she smiled, beautiful teeth broke through the monotone of her face like light, and a sudden dimple dented the smooth oval of her cheek; but the fire was not warm enough to kindle the remainder of her face, and her blue eyes were cold by contrast. At the flash of her smile many a wave of feeling went out to her, only to be returned like an undelivered letter. Had teaching blanched her like a frost? Did it do it all at once, or after many years? Had she ever been ardent, overflowing, like our friend Lucile? Would it chill Lucile in the same way? Once a teacher, would Lucile's humor become skimmed and thin? Would her laughter dwindle into a driven smile?

Teachers never loosened; when two of them walked together in the halls during recess, they backed into their spines, away from each other; never did a fresh laugh break from one of them. Miss O'Brien was fluffier, but it was a wiry fluff. Nobody in "the department" was ripe and spacious. Lucile was the only teacher I knew outside of school and she had not taught long enough to set in the mold.

When Lucile unexpectedly appeared at our door, we knew that she had learned of a possible vacancy in the Girls' High School, and had hurried up from her school in Los Angeles to call upon members of the Board of Education. There were twelve members, each to be sought in his own shop or office. The applicant often had to call again and again before he was free to receive her.

When Lucile burst upon our home to report one of these visits, the work of the house stopped. If we were in the kitchen, Mother quickly basted the roast and slammed the oven door. The dishrag in Maggie Doyle's hand lingered over the surface of the dishpan. Nobody was willing to leave the room, or miss a word. Lucile acted all the interviews. She was the cast, the school directors, chance visitors, and herself. On rainy days she arrived dripping and tired. In a moment her raincoat was over the back of a chair, her umbrella in the sink, and she was on her feet in the heart of a scene.

Sometimes she would not know the occupation of the director before she arrived at his place of business. One member of the board was a coal dealer who lived out in the mission district. He looked kind, and she was not afraid of him. "Just a minute, Miss, and I'll be with you. I have to pay off some gentlemen outside." Five heavy men, black with coal dust, lumbered into the yard and received their pay. When they left, Lucile explained that she was an applicant for the position of French teacher in the Girls' High School.

The coal dealer was very polite. "Well, Miss," he said, "if your French is anything as good as your English, and I don't doubt that it is, you surely ought to have the job."

He confided that the only rival was a dried-up schoolteacher from Chico, sister-in-law of Tim McCarty, the saloonkeeper, lieutenant of Sullivan, political boss of San Francisco. He was sure she had never been closer to France than Sacramento.

"You can reckon on my vote," he said. He did not ask for credentials, just took her as she stood.

That was one vote, and we were encouraged.

Her visit to the doctor member of the board stirred my curiosity and heightened Lucile for me as a person of worldly experience. She had to wait in his office all afternoon until his last patient had gone. He talked much of himself, and encouraged her to talk. When she arose to go, he followed her to the door and put his arm around her shoulder.

"You're a nice little girl," he said. "You must come again to see me."

Surely he would give her his vote. Mother was indignant at the recital and threatened to go down and report him to the president of the board, but Lucile, alarmed, begged Mother not to antagonize him. She, herself, had not let him see how she had resented the liberty.

That the banker-director would respond to her personality and exquisite speech we felt secure. The superintendent of schools himself took Lucile to call upon him.

"An educated man," he told her. "He speaks French. He will appreciate your accent."

The banker received her graciously. If the superintendent had such confidence in the young lady, he would do all in his power to secure the position for her.

Suddenly he turned to Lucile. "How do you pronounce 'marquis,' mademoiselle?"

84

And when she pronounced it, "Oh no, no, no, not at all," he cried. "It's like this—'Mackay.' The French company, who played at the Bush Street Theater last month, pronounced it so many times, 'Mackay,' he repeated, "like the mining magnate, 'Mackay.'"

Lucile dared not contradict him. She was disheartened, and looked to us for help. We could give none.

"Never mind, let me tell you about Miller, the chicken man." Lucile lifted her head, jerked a finger toward our dining room, and the sausage man at the entrance of the California Street Market was answering Lucile's inquiries for I. Miller, school director.

"Over there to the right, the tall man," the sausage man pointed.

Lucile walked across the market to find herself before the stall of I. Miller, Chickens and Poultry. Behind a marble counter a man was stooping over a pail, plucking a hen. He, too, was young.

"Cut it short," he grinned. "Just tell me what you want." He promised to vote for her when the matter came up.

What I liked best was the visit to the undertaker. Lucile had not known the special character of his occupation, and when she saw the sign above his parlors, she did not have the courage to enter, but walked up and down the street trying to force herself to open the door. When, over the half-curtained window, she saw a man inside, watching her, she walked to the door, which opened for her.

"You're afraid to come in, now aren't you?" he asked, and led her to a rear room, dimly lit, where he said they could sit down and talk more cozily. As she started to explain her presence, she became aware of something between them, long lines that gradually gave shape to a coffin raised on supports. In the half darkness she could not tell whether it was open or covered. She looked for escape.

"Don't be afraid," the undertaker said gently. "The dead," and she jumped, "cannot harm you."

We counted the votes promised, and felt secure that this time we had reason to hope. This time the directors had not hurried Lucile; they had listened to her with interest, and had been moved by her youthful enthusiasm. We waited with assurance until the day we read in the newspapers that the selection had been made. The dried-up teacher from Chico, sister-in-law of Tim McCarty, the saloonkeeper, received the appointment. Every director had voted for her.

After Lucile left the city, I stopped wondering about teachers, what they might have been, and would become. The possibility of a change of temper did not occur to me. The same teachers had been in the school in Addie's day and would be there down the years— isolated figures, never touching each other, never changing trait or gesture. I accepted, as changeless, the dry cough of Miss Anderson, which would be forever stealthily stifled beneath the folded handkerchief; Miss Hayden's smile, which would never extend beyond its tide line. "The Susquehanna River?" Miss Hayden would command, and a new generation would answer, as I was answering, "Takes its rise in the Appalachian Mountains, flows in a southeasterly direction, and empties into Chesapeake Bay."

> "Come and trip it as you go,
> On the light fantastic toe;
> And in thy right hand lead with thee,
> The mountain nymph, sweet liberty."

Miss Anderson would read in melancholy tone to our children and grandchildren. "Accent the trochee." And, in unison, they would bear heavily upon the first syllables.

> "Come *and* trip *it* as *you* go
> On *the* light *fantastic* toe."

I enjoyed dropping the weight on syllables, as I liked swinging rivers to the sea; and, if I noted the resemblance of Miss Anderson to the apothecary in *Romeo and Juliet,* and wished that she might have been riper and more jovial, I was impressed by a knowledge that could deliver to me the lines of George Eliot which gave the lofty conclusion to my valedictory address.

Although Elsa Schmidt had been running a close second to me in scholarship, and I had been warned that I was too short to make an appearance upon the stage, that my voice would not carry in the great theater, I was not surprised when I was chosen valedictorian. The family declared that they had not been in doubt for a minute. Even Mother showed approval of the honor to our house, and my dress was bought fresh in a store, not made of left-over material from one of Addie's dresses, or cut down from one of Polly's.

The graduation exercises were held amid the splendor of the Grand Opera House. The theater was kept in semi-darkness until the audience was seated, and we sat waiting on the stage, trying to distinguish outlines in the auditorium. At last came one sputter of light, then a second, and a third, when the great chandelier took fire, and a hundred gas flames, reflected in crystal, called out of the darkness an orchestra, a dress circle, two balconies, and a gallery crowded with people brilliant in color. Floral tributes banked the curve of the footlights, an open book of pink carnations; a swan of white roses; cornucopias pouring forth geraniums and fuchsias. I recognized among them two huge bouquets of tightly packed yellow and red roses, one sent by Maggie Doyle and another by Hink, the grocer. There were set pieces from relatives. The tall structure that began as a boat and ended high in a burning torch of yellow lilies expressed the complexity and richness of Father's emotion.

Behind the hedge of bloom the class sat on raised tiers, massed rows of white. From the first row where I sat, clasping my address, tied with ribbon of the same blue satin that fastened my long black braid, I examined the audience, hoping to locate Father. I knew my address by heart, but Miss Anderson considered it more modest not to claim full confidence, rather retaining the manuscript in acknowledgment of human limitation.

Admonitions had pursued my entrance upon the stage. I must speak slowly, enunciate clearly, raise my head, lift my voice, not let it trail off at the end. I looked up to the distant ceiling, and knew that my voice could reach it; at the auditorium, and was confident that I could fill it. I was composed by the dignity of my theme: "Spiritual and Material Love." The principal's address ended and, when I heard my name, Hattie Levy, I arose and, without perturbation, faced the great audience.

As introduction, I had chosen the dying words credited to President Garfield, "I shall live." Grosser minds might read into them a prediction unverified by fact, but I drew from them our President's conviction of immortality. From this high note I moved easily to the theme of my essay. Intuition, rather than experience, supplied the body of my talk. As I approached the concluding lines, the verse of George Eliot, I rose on my toes, raised my head and, with my eyes on the great chandelier, I lifted my voice:

> "O, may I join the choir invisible
> Of those immortal dead who live again
> In minds made better by their presence; live
> In pulses stirred to generosity,
> In deeds of daring rectitude, in scorn
> For miserable aims that end with self,
> In thoughts sublime that pierce the night like stars,
> And untie their mild persistence urge men's minds
> To vaster issues."

Glued to the stage by the applause, I did not move until the principal came and led me to my chair.

"Could I be heard?" I whispered.

"In heaven," he said.

The following day relatives and friends hurried to our house to offer congratulations. It was wonderful, everybody said: "Yes, it was, yes, it was." The family did not conceal its excitement. The volume of my voice had lifted them off their feet.

Father brought word from downtown: Heller, up in the gallery, had heard every word; Daniel Meyer, the banker, standing behind the back row downstairs, had not missed a syllable, not an A.

"Well!" our uncle Konig said to Father. He gave him a jocular push. "An orator in the family. Don't say nothing, yes, Levy?"

"Yetta," cried our full-flavored Cousin Flora, drawing Mother to her heavy bosom. "Yetta! What do you think, Yetta? Little Hetchen! What the dickens, what the dickens!"

Lawyer Reinstein took Mother aside. "A fine delivery," he told her, the corner of his eye upon me.

"An unusual flow of language," Dr. Hoffman affirmed with finality.

I had heard Adelina Patti sing "The Last Rose of Summer" in the Opera House a week earlier. She had received no louder applause than I. I thought it a pity a valedictorian did not acknowledge an ovation with an encore.

A few days before graduation, Daisy Duffle and Sophie Brush told me that they were going to the University of California. They urged me to go with them. I was surprised at the girls' sudden ardor for higher education; their interest had been more in clothes than in learning. Daisy said that they had known right along that they were going.

"It isn't necessary to take the full course. You can go as 'a special' for as long as you want to stay," she explained, and rolled her black plush eyes.

I had never considered a university education, as girls whom I knew had not gone to college. The proposal, coming suddenly, associated itself with no image. I knew nothing of qualifications for admission, or of entrance examinations. I had not even seen the University of California, nor been to Berkeley.

I told Father. He would have to think it over, he said. He liked the idea, and would consider it. He would ask the advice of Nathan Sachs, the wholesale dry-goods merchant. Mr. Sachs told Father that education was fine for a boy, but would spoil the chances of a girl. Men did not like smart wives. Father looked at me over his glasses, explaining the risk. He had never thought of it before, but now he wanted a university education for me. We decided to take the chance.

The following day I went across the bay with Daisy Duffle, who wore her best taffeta silk dress. When I asked if I should have dressed up, too, she said that it was not necessary, she just liked being dressed up. I had never seen a university, and did not know what to expect. We got off at the Berkeley station. A long, narrow path led up an incline into the grounds of the university, among woods of maple, bay, and tall eucalyptus trees. We came upon oak trees, large and wide-spreading, more beautiful than any I had ever seen. I seemed to be walking in a lovely park. The space between the trees made the grounds look like a cultivated estate. The low wooden building among the foliage was the gym, Daisy said, and explained that "gym" stood for gymnasium. College students had college names for things. They called it "gym" just as they called examinations "ex's" and professors, "profs." She rewarded my excited interest with more inner knowledge. "The president is called 'Prexy,'" she shared with me.

Straight ahead a tall brick building, with a clock in the turret, stood against the high brown hills. It was the library. To the side and rear of it was the chemistry building, Daisy told me, appropriating them as she explained. We stood at the top of the incline, regarding the grounds. The lawn leading down toward us from the library was the campus proper. The two long, three-storied brick structures, with stone foundations, to our left and right, were North Hall and South Hall. Daisy indicated them with a gesture of her arm and hand, and looked to me for some emotion.

"It's grand, isn't it?" she asked.

"Is this the whole university?"

"Isn't it enough?"

We turned to the left toward North Hall, the steps of which were black with boys. More poured from the basement door. "The Coop," Daisy instructed me as we approached the building, reserving the precious knowledge that the Coop was the co-operative bookstore.

Boys with battered white top hats hurried across the lawn from the red brick building; a girl, with a mortarboard on her head slowly walked by the side of a boy with a black stovepipe.

"A senior," Daisy whispered excitedly.

We stopped at the foot of North Hall steps and waited for the boys, seated there, to move for us. Daisy asked one for the location of the president's office. She rolled her black eyes when she talked to him; he stood up, and was polite to her.

"Why didn't they make room for us?" I asked.

"University men don't approve of co-eds," she said, and smiled.

The president received me kindly when I told him my name. He had heard my valedictory address at the Grand Opera House, and praised me for it. He dissuaded me from taking a special course, and encouraged me to enter as a full student. I could enroll for a degree of Bachelor of Philosophy, for which neither Latin nor Greek was required. The university had need of serious students like me. The examinations were being held at that moment, he told me, and suggested that I take one that day.

"You need not worry about the questions you cannot answer," he said.

Just as I had never heard of entrance examinations, so was I ignorant of the customary preparation for them. I arranged to return the following day.

Daisy Duffle was not going to Berkeley the next morning, and Mother would not permit me to go alone. The family agreed that Polly should go with me and sit in the classroom while I took the examination.

We crossed the bay early in the morning. I wore my green-and-red-plaid woolen dress, my best dress. It was short to my knees, but I would have a longer skirt when I was sixteen. The clock struck the hour as we entered the university grounds, and the empty campus suddenly swarmed with boys. Polly was not afraid. She asked for directions of a tall, black-bearded man in a white top hat, and we found the classroom in North Hall, where examinations were being held. When she opened the door, I saw a large room, crowded with boys seated at desks, a few girls among them. Polly took a vacant chair and seated herself near the entrance. On a platform facing the room stood a red-haired man who I felt sure was a professor. I walked up to him and told him that the president had asked me to take the examination, and had told me not to worry about what I did not know. He said that the subject was word analysis that morning, and gave me a paper with written questions, which I took to a desk near a window behind another girl.

I could not answer the questions. I had not studied word analysis in high school. The girl in front of me was writing fast. She looked older than I, much older. Her hair was high on her head, not down her back in a braid like mine. I sat for a moment, rereading the questions, then I returned to the professor.

"I did not study word analysis in Girls' High," I said. "I can't answer those questions."

"What did you study instead?"

"German," I said.

"Quite all right," he said gently, and thought a moment. "Do you know Gray's 'Elegy Written in a Country Churchyard'?"

When I nodded yes, he said, "Very good; translate the first three verses."

His deep blue eyes looked down into mine kindly, as if he liked me. I thanked him and returned to my seat.

> *The curfew tolls the knell of parting day;*
> *The lowing herd winds slowly o'er the lea;*
>
> *The plowman homeward plods his weary way,*
> *And leaves the world to darkness and to me.*

The verse readily sprang to my mind, but when I tried to translate the opening line, the first word halted my advance. In a moment every word lost its friendliness and acquired a strange physiognomy.

> *Curfew—tolls—knell. . . .*

I seemed never to have met them before. One by one they retreated, challenging me at a distance. "Day" was the only word that remained familiar. I would write the words that I could translate:

> *Der—des scheidenden Tages*
> *Der—Herde windet langsam—*
> *Der—heimwarts—sein—weg*
> *Und lässt die Welt zu—und mir.*

It wouldn't do. I tried again. I tried three times.

Gathering my paper and bag, I resumed to the professor. "I can't translate Gray's 'Elegy Written in a Country Churchyard,'" I told him, and waited.

"Think of that," he said. "Not 'curfew,' or 'tolls the knell'?"

"No," I said. "I don't know the German words for them."

His brows knitted. "Not 'wheels its droning flight'?"

I shook my head.

"Nor 'Drowsy tinklings lull the distant fold'?"

"No, I don't know those words either. They weren't in anything we had in Girls' High. They weren't in *Nathan, the Wise,* and I am sure they weren't in *William Tell,* either."

"Too bad," he said, and seemed to reflect. "What can you translate?"

92

"I can translate *Du bist wie eine Blume,* or *The Lorelei.* But that would be from German into English."

"That will do nicely. Translate *The Lorelei,*" he said, and added, "Try to catch the spirit of Heine."

"I'll try," I said. I translated *The Lorelei.* I tried to catch the spirit of Heine. It was a good translation. Anticipating the reading of the examination paper by another professor, I wrote at the bottom of the page: "I did not take word analysis at Girls' High. The professor told me to substitute a German translation."

Every day for a week Polly and I crossed the bay to Berkeley, and I took an examination. The great number of boys remained a single mass, inspiring no fear in me. On the last day, when the boy behind me pulled my long braid, I did not turn around.

As I handed in the final paper, I realized I could not expect a high mark; however, when the report arrived marked "2," I was disappointed until Daisy Duffle explained that "2" was higher than "3" or "4."

When he learned of my admittance to the university, my father kissed me. He gave me sober advice about crossing the bay alone, and presented the disadvantages of intermarriage.

In the fall I returned to Berkeley, a regular student. I hoped to be in the class of the kind professor who had conducted the examination in word analysis, but I did not see him again. When the truth came home to me, weeks later, that he had been making sport of me, my feelings were hurt, but I did not tell my father.

"What became of the red-haired professor who conducted our examinations in word analysis?" I ventured to ask a girl who had taken the examination with me.

"Josiah Royce? He wasn't a professor, he was an instructor. He went to Harvard."

I did not betray to anyone my hopes that for his doctorate, Josiah Royce would be asked to translate into Russian the first book of *Paradise Lost.*

Reverberations of my valedictory address at the Grand Opera House reached the ears of the entertainment committee of Temple Emmanuel, who invited me to take one side in a debate to be given in the Sunday-school rooms of the reformed synagogue. The subject, "Are the Jews Responsible for the Prejudices Existing Against Them?" echoed down the corridors of my mind and evoked a chorus of conviction, and I whole-heartedly accepted the invitation to assume the negative side of the debate. Isador Newman, prominent in the business world as a fruit grower, and in the world of fraternal organization as executive and after-dinner orator, was my opponent.

I had never encountered prejudice against the Jews from without, only having observed the cleavage within the Jewish social body itself; and I was aware of such sentiment only as the dark hostility associated with abuse and persecution of remote ages. However, if prejudice against the Jews did exist—and the presentation of the subject for discussion was proof that it must—I was ready to prove it unwarranted. Even before J.B. Reinstein came to see me, something within me told of the groundlessness of such a sentiment. The prospect of a debate kindled my interest.

I had never taken part in one, but I understood a debate to be the combat of argument against argument and that to the possessor of the unanswerable argument went the victory. The subject inspired no hesitation in me. Complete ignorance of historical as well as of contemporaneous data left my thinking free. All I would have to do was to trust to the guidance of my feelings; the more I turned to my feelings, the surer I would become of my position.

I felt no need of a library. J.B. Reinstein, the highly esteemed attorney, later regent of the University of California, familiarly known as J.B., was to coach me. I was afraid of J.B. To me he was a grumpy man, silent and reserved when not stirred to argument. His irritability was ascribed to headaches, which necessitated frequent retirement. People spoke of them as a personal possession. When he failed to appear at a dinner party, J.B. was said to be having one of his headaches.

J.B. came to our house to supply me with arguments for the debate, which he called "points." He gave me three, which he said would be enough. Newman might need four. He mumbled something to himself about talking against the Jews to a Jewish audience. He chuckled as if the idea pleased him. He wrote the points on a slip of pink paper and left them with me. He cautioned me to talk slowly and distinctly, and to put conviction into what I said. I told him that I would, that I knew from something within me that the Jews were in no way responsible for existing prejudices, and that I was glad to defend them. He was pleased that I felt as I did, but told me not to forget that a few arguments would help the feeling. He counseled me to have no fear (I had none); mine was the popular side, and I would find support in the sympathy of the audience. I asked whether Isador Newman was a good debater, and learned that he was a fine debater, but that he would not have a chance.

"Listen carefully to him," J.B. advised, "and take note of his arguments in the order in which he presents them. Don't leave any of them unanswered. I have given you the answers."

I did not see how he could know in advance, but I said nothing. The three "points" convinced any unsuspected doubt. My instinct had been true. I felt no obligation to explore the subject beyond the information given me by J.B. He knew.

When the evening of the debate arrived, I took my seat on the platform in full confidence. I had J.B.'s points and my feelings. The audience smiled upon me. They had probably heard my valedictory address. Isador Newman, a broad, heavy, pompous young man, opened the debate. Unperturbed, I listened to the swing of his sentences. Argument followed argument, as if playing into my hand. I listened carefully, undisturbed by the grand manner of his professional address. How J.B. had anticipated his words! I held the answer to every point. He spoke quietly, in measured clauses, accenting his points with his index finger. As he continued to speak, casting slurs upon his own people, exposing weaknesses of no practical import, revelations that might have been left to enemies of his race, resentment possessed me, and I refused to listen further.

When the time came for the negative side, I arose in full command of my material. I began, slowly and distinctly, to deliver J.B.'s points with authority. I outdid Isador Newman's measured phrases, but it was not easy to continue calmly against the emotion piled up against my door. As I spoke, my theme awoke to a life of its own; it cut loose altogether, and was off under its own power; I could not stop it.

This prejudice against the Jewish race—what was it, I asked? What righteousness could there be to a feeling that discredited a people who had given to the world the best part of its culture: its music (witness Mendelssohn); its literature (witness Heine). I felt the need to include its philosophy, but had failed to provide a witness. What was my opponent, I asked, but an expression of that injustice which, for centuries, sought to extinguish the torch of world enlightenment? Indignation caught me up and carried me along a smooth road. Just such injustice it had been, injustice such as this, which had led one nation after another, since the days of ancient Rome, to imprison the Jews within the narrow confines of the Ghetto, cheating them of the broader contact that comes with travel (J.B. had told me that the injury to them from the lack of travel was incalculable).

And tonight, I cried—and the words came so fast I could not hold them back—*tonight* they are accused of possessing a character created by the very nations who accuse them. Is it fair, I asked for the third time, and now I spoke to an audience which extended beyond the walls of the synagogue, to Moscow, and to Rome: is it just, is it honest, to cripple a people, and then taunt them with their infirmity? I paused, not only from lack of breath, but because I could not continue. I had soared too high. One point of J.B.'s remained unutilized. I did not know how to get down to it, or how to draw it up into the ether of my elevation. As I stood, poised in space, a small boy in the audience came to the stage and handed me a slip of pink paper on which was written the word, "Quit." I bowed to the audience and took my seat.

To the rebuttal I gave no heed. No member of that audience could have lent an ear to it. I won the debate. Women embraced me; men shook my hand warmly; I had exonerated the race. When Isador Newman congratulated me, he looked shamefaced (I thought); he never should have taken that side against his own people. I returned home on the shoulders of the congregation, so to speak. Before I left the synagogue I looked for J.B., but he had gone home. My threatened leap from the zenith must have given him one of his headaches.

To the morning call of Dr. Brownell, the new physician who was attending Father, Maggie Doyle gave hostile acknowledgment, lowering her eyes upon his entrance and lifting them to regard his back reprovingly as he mounted the stairs. She could tell a thing or two about Dr. Brownell, she said.

When the Wagner house on Eddy Street was dark at night, he stole up the back way to visit Faithful, the oldest daughter. Katie, the Wagners' upstairs girl, had told Maggie Doyle. Didn't she know that he had a wife and children?

The effect of the story upon me was a change of route to town, from O'Farrell to Eddy Street, that I might examine the handsome premises of the Wagners' and reconstruct the nocturnal adventure: the rapid opening and closing of the garden door, the stealthy ascent of the basement stairway, perhaps a lantern. The clandestine visitor, his face shielded by a lifted cape, became integrated into the architecture of the residence. Disposition of his coupé provided occupation until I concluded that he parked it in front of the Bohemian Club.

That the features of the oldest daughter of the Wagners' displayed no evidence of the illicit adventure disturbed my belief in a chartered map of character within the skull. The smile of girlish sweetness that isolated her face from the harder features of other members of the family continued to exhale a springtime serenity.

Dr. Brownell was said to be a man dangerous to women, one who played fast and loose with a girl's affections, compelling her to his will by his fascination, only to cast her aside like a soiled glove. My curiosity played upon the stories of his transgressions, striving to understand a marital relationship maintained in spite of a wife's awareness of her husband's infidelity. Far from living in retirement, Mrs. Brownell held a prominent position in literary organizations and in the social life of the city, refusing to limit her activities to ingenious concealment of a secret sorrow. Her face betrayed neither pain nor resignation. Life was indeed baffling!

When Father asked me to go to Dr. Brownell's office to ask for his bill, I welcomed the opportunity for closer inspection of the scene of the Brownell family story. The doctor's office was in his home. The entrance to his apartment in the three-storied, somber-hued residence was through a small street garden. I obeyed the sign, "Enter without knocking," and opened the door into a dim, unlighted corridor. It was so long that, as I walked down it, the isolation of the apartment from the remainder of the house came upon me with disquieting realization, and my steps grew shorter. Before a door bearing the name of the physician I stopped, hesitating.

Almost before I knocked the door opened, and the doctor stood before me, a hand outstretched in welcome. He motioned me to a seat at one side of a long, heavy table, and seated himself opposite. A single lamp on the table lit the large room. The room was wonderful, like a library. Books were everywhere; up the walls to the ceiling, and down the walls to the floor; more were on the table and chairs. The doctor looked broader and heavier than he had appeared in our house. And different! Spread in his chair, his blond-bearded face became jovial, his eyes friendly and inviting ease. In spite of the great size of the square room, the high ceiling, and the heavy oak furniture, the place was cozy. I drew back a little from the edge of my chair and returned the smile inviting me.

"Well," he said, "what has brought you here?"

At once I felt thoroughly at home. It was good to be there, to remain there for a long stretch. I need not hurry to say anything that I had to say, but might sit at my ease, assembling my thoughts before presenting them to a listener, who had no occupation beyond sitting before me, waiting for my word. My body drew back farther into the chair and subsided into the cushion. All the while the doctor's eyes looked at me from depths of smiling kindliness.

"Well," he asked again, and his voice was deep and rich, "what can I do for you?"

"I have come for my father's bill," I said, and was startled by his heavy laughter.

"Why did you have to do that?" he asked.

"Tomorrow will be the first of the month, and my father always pays his bills on the first."

"But why?"

"Don't people pay their bills on the first of the month?"

"Some do, but why should you?"

"Why should I what?"

"Why should you pay the bill?"

"When my father is sick, I attend to his affairs," I said. "I deposit his checks at the London and Paris bank, and pay his bills."

"I mean why do you have to pay the bill at all?"

I stared at him.

"Let's call the account settled," he said, "and talk a little."

"No, I shouldn't think of it. We always pay our bills."

"Can't you understand that your coming here more than pays for my service to your father?"

What strange talk was this? "We always pay our bills," I repeated. "I came to find out how much my father owes you."

"Fifteen dollars," he answered, and laughed aloud again. "Now is that settled?"

I started to get up, but he motioned me back to my chair. His voice was low and quiet.

"Let me talk to you. I have something to say to you." He leaned toward me. "You don't know yourself. You are an attractive girl, an intelligent girl, the kind of girl to whom life offers interest and delight." He stopped, but I had nothing to say, and he began again.

"Some gifts are offered once, and never again. You can open the door to them, or you can close it upon them. You haven't yet learned how to accept. You must be educated to accept." His voice was sober and urgent, deep reaching and beautiful.

"Do you know what I am saying to you?"

I shook my head.

"No one else will tell you what I am telling you. Life is rich, rich with joy. It is not for everyone, but it is for you, if you will take it. I know. I know you. Let me teach you. Let me show you the way."

I was silent.

"Let me teach you living, real living. Teach you how not to be afraid. You will come and let me teach you? You will—won't you?" His voice was heavy with feeling.

"I am going," I said, and arose from my chair.

"But why?"

I did not know. I knew only that he was talking about good and bad, and that he was telling me that bad was good. I knew, too, that one did not permit words like these to go by without rebuke.

"Is this what you teach your daughters?" I asked above the beating of my heart.

"Surely," he said quietly.

There was an answer to this. I searched for it, but before I could find it his powerful arms were about me and his warm cheek pressed against my face.

"There," he said, with a laugh, and released me. He opened the door of his office, and I moved toward it.

"Think over what I have told you before you come again," he said, and I was in the corridor.

I pulled the brim of my dislocated hat over my forehead; again I pulled it lower in the street. I did think over what he had told me. I thought it over and over in the days to follow.

When I returned to his office to pay the next month's bill, I took Mother with me.

*Henriette and Benjamin Levy on O'Farrell Street, before 1900.*
*Photo courtesy of Albert S. Bennett.*

*Benjamin Levy with grandson Jeffrey Salinger in the garden at 920 O'Farrell Street, before 1900. Photo courtesy of Albert S. Bennett.*

*Benjamin Levy with granddaughter Ruth Salinger at 920 O'Farrell Street, before 1900. Photo courtesy of Albert S. Bennett.*

*Harriet Levy and Alice Toklas, Fiesole, Italy, 1909. Photo courtesy of The Bancroft Library.*

*Congregation Sherith Israel, San Francisco, ca. 1875. Photo courtesy of The Bancroft Library.*

The descendants of Benjamin and Henriette Levy, in the dining room of the Salinger home (1504 Oakland Avenue, Piedmont) on one of four annual formal dinners: Thanksgiving, Addie Salinger's birthday, Albert Salinger's birthday, or their wedding anniversary, before 1927. Photo courtesy of Albert S. Bennett.

*Clockwise from lower left: Addie Levy Salinger, with Robert Elkus on her lap, Albert M. Salinger, Jeffrey Salinger, Robert Salinger, Benjamin Elkus, Polly Levy Jacobs, Frank P. Jacobs, [Little] Ruth Elkus (Prosser), Lena Sickles [Albert Salinger's sister], Herbert Salinger, Ruth Salinger Elkus, Charles Elkus, Sr., Harriet Levy, Garry E. Bennett, Sylvia Salinger Bennett, Charles Elkus, Jr.*

*Harriet Lane Levy, ca. late 1880s. Photo courtesy of The Bancroft Library.*

# 7

# *The Parlor*

No one saw the parlor with unbiased eye, but through a mind excited to appreciation by the splendor of the mantel. To see the parlor first and then the mantel was impossible. You opened the door and there it was, bursting upon you with a shock that made you take a step back into the hallway. It should have been approached by a long nave, with slow steps and many hesitations, for its brilliancy was that of an altar with all the candles burning. The marble sent forth no chill and vibrated with light and life from base to summit. "Oh, oh," one exclaimed, and then sat down to break it into segments of joy.

The fireplace was translated into beauty so enhancing that not until I was a grown woman did I suspect that it contained a grate, a practical iron grate. Nobody, not the most astute, could know, I believed, or ever could discover for himself, what the fireplace really was, for the opening was completely covered by a sheet of polished black japan out of which shone a mirrored disk. Would anyone have dreamed of a mirror in a fireplace? No one. Yet there it was, confuting the incredulous by its presence. Heavy bands of gold framed the black surface while others, equally gleaming, made a circular railing that divided the parlor proper from the hearth. The mantelshelf bore no concealment, no heavy gray corded macramé lace with knotted fringe covered its cool length.

From a white base rose, sheer and august, the mantel mirror. Occasionally a departing visitor ventured to approach it to tie the strings of a bonnet or adjust a turban, but the act shaded into awkwardness and, if she caught Mother's eye in the glass, into consciousness of impropriety. The glass (the plate glass, we called it), rising so broad and high, was but an excuse for its frame. The frame was the thing—pure ornament. Deeply and widely fluted, it rose nobly, pausing twice, in its ascent in shelves of gold, and losing itself in the heights of the cornice. Each pair of shelves held its sculptured romance. In pale tinted bisque, shepherd beckoned to shepherdess across the mirrored field; higher, where a terra-cotta gypsy, gallant in gilded doublet and hose of many colors, lifted a pointed toe to the strumming of a lyre, his lady stepped in graceful accord.

I watched the eye of our visitor slowly rise from the carpet to the mantelshelf, stop to acknowledge two stern-faced marble youths, each lifting a torch of frozen flame; then rise again, from one charming figure to another, until vision lost itself in garlands of roses woven upon the frescoed ceiling; then down again, shelf by shelf, until it reached the floor where, startled, it remained fixed upon two extraordinary objects. On each side of the fireplace, on short legs of gold with widespread feet, stood two stools—round cushions of red brocaded satin tucked into broad rims of metal. From each a tongue of gold shot forth, looking like crimson tortoises tranquilly squatting and guarding the hearth. What were they? Nobody ever guessed. Nobody asked immediately, but after a little interval curiosity ventured the question. Then Mother walked proudly to the mantel and placed a foot upon the golden tongue. The crimson brocaded satin cushion parted; the cover rose and disclosed a white porcelain cuspidor. Marvel upon marvel! Everyone gasped in astonished pleasure.

Nobody lingered after that surprise, but each visitor hurried home to spread the tidings that the Benish Levys owned spittoons covered with satin which could be pressed with the foot, when they opened miraculously, and that there were two exactly alike. After one experience a friend, upon a second visit, would ask the privilege of pressing the tongue that she might, in turn, astonish a guest still unaware of the amazing content. It is surprising that no daring mind ever was tempted to establish the utility of the two little squatting guards, but throughout the twenty years of Thursdays at Home no one ever did, and when the great earthquake closed the chapter of their uneventful lives, it was as unsullied virgins that they mounted into flame.

The double parlors were endless; palatial was the word used by our visitors. Huddled in long sealskins and tawny mink capes of countless tails, they surveyed the full stretch of color, insensible to the cold of the atmosphere. All parlors were chilly, and they were persuaded into a sense of cheer by the richness of tone and texture of carpet and upholstery and the gleam of mirror and picture frame.

The room was exposed to the south and a deep bay curved in hospitality to the warm sunshine, but no enemy was more closely guarded against by Mother. Inside shutters stopped its advance, opaque shades snuffed out the surviving beam, and from the inner arch of the bay hung heavily designed net curtains and crimson satin portieres, looped up on each side by gilded brackets of walnut. If, upon window-washing or cleaning day, the blinds were raised and the shutters opened, newspapers defended the exposed area of carpet.

Every article of furniture had its allotted space, and securely rested in inviolable permanence. If I, or one of my sisters, altered the position or angle of a chair, we found it mysteriously restored to its original location. Each piece of furniture lived under the observation of its double. A walnut armchair with seat and back of crimson brocade was here against the eastern wall and there against the western. A cushioned taboret stood on this side of the slender onyx table in the center of the room, and again on that side. Two long, high-backed sofas austerely regarded each other from opposite side walls; even the bronze chandeliers were twins. Along the same wall, balancing the first mantel, second mantel owed its reputation to the baby turtles clustered on a mossy green stump under two oval glass globes. When I shook the globe, as I did on cleaning days, the turtles quivered in head and tail.

The symmetry of the furnishings extended to the walls. On one side of the front mantel a broad, gold frame enclosing a crayon portrait of Mother was companioned by the equally heavy-corniced frame of the portrait of Father on the other side. When the bronze chandelier was lit and the light of the sixteen gas jets kindled the gold of the crusted moldings, the frames doubled in magnificence. Everybody agreed that the portraits were speaking likenesses; few failed to count the stones in Mother's earrings and brooch, marveling at the accuracy of the reproduction.

When we had visitors I used the opportunity to sit beneath Mother's portrait, so that I might have a full view of the canvas on the opposite wall, on which was painted in oil a sad-eyed girl, standing before a mirror, trying on a jeweled necklace and earrings. Strings of pearls hung from the casket on the table beside her. I was puzzled by the sadness of her face as she regarded herself in the mirror. Nobody explained her sadness. Our guests stood before the painting, made note of the long gold braids and the casket; then, flattered by their recognition, turned to Mother.

"Marguerite?" they ventured.

Mother made gracious assent. "Marguerite."

Mother had purchased Marguerite at an auction sale. All the art treasures of our house were trophies of exciting battles in crowded parlors and dining rooms and hallways of dismantled mansions. George Washington and Lady Washington would never have held their levees on the rear wall of our parlor, nor would Macbeth, on our eastern wall, have clutched the dagger that he saw before him, had Mother not carried off both expensive steel engravings from competitors at historic sales.

Mother never missed an auction sale on aristocratic premises. If Father accompanied her, complications were likely to occur, involving mutual reproaches and scars that never healed. No visitor climbed the twenty-three steps to our second story (we counted them as if distinction lay in their number) who did not stop in admiration before the rich dark canvas that covered six feet of wall. Not even the niche above, at the head of the stairs, which held the white plaster of Bacchus, could prevent him from stopping long enough to enjoy the vista of the timbered chain of the Rocky Mountains. No appreciation of guests, however, could compensate for the pain associated with its history. Mother and Father had attended that auction sale together. Separated by the crowd, they lost sight of each other. The beauty and dimension of the landscape called with similar urgency to each of them, and from different angles of

104

the huge room they bid against each other. Father captured the prize, but at what a price! Nineteen dollars and fifty cents, and Mother's everlasting accusation!

It was only after my sister Polly was "out" that the parlors were opened informally to visitors. Before that time they were occupied only on Sundays and on state occasions, such as Addie's engagement reception, when floral offerings, horseshoes, interlaced hearts, and cornucopias grouped around the mantel gave the room something of the aspect of a popular funeral.

I never entered the parlor unmoved by awe. If I were sure Mother would be away all afternoon, I ventured in alone. I turned the key, pressed the door open (it stuck a little from disuse), and let my feet sink to my ankles, so deep it seemed, into the soft silence of the carpet. I never dared to walk the full length of the room, but stood still, frightened by the shadows that clung to its farthest reaches. If enough sunshine percolated through the shutters to moderate my fear, I walked across to the mantel, pressed my foot heavily upon the tongue of the cuspidor, and observed the cover slowly rise, reveal the lustrous white interior, and slowly descend again. Then I stole out of the room, carefully locking the door that no sign of disarrangement might betray my invasion.

# 8

# *The Music Room*

The music room was redolent of gentility; indeed, it was something to say, "You will find her in the music room," and I sometimes strained opportunity for the pleasure of the designation. To its distinction as a room reserved for music was added the innovation of an alcove, not accidental, but built with the house, to receive the Steinway square piano. Of all our friends, we alone possessed a piano that fitted into an architectural frame, and we waited for our friends' unfailing exclamations of surprised approval. When the Swedish painter added cupids to the alcove wall, the music room almost rivaled the parlor in interest and elegance. Later no one could remember in whose imagination, Mother's or the Swedish painter's, the idea of the cupids had birth, but the vision, once entertained, was not to be relinquished.

We regarded, as a miracle, the way we came to have the interior of our house painted. The Swedish painter, a frescoer, had come to California expecting to find work. Failing to find any, he had consented to decorate our ceiling at a moderate price. The extensive ceilings of the parlor alone were to be covered, but when he suggested for the ceiling of the music room a lattice of bamboo intertwined with garlands of tea roses and autumn leaves, and burnished birds of copper and blue winging their flight across the area of the firmament not occupied by the base of the chandelier, the improvisation was irresistible. Mother said, "No," but in the end she gave her consent. The result was entrancing. Even Mother did not regret the outlay.

106

Each member of the family, in turn, lay upon the sofa, surrendering himself to that picture of rural delight. Each discovered a bird which the others had failed to descry, and each declared that he could lie there forever and ever, just looking. To this uplifted state of mind, the cupids on the alcove were proposed and met with enthusiastic approval. They could not be too numerous nor too voluminous, so expansive had become the emotion of the family. After conference and discussion, we decided that there should be three, the dimensions of the composition and the figures themselves to be left to the judgment of the painter.

Later, however, Mother pointed out that, as long as the space above the piano was there and the expense the same, they might as easily be painted large, and so they broadly spread into life before our enchanted eyes. Under the magic brush of the painter, where blank walls had been, appeared three plump pink cupids, a trio of innocence and playfulness, each contributing, through horn, or clarinet, or flute, his individual note of gladness. If the niche had pleased by its novelty, the cupids painted upon its walls dissolved the onlooker by their grace and charm, and although we accepted with restraint the admiration they excited, our shining eyes betrayed our exaltation.

After dinner it was our daily habit to go into the music room. "Let us have a little music," Father said, and we all arose from the table; all but Mother, who remained to instruct the servant concerning the disposition of the fowl left on the platter, safeguarding the reappearance of certain portions, unmolested, upon the morrow.

In the language of the day both my sisters were musically inclined. Polly, who played the piano, "had a fine touch"; Addie sang "with feeling"; Polly played "by heart," and could transpose into any key any melody that she had heard once. She spent hours daily, practicing scales and five-finger exercises for a teacher whom she hated. Strange composers were coming into vogue, Beethoven and Chopin, but she preferred Offenbach and saw no reason to change. Addie also played, and it was pleasant to listen to their duets, *Poet and Peasant* and *William Tell*. I would wait for the storm in the Alps, and when the twenty fingers ran up and down the piano in galloping crescendo, I felt excitement and wildness, as of horses racing around a circus ring.

Though Polly had a moving contralto voice, she would take no singing lessons. Addie, who had no natural endowment, submitted to laborious training. She was a sober girl, reticent and without coquetry, a gentle, kindly girl whom everyone liked. Addie was Father's favorite. Everyone said, "A nice girl," and "She is her father's favorite." They said of Polly under their breath, "Such a devil," their eyes following her with approval.

After dinner it was Addie who sang to please Father. However, if young men were present, Polly would entertain them. People said of Polly, "She's a girl who can entertain at the piano for hours." Some of the arias were introduced by a stately recitative like an avenue leading to a palace. We called them "retchitateefs," accenting the word sharply on the last syllable, savoring the explosive violence of foreign sound. Addie's great number was the aria from the *Barber of Seville, "Una voce poca fa."* We settled back for that. Father, in his armchair, folded his long woolen dressing gown around his knees. I sought the shadows of the couch where my emotion would not be observed. Mother, on the edge of her chair, alone sat upright.

When sung by Addie, the aria opened with notes that plumbed tonal depths of solemnity. We listened earnestly, realizing that it was a difficult number, making heroic demands upon the vocalist, and were impressed by Addie's ability to take the breakers, as it were. Of ourselves, we would not have expected the aria of Addie's limited vitality; but *"Una voce poca fa"* was the touchstone of vocal skill and Miss Tourney, Addie's singing teacher, in pride of spirit, whipped up Addie's mezzo-soprano to an incredible height from which it ascended afresh in tenuous sprays.

I did not altogether enjoy the number. The cadences *ad libitum* hurt me. Even when curled upon the couch in Mother's bedroom, the shrill jets of sound could discover my ears, after having penetrated timber and plaster and the double interlining of the heavy Brussels carpet. I tightened, too, with suspense for fear that Addie might not have reserved enough breath to last to the finale. But as she achieved the spiral ascents and perilous returns, and still had a reserve for the sustained note of passion, Father turned to us as if to say, "She's going to make it."

When Addie planted a foot upon the summit ("S'largo giubilazione"), our sympathies closed upon her in fond rejoicing. The final chord of Polly's accompaniment was a flag flying. No one would have demanded another number after an effort so arduous, but "What now?" Addie herself asked, and interpreting the look in Father's eyes as the desire she knew it to be, she sang, not without genuine feeling, the beautiful aria from *The Marriage of Figaro*, *"Die Ihr die Triebe des Herzens kennt, Sagt ist es Liebe was hier so brennt?"* I, too, loved that moving melody and understood the moisture in Father's eye.

Excited by our admiration, Addie struck a gayer note with "Il Bacio (The Kiss)," Arditi's waltz famous as an encore by Adelina Patti. Galvanized into sudden liveliness, she bent her head with a little birdlike twist, fluttered her eyelids, and began in saucy staccato, *"Sul-le Sul-le labra,"* wandering into seductive legato, panting in her efforts to keep up with Polly's relentless acceleration, and ending on a note of accomplishment that justified all the money paid to Miss Tourney for her instruction. Father beamed his pride, and Mother rearranged the tidy back of his easy chair detached in his emotion. Now Addie sang ballad after ballad, defending the claims of the heart against worldly prudence. She was possessed by a compulsive predilection for shepherds, and passionately disclaimed the suits of landed gentry though they came laden with treasure like the three kings of the East.

"They say I may marry the laird if I will," she confided, her eyes far away in distant reminiscence.

> *"The laird of high degree,*
> *And jewels so fair*
> *I may twine in my hair*
> *And a lady I'd surely be,*

"But oh!" Addie cried with sudden shrillness, and I jumped.

> *"But oh where would my heart be*
> *In spite of the gems so gay?"*

109

Her hand rose to the invisible brooch upon her bosom.

> *"My heart it would break*
> *For somebody's sake."*

I crinkled under the circling, coquettish glance that looped the music stand back of Father.

> *"So I think I had better say nay.*
> *And . . ."*

A pause, and Addie, swinging her head from side to side in happy abandon, confessed her decision:

> *"I will marry my own love,*
> *My own love, my own love;*
> *And I will marry my own love*
> *For true of heart am I."*

It may have been disapproval of the sentiment of the song from a native reluctance to encourage an unworldly alliance, or merely a mechanistic reflex that impelled Mother to rise before the end of the ballad and pull a chair back from its threatened encroachment on the newly painted wall, while Father and I sat lost in the glow of Addie's tender fidelity.

An inevitable number of the musical program was drawn I from a touching story of war history. A young soldier hears the song his sweetheart used to sing, is overmastered by longing, flees to her, is captured and shot. I loved the song, but could scarcely bear the pain of its tragedy. The ballad opened with a single statement, charged with prophecy:

> *"Roses blossom on an early grave."*

I repeatedly nourished the hope that the tragedy might be averted, that a reprieve might have been secured since my last hearing of the song, but when I saw that the story was moving on to its merciless end, I fled from the room. Outside the door I could hear the chords of doom:

> *"A soldier's heart doth beat no more."*

While I choked and Father blew his nose, and Mother readjusted the bronze cow to its original angle on the mantelpiece, Polly's hands ran off into inconsequent melodies from "Le Petit Duc" and "La Fille de Madame Angot," publishing her release from enforced service.

A duet would draw her into the family again. She had an unshakeable sense of pitch. No matter how the soprano threatened, Polly held her own. The soprano might hover, approach, engulf her; Polly held her course, as if steering by an invisible compass. As for me, no matter what I was when the duet began, I was the other voice before the song had ended. I prayed that I might be able to sustain a pitch, so that I, too, might be included in the rapture of a duet.

"Do let me try," I entreated, and if Addie were absent and no one was there to take her place, Polly ungraciously consented. Then I turned my back to the piano, fixed my eyes upon the chandelier, by a psychic twist turned off all sound, and began:

> *"What are the wild waves saying*
> *Sister, the whole day long*
> *That ever amid our playing*
> *I hear but their low lone song?"*

Polly answered:

> *"Brother, I hear no singing*
> *'Tis but the rolling wave*
> *Ever its lone course winging*
> *Over some ocean cave."*

All was going well. Our voices rose in unison:

> *"No, no, no—no, no, no.*
> *It is something greater*
> *That speaks to the heart alone,*
> *The voice of the great Cre-a-tor*
> *Dwells in each mighty tone,*
> *The voice of the great Cre-a-a—"*

A crash from the piano brought me to earth. "You're off, you're off, can't you hear it yourself?"

"Let me try once more," I pleaded. "I'll close my ears." Then with my fingers in my ears, my eyes closed, and every muscle taut, I began afresh. A wave of fervor (the voice of the great Cre-a-a-tor) carried me to the end successfully. But when I opened my eyes the piano was shut and Polly had disappeared.

To Addie's singing teacher we gave unreservedly of our gratitude for the flowering of Addie's talent. With disturbed curiosity, I regarded her—a tall, vigorous, huge-bosomed, middle-aged woman. She had been on the stage in her youth, and the pleasure of our association with her was enhanced by that experience. It was as good as if James O'Neill or Richard Mansfield were directing our recital of "The quality of mercy is not strained," or "Blow, bugle, blow! set the wild echoes flying!"

Miss Tourney was single and she lived alone. How could she be so old and yet unwed? I knew no other unmarried woman of her age. I knew that there were old maids; a cousin was fast becoming one. I heard my mother reproach her on her twenty-first birthday, but that did not mean that girl would not eventually marry; it meant only that she would have to go to the country to live, to the interior. The interior was the market for all marriageable material that could not be advantageously disposed of in the city.

Shopkeepers came to the city from the interior, from towns of the San Joaquin or Sacramento valleys, or from the mining towns, Grass Valley, Calaveras, or Mokelumne Hill to buy goods. Their quest often included a sentimental hope, confided to a downtown wholesale merchant. If a man's appearance was agreeable and his credit good, he would be invited to the merchant's home to dine and meet the unmarried daughters. To my faith that conceived the interior as broad enough to take care of every unmated daughter, the celibacy of Miss Tourney was disquieting.

She deviated from the accepted in other ways. The threat of a mother to a fastidious daughter was the prophecy that she would dry up into an old maid. I believed the shriveling processes attending delayed matrimony to be a visible law of physiology. Yet here was Louise Tourney flowering and redundant. Again, she was the only woman I knew who lived alone. Everybody lived with somebody, a mother or an aunt, or even another sister. But all alone! I tried to imagine such living. All my fancy could draw was a thin, solitary figure, standing at an open window, looking forlornly out at the world, a picture suggested by the German song that Mother sang as a warning to her "particular" daughters:

> *"The long, long day*
> *I know only pain*
> *And in the night*
> *I weep again.*
> *When I wounded him*
> *He would often say*
> *You will weep for me*
> *Many a day."*

But Miss Tourney was too bristling for so delicate a setting, and my imagination could not bend the robust figure and enormous bosom to an appropriate droop of desolation.

# 9

## *The Dining Room*

Father sat silent in the tufted maroon armchair that stood in the corner of the dining room before the folding glass doors leading into the music room. Father had been growing quiet of late. He asked no question about our work at school, not even teasing me with his monthly wager that I would not have a number one on my report card. If he were spoken to, he answered in short sentences.

Something was wrong downtown. Mother said nothing, but from time to time she sent glances of inquiry toward him. Father grew worse as the days passed. One night at dinner he suddenly dropped his knife and fork, got up from the table, and sank into the armchair in the corner. We continued to eat in silence, but we no longer knew what we were eating. I stole a glance toward him, where he sat motionless, until, in answer to some disturbing thought, he raised a hand and brought it down flat upon his knee. We jumped at the noise.

"What is it?" Mother asked. "At least tell me what's the matter."

No answer.

"*Stumm* [mute]," Mother said. She tried again, "Is anything wrong downtown?"

"No, everything is fine, wonderful," Father answered with a quick bitter smile.

"It isn't Blumenthal?"

"No, it isn't Blumenthal." And then it came. "It's Fulda. Fulda is shaky."

Mother said nothing. She understood. Father had ten thousand dollars invested in the firm of J. Fulda & Company. A failure!

Nothing in my whole experience could compare with it, nothing could so at a stroke take the edge off of living and envelop a world in shadow. We were never completely free from the fear of it; Father's face had only to show a deeper line, and we framed one inquiry.

We had had no experience to serve as a measure of its significance. No sudden or untimely death had entered our lives, no serious illness or accident, nor had we known vice or intemperance in our family; so that a failure stood alone as the great calamity that might bear down upon us at any hour, and that was not to be avoided.

The desolation that it brought to pass invested it with power for me. Not that the loss of money affected our way of living; no change in our lives had followed upon a loss. A possible failure was terrible only because of its effect upon father and the consequent effect upon us. To him it was a catastrophe, and so it became a catastrophe to us forever. Forever, because it gave to money a precedence that it never lost in computing relative values in life, making of it the basis of serenity and confidence. With the loss of it, we saw strong natures reduced to helplessness and confusion and enveloped in gloom. Seeing that, money came to denote not a means of securing agreeable living, but something whose loss produced emotional havoc. I deduced that every caution must continually be exercised to avoid a loss that entailed such serious consequences. The conviction followed inevitably that money is security.

I did not suspect that there might be another viewpoint. I did not know that there were people who measured their security by the assurance of power they felt within themselves, and to whom experience was zest and confirmation; that to stand alone, backed by no negotiable note against the hazards of life, was in itself an attitude by which unsuspected resources might be evoked. Nothing of the refreshment of a plunge-and-trust attitude did I dream of, until the habit of dependence upon possessions for confidence had caged the impulse to experiment, and adventure was no longer possible as a joyous exercise of strength. From whom could I have learned such a strange doctrine?

115

Beginning with Louis Levison, our right-hand neighbor, at 922 O'Farrell Street, down past two solid blocks of houses to the Kauffmans', the heads of the two-story-and-basement wooden houses were as identical in cast as the buildings they owned and occupied—solid merchants who had left villages in Germany and Poland to come as boys to America, sailed around the Horn to California in the early fifties, and started a business in small towns of the interior, in the mining settlements of the Sierras, or in the fertile valleys of the Sacramento and San Joaquin rivers. As soon as they accumulated a little money they came to the city, became wholesale merchants, jobbers, or manufacturers, acquiring prestige and complacency as they rose. There was no deviation from the one standard of excellence. Each had a paying business, a family, a house and lot, and some money in the bank. Each stood firm on his feet, looked the world straight in the eye, and knew that he measured up well by the standard of God and man. They paid their dues to the synagogue, observed the Sabbath, gave to the charities, supported poor relations, and among men in business their word was as good as their bond.

They stood for solid possessions, acquired by solid worth, upon adherence to solid principles. They were all strong men in muscle and in moral fiber. They obeyed the law; they spoke the truth and expected it. Rooted in favorable soil, they were destined to live the full years of their allotment. Not one died under seventy; not one was disabled before the end. They inspired confidence in natural law by which one came into the world, grew, flourished, and passed away. A regiment presenting a solid phalanx resolved itself into Greens, Loebs, and Lilienfelds massed into invincibility. The world of successful merchants was our world, and I did not know that there was another.

In their presence there was no place for doubt or inquiry. One standard of prestige existed as did one God: to have money was to be somebody; to have none, was to be nobody; the man who had more was better than the man who had less. To have little, but to be on the path to acquire more, was to be ambitious and praiseworthy; to have much with a prospect of acquiring much more was importance and distinction. All this I accepted, and gauged our status by this measure. The name Weil was spoken—and B. Weil of Weil Brothers, wealthy tanners, came to mind accompanied by a quick "better than us." Everyone was "better than us," "not so good as us," "just as good as us," according to the measure of rich or poor, Bavarian or Pole. The pleasure I felt in our excellence was insignificant, but the pain that I suffered from our inferiority was intense. Moreover, so busy was I kept securing barriers to pain or trying to make good in the eyes of superiors that I sacrificed my sensibility to living as it unfolded before me, and estimated people largely by their capacity to produce in me confidence or discomfort. The sensitiveness to pain was an exaggerated one, and the impress was often for life.

Once, when I was a mature woman, returned home after years of absence, I found myself alone in the dining room of a large hotel. A man and a woman whom I had not seen since I was a girl entered; they had both grown white-haired and old, but I recognized them as wealthy leaders of social life with whom my parents had had no contact during my childhood. As they passed my table the woman looked squarely at me, and my eyes dropped. "Better than us."

If Father had failed in business, and we had tasted the worst that pecuniary misfortune can do to a capable man, no doubt we should have made a readjustment to changing fortune and enjoyed the confidence inspired by survival. But the experience did not occur, and the sudden loss of money remained for me the one catastrophe threatening a solid universe. There were few ups and downs in the lives about us. There were good years and poor years; money put aside from business that might go someday to the purchase of a carriage and horses; or a more imposing home; or, at worst, a loss. But of the real hazard of life there was none.

Any capital not invested in Father's business was loaned to individuals or firms on personal notes. Later, when he retired, all his capital was loaned in this way. The downtown world was a small one, and there was no need of Bradstreet. If a firm was sound, it was likely to continue so, free from the suspicion of risky speculation. Father might take a fling at mining stocks, of course, but his muscles were not trained on a broad arc, and the risk would not be dangerous to his capital. Notes were made out three months or six

117

months after date. The rich firms gave notes written one day after date, which was impressive. There was no other security than a man's business rating and his integrity—good security for the most part. Uncertainty more often concerned itself with the return of a note than with the failure to pay it. If there was no "A-1" firm available, Father would sow the seed of wakeful nights by loaning money to someone in whom he had not complete confidence.

Sometimes the fear would grow with rumors downtown, and after much hesitation and embarrassment he would force himself to ask for a return of his money. If the merchant returned it with resentment, Father was satisfied that he had acted wisely in withdrawing it. On the other hand, if it were restored with unconcern, Father became depressed and reproached himself for his suspicions. His capital was made of the earnings and savings of years, and all his imagination had to play with was the balance of saving over expenditure. On the first day of every year, as he counted his two columns, he already anticipated the larger balance of the next year. The contraction following a loss was the contraction of a vision.

Fulda & Company caused him no end of anxiety. The rumor of their instability came as a surprise to him. Ten thousand dollars was a big amount to lose, if the rumor were well-founded, and would be a difficult sum to reinvest if it were not. The strain finally became too great, and he asked for the return of his money. It was given to him, but Mr. Fulda turned his head away when he met Father on the street. A month later J. Fulda & Company failed in business, and paid their creditors fifty cents on the dollar.

"Better that he shouldn't talk to me than that I shouldn't talk to him," Father said when he told the story.

# 10

## *The Front Bedroom*

The front bedroom was the only room in the house that offered sunshine and warmth. Entering it from the shadowed hall was like stepping out into a garden. The tall windows of the bay, opened to the southern sky, received full drafts of light from sunrise to sunset, drawing us all into the comforting embrasure. All day long the shades were high, and we might sit at a window thawing deliciously or, if the time were short, stand for a moment warming our backs, or enjoying a glimpse of the drama of the street. A gay room: sunshine, walls of rose-embossed satin (paper, yes, but of a texture!), mantel cover, and long drape of honey-combed, rose-lustered wool, a carpet of cool gray velvet with slow-moving scrolls and garlands of roses. Not even the heavy weight of bureau and bedstead could diminish the glow. Rather did they unbend in playful detail to the color of the environment.

The sumptuous bureau of walnut with its tall, narrow mirror up to the cornice, the low, broad drawer close to the floor, and the succession of small drawers high on either side, solidly settled into place between mantel and bay, secure of tenure as long as the house should stand. Not mere bulk of wood and solemn breadth; not pompous, but genial, with smiles of ornament and gay bands of curly veneer, and chubby handles dangling from smoothly sliding drawers. The marble tops were softened by tidies of creamy lace, edges and design outlined with piping of red. On one side stood a silver-plated jewel box, which rolled back like the lid of a desk, disclosing rich puffing of deep blue satin. On the other side prongs of silver clasped a frail glass vase, which never held a flower lest the water imperil the daintiness beneath.

To stand before the tall mirror and see all of myself at once, especially when my hair was let out, was intoxication. The night before a party I knelt before Mother's chair while she divided my long, heavy hair into twenty strands and plaited each tightly into a narrow, stiff braid. They began painfully close to the scalp and ended in ragged wisps. "Many more?" I asked, sharply twisting my head to see.

"Enough! Hold still." And Mother pulled my head back into line.

My knees and back ached long before the last rigid plait was fastened to the long white string that held them all together. It was hard sleeping on the knobs that night, but next morning, after the strings were untied and the braids opened and combed ("You hurt, you hurt!" "Be still, be still!"), the discomfort of the night was forgotten. I shook my head and the great, black, crinkly mass leaped wide, as if charged by a hidden battery.

Crimps were for an occasion only; so was the white piqué dress, my party dress, that lent to me, I believed, something of the state of my sisters, who had worn it and, in turn dropped it upon my shoulders as they ascended. Blue-ribbed cotton stockings and soft black shoes supported it. When Mother unrolled the broad grosgrain ribbon of the sash and tied it around my waist, I could scarcely wait to reach the mirror. I stood before the long glass, regarding with satisfaction a white dress starched to the breaking point, its circumference reinforced by petticoat and starched drawers becoming visible as I swayed. A large bow of sky-blue ribbon sprang smartly from my back. I shook my head slowly, and my long hair opened like a black fan. Then I ran downstairs to the kitchen to show myself to Maggie Doyle that she might tell me how fine I was.

The bedroom was so large, so rich in adornment of wall and carpet and furniture that the satisfied eye came with a start to its most distinctive feature. You were looking with pleasure at the bureau or the heavy lace curtains emphasizing the bay; or you were stirred by sadness, sensing the humiliation of Napoleon III who surrendered his sword to Prince Bismarck in the steel engraving

120

over the mantel. Father hated the picture and entreated its removal, but Mother, remembering the price, was relentless); or you were admiring the bronze storks and dark, veined onyx clock upon the mantelshelf; or corroborating with a tracing finger the white scroll pattern raised from the rose satin ground of the paper that enriched the walls—elegance associated only with palaces of French kings— when, turning to tell of your admiration, you beheld the Alcove— or rather the Bed, for the Bed *was* the alcove.

The bed filled the alcove, leaving just enough space on one side to walk to the lace-draped window, which gave upon the little porch, and on the other side to the closet called Father's closet. The bed was of walnut—solid walnut, we said; the prefix was inevitable as the George before the name of Washington. Mother would knock upon it with the knuckle of her second finger against any unspoken suspicion in the mind of a visitor. It was broad, broad enough to have housed a king, queen, and three little princesses comfortably. On stormy nights, when the house shook, a child could crawl into it and sleep at the foot and never touch a toe. The long sides were low, and the headboard rose superbly to the crest, but the eye rarely reached the top at one glance. It was arrested by a great moon of polished walnut; swirls of mellow luster glimmered through the surface as through glass. Slender rectangular columns on either side were crowned by festal cupolas, like the ornament of bells upon the white satin cover of the Sephar Torah, the Scroll of the Law, in the synagogue. The base of the bed was ornamented by a broad rectangle of veneer, also beautiful but not so imposing. If Mother was out on a visit, I would push the sofa aside and kneel to see my image, or I would draw a finger slowly over the smoothness. Then I hurried to the commode for the dark red felt bag that held the silver teaspoons, and carefully rubbed away the marks of delinquency. A beneficent bed, even the low posts at the foot curved into knobs that fitted into the hollow of the hand comfortingly.

The bed, dressed, was unapproachable in its ceremonial stateliness. It stood there, an object so fixed that daily experience with its morning disarray could not interfere with the later illusion of a permanent dignity. Through the meshes of the heavy lace spread and pillow shams glowed the bloom of rose sateen. The pillows rose, stiff and high, like Mother's rigid pompadour. To sit upon the bed was an act unthinkable to the most wanton child; to place a hat or coat upon it was to witness their instant removal with a sharp reproof from Mother. I have seen Father's top hat rise, as if borne by a wind, from the pink bed to the high shelf in his shallow closet. In the morning the bed was unrecognizable. It had burst confinement; it was uncontrolled, loose, ribald—a fat woman who had chucked her corset. The scarlet mattress of feathers protruded here and bulged there from the restraint of sheet and blanket in deep, rich disorder. It is inconceivable that Mother should have found relaxation and repose among those voluptuous billows. Did the rigid spine yield to its sensuous hollows, or did she lie upon the crest, resisting this appeal as she did all the blandishments of life?

To the embrace of the sunny bedroom I should have run wholeheartedly but for the disturbing and mysterious objects which it housed.

There were Mother's teeth. I did not know whether my sisters knew the truth about them, and if they shrank from them as I did. Even to myself I did not admit that they were unlike my own; but if I ran into the room in the early morning I never failed to send a quick glance to the chair beside the bed to assure myself that the glass upon it contained only water. If I saw the shadow of a darker object within it, I pretended that I had forgotten something and retreated to my room. Occasionally I intercepted a swift movement of Mother's arm reaching out and returning from the chair, and I heard a strange noise as of a sparrow at his bath. Once I burst into the room a second too early. Mother's eyes met mine in consternation, made up of guilt, entreaty, and accusation. Even before I fled, we had silently agreed to repudiate the revelation.

Toward Father's side of the bed I also looked with sidelong eyes, lest I see the high martial boots which disquieted me. If he was pulling them off I turned away, conscious of an obscure indelicacy. Sometimes I looked squarely and beheld him sitting on the edge of the bed stretching back, his cheeks blown and coarse, his muscles straining as he drew on his boots with steel hooks like piano-tuning hammers. Furtively I made my escape.

To look into the shallow closet beside the bed and examine all of

Father's belongings, every object familiar from long use or concealed for occasion, was a morning's pleasurable occupation. First, however, I had to obliterate the dark shadow in the corner of the high shelf if I were to enjoy the elegance that moved upon the glossy surface of his black broadcloth and the parade that sprang from the red flannel underwear, piled upon the lower shelf, close to the floor. On the high shelf, safeguarded by cardboard and tissue paper, waited the stovepipe hat of unblemished polish and the piqué vest with glass buttons, which bided the coming of a holiday. I regarded them with grave interest, investing them with something of the solemnity of the days on which they would be unveiled and worn.

In the dark corner of the shelf, coiled like a snake, lay the phylacteries. I could not talk about the phylacteries, and my fingers shunned contact with the long, narrow band of black leather that Father wound around and around his upper left arm, and the two narrower bands with the small, square, leather box in the center that he wore every morning in the middle of his forehead while he said his prayers.

The box and its contents puzzled me, but I asked no question, fearing that knowledge might add to my uneasiness. Nobody made mention of the phylacteries. Father just wore them and, when he had finished the reading of the morning prayers, returned them to the closet like tools. My surprise would have been great, my fancy delighted, could I have invested them with the hues of their ancient origin and have known that the tiny box held, in miniature, the "Hear, O, Israel: The Lord our God, the Lord is One," could I have heard in them the echo of "And these words which I command you this day shalt be in thy heart. . . . And thou shalt bind them for a sign upon thy hand, and they shall be for frontlets between thy eyes." Instead, the phylacteries continued alien objects, stirring distaste and an unspoken entreaty that they would disappear from Father's closet forever.

However, Father never relinquished the offices of his daily devotion. Clad in red flannel underwear, his legs encased almost to the knees in the black boots, the stovepipe hat tilted back on his head, the Law between his eyes and encircling his arm, Father silently read the morning service. Nor did we think his raiment inappropriate or amusing. Occasionally, as he read, he wandered into the bay and approached the window, looking up and down the street.

"Levy," Mother called sharply to him. "Come away. What will the neighbors think?"

Whereupon Father looked at her over the spectacles he was not wearing, and reluctantly retired into the room with no interruption to his devotion.

He slept in his heavy red flannel shirt and drawers. With a helmet and a hatchet added, he would have been ready to leap upon a hook and ladder. Sitting up in bed, his strong, heavy marked face outlined against the white pillows, he looked like an early American statesman. In the early morning I peeped into the room to see if he were alone. If Mother was already in the kitchen, I sat at the foot of his bed and we, Father and I, talked of plays and actors—talked until Mother's voice sharply reminded us of the late hour, and I hastened from the room to breakfast.

If I remembered in time I left the bedroom without seeing it but, unless I was alert, the corner of my eye caught the small metal case that clung, as by pores, to the jamb of the door leading into the hall. Years passed before I was able to look at it with free eyes. I asked no questions, fearing that here again I entered a forbidden zone. The distrust, awakened by the object itself perched up there like a talisman, was deepened by its name: Mezuzah. Invasion of our intimate life by an object so estrangingly named—Mezuzah—confirmed the accusation that we were a peculiar people, and I did not wish to be peculiar. I wanted to be like. As no question was asked, the explanation was not provided that, upon a tiny scroll of parchment within the case, was inscribed, as upon the tablet of the phylacteries, the Sh'mah, the unity of God. "And thou shalt write them upon the doorposts of thy house and upon thy gates."

I knew that, in homes more orthodox than our own, the men of the house, as they came and went, placed a finger on the lips and upon the case. At least, I thought, we were spared that added isolation. I did not know that the act accompanied the gentlest of silent prayers: "May God guide my going out and my coming in." I continued to dislike the metal box and, although my sisters later referred to it without visible embarrassment, I did not lose my distrust nor would I have touched it any more than I would have put a finger to the phylacteries.

But all these shadowed areas were as nothing compared to the mystery of the big bedroom closet. Here was prohibition unbroken over fifteen years, mystery not even second to the Great Mystery. For of sex I feared only enlightenment, while the closet threatened anger and punishment. It was as secure against invasion as if Thou Shalt Not were burned above the door. My imagination danced before its promise; no limit to the surprise it might conceal nor to the unpredictable riches it safeguarded. Father never entered it; Mother was the sole guardian of its mysteries.

Treasure came out of the closet; a heavily fluted soup ladle of solid silver; a broad cake knife, chased and perforated into design so thin that it threatened to break under the pressure of a finger, yet bearing without injury the strain of deep slices of triple layer cake; a sugar bowl with delicately curved handles, the cover crowned by a little globe that tempted rubbing, so brightly could it be made to shine. If I came into the bedroom, I might see heaped on the sofa all the smooth satiny metal—dull, ready to be taken to the kitchen, or lustrous like a mirror, renewed under the palm of Maggie Doyle. I never saw Mother in the act of carrying the silver into the closet or removing it; but I knew that, with my retirement, it would be restored, and understood that I was not to betray that I knew its abiding place.

When Mother paid formal calls, she carried a rectangular cardcase of finely threaded silver filigree that I admired and was sometimes permitted to hold. Between calls I never saw it. There was also a flat box, covered with polished gray-and-black-plaid paper, that opened on a hinge and exposed a pink rose pasted upon the inner surface. The box held precious objects all of a hereditary complexion: a handkerchief and collar of rose point, firm but exquisite and, best of all, the cream-colored, polished dance program of Mother's wedding party, bearing record of bride and groom, the members of the reception and floor committees, and the order of dancing: march and waltz, quadrille, schottische, mazurka, waltz, and polka. If permitted to hold and read the program, I would try to draw Mother into romantic remembrance. But it was useless; she only withdrew

125

the card from my hand and let the lid of the box drop upon it. Then she put the box into the bureau drawer from which it would vanish upon my departure from the room.

A wedding or a party, and the closet yielded even greater riches. Early in the afternoon an evening dress of black velvet or grosgrain silk, high-necked and long-sleeved, stretched a trailing length upon the couch as in a swoon. Later, gowned, Mother stood before the mirror regarding her image coldly; never a quickening of pleasure or excitement. If we observed the slenderness of her waist, she waived the praise; it had once been small—twenty inches could have spanned it. She said this often until I could not think of her waist, except as encompassed by interlocking fingers.

"Your eyes are beautiful," I said.

"They said that they were like the eyes of Lola Montez," Mother answered, unmoved by the memory.

As she stood there, her eyes upon the mirror, her arm moved out and from nowhere, as if clasped from the air by a prestidigitator, her hand had drawn a pair of pendent diamond earrings: three stones, the largest a huge diamond encased in a cup of yellow gold. Now I looked at the bureau, and without surprise, as one habituated to the miraculous, I saw, where a moment before there had been nothing, the great round diamond brooch, each of the fifteen diamonds standing high, detached, grouped around the central stone like satellites around the sun.

In like miraculous fashion appeared upon the bureau top a green velvet box holding a heavy gold watch chain and a watch of crusted gold in the center of which, ringed by embedded pearls, gleamed a diamond-flaked disk of dark blue enamel, a sky dotted with stars.

To behold the surface would have been enough, had I not known what it concealed. If I asked Mother to open the case of the watch, she said no; if I insisted, she inserted the nail of her little finger into an invisible crevice, lifted the lid, and there, under glass, was a picture of Father. The wonder never grew less, and the delay before the revealing seemed appropriate to so momentous a happening. I did not recognize Father in the gaunt face with the hollow cheeks and the heavy black beard; the unfamiliar aspect gave me a feeling of uneasiness, and confirmed Mother's taunt of "agitator."

126

The diamond set, the watch and chain, and the bracelets broad as manacles, which fitted so tightly that they added to their breadth a narrow roll of displaced flesh, were all the jewelry I had ever seen Mother wear. I felt sure that they were but a few of the countless gems and ornaments which she might draw at will from their place of concealment.

One day I ran into the bedroom to call Mother downstairs. The gas man was at the door with his bill. When I entered the room I found it empty, although I had heard Mother's step there a moment before. Turning about, I saw something that made me tremble. The door of the closet was open. Within it, shrouded in the folds of long black skirts hanging from their hooks, Mother was kneeling before a low, wide-opened door. In her hand she held the green velvet box. She looked up and saw me, and her face grew red. Instantly she was on her feet, bearing down upon me.

"Promise me, promise me," she cried, pointing a finger at me, "that you will never tell anybody!"

She did not name what it was I was not to tell. Terrified, I promised. Then, while I stood motionless, she returned to the closet and closed the low door. I heard the turning of a key and saw her raised arm reach to the high shelf and slide something under a newspaper lining. As she straightened the long black dress skirts, the low door disappeared behind them. Without a word to me she left the bedroom, and I could hear her voice below, raised against an excessive charge, and the gas agent protesting. After that day the closet was more urgent than ever, and the secret, half-disclosed, possessed me. Neither Mother nor I mentioned the catastrophe of my discovery.

One afternoon, weeks later, when we were expecting company for dinner, and Mother was busy in the kitchen, she asked me to go upstairs and bring down the soup ladle and vegetable spoons. I looked at her, unbelieving, but there was no sign of anything unusual in the command, except a voice lowered below the sensibility of Maggie Doyle's cocked ear. (Maggie Doyle could hear, Mother said, even when, as now, she was in the basement.) She explained to me carefully what I was to do.

"Be sure to lock the bedroom door," she called after me as I flew up the backstairs.

I could not wait to reach the bedroom; but, when I had closed the door, turned the key, and slid the bolt above, I was afraid. Locked in alone in the large silent room, I stood with my back against the door, as if an invisible intruder were pressing to enter. The closet before me was a mask, aware. I stood a moment looking at it; then I turned the knob and opened it.

A strong smell of camphor came to meet me. The closet was crowded with clothes; long dresses, all black, fell straight down from the iron hooks; three walls were hidden by them. In one corner square white bandboxes were piled one upon another. To one uninstructed, the closet would have differed from any woman's wardrobe only in somberness, but I knew. I rose on tiptoe and stretched an arm that hardly reached the high shelf; my fingers felt under a flattened newspaper until they touched and closed upon a key. I moved the curtain of dresses apart as I had been told to do, and halfway up the wall a shelf disclosed itself; below it was a key-hole. I inserted the key, turned it, and pulled out a deep drawer.

Here they were—all the familiar objects of splendor: the green brocade Japanese case, lined with scarlet, that contained the filigree cardcase; the wine-colored leather arched cover that would lean back and reveal the diamond brooch and earrings; and the polished gray-and-black-plaid box with the laces and wedding program. They looked strange in the unfamiliar setting, but genial, and I felt myself being led to the very heart of treasure. There was nothing else in the drawer, except a small piece of curved iron, a hook which I withdrew.

I looked down the face of the wall and marveled. Nobody would have known that it was anything but a closet wall. Nobody would have observed the little raw-edged hole, halfway up from the floor, or expected what lay behind it. I fitted the iron hook, and hesitated. It would have to be drawn slowly, so that the door would not open too wide, for I might be met by a rush of gold and silver when the door swung open. I pulled the door out cautiously. Before me was a cupboard with two shelves. On the upper one the green velvet box stood upon its ivory legs, the bracelet casket beside it. On the lower shelf my hands touched the fluted ladle, the vegetable spoons, and a bunch of tablespoons, held together loosely by a white string, the sugar bowl, and the creamer.

I placed each object beside me on the floor. Then I felt in the corners, and drew out an oblong block of heavy silver. Words were engraved on it. "From Jacob Meyer to Benjamin Levy, Virginia City, 1861." From another corner I drew a limp, dirty bankbook, and something that shone. It was a set of teeth, the plate of thin copper-colored gold. I returned it quickly to the shadows from which I had taken it. That was all. Nothing more! I strained my arm and my fingers, and again felt about into the dark recesses into which I could not see. Nothing more. I sat there alone, alone with the emptiness that was heavier than all the weight of gold and silver that I had expected to uncover. Then I returned the objects one by one, closed the cupboard, slid the drawer into place, locked it, and re-placed the key under the newspaper on the high shelf. I spread the thickness of black dresses over the wall and closed the closet door. The sunshine dazzled my eyes as I turned back to the room; I turned the key, drew the bolt, and walked down the backstairs.

"Did you lock it up again?" Mother asked me as I came into the kitchen.

I nodded.

"Where is the ladle?"

I looked down at my empty hands.

"And the vegetable spoons?"

I had forgotten to bring them. I did not explain, because I could not speak. I ran from the room.

# 11

## *The Back Bedroom*

In the early days of 920, when the back room was Addie's bedroom, and long before its contamination by Cousin Gustav's brief, catastrophic occupation, and the subsequent introduction of the sewing machine, agitation habitually emanated from its walls. Behind its locked door conferences were held, interviews of Mother with an affronted blood relative, of Mother with an old friend in trouble, come to confide a secret physical malady, a threatened disgrace from wayward daughter or lawless son, or an impending financial disaster. A certain cordiality of temperament in the room invited the fervors of the heart to unburden themselves.

In that room Mother and our beautiful cousin were closeted whenever Rosalie came to San Francisco on secret visits from Virginia City, Nevada. Rosalie was young and so like Mary Anderson, the beautiful actress, that an illustrious destiny of some order seemed to Mother a fitting and not extravagant hope for our cousin. But she could not be made to appreciate her endowment; she visited us again and again, in successive throes of love affairs with men of a degree so out of keeping with her beauty and our predicted destiny for her that Mother was forced to tears in her repeated efforts to halt the stride of her niece toward a calamitous marriage.

Rosalie enjoyed intermittent wealth. Each visit to us followed upon the wake of a tip from some mining magnate which, successfully acted upon, brought riches, but simultaneously touched off a floating passion, directing it toward the most immediate suitor. Jim

Fair's whisper toward Consolidated Virginia netted ten thousand dollars and a passion for the locomotive engineer who ran the train from Virginia City to Reno.

Mother entreated Rosalie to pause at this moment of maximum wealth and physical flowering, to take inventory of her assets and realize how desirable a husband she might hope for. Rosalie protested the strength of her own feeling, the manliness of her lover. Mother argued for worldly advantage, for a home in San Francisco, a cook, and a second servant. Finally the bedroom door opened upon a tear-stained, acquiescent girl, and a counselor not the less worn and red-lidded for her triumph.

The emotional life of the back room swelled into its fullest tide with the coming of Miss Lauber. When Mother opened the latest bill of Miss Denny, dressmaker to the exclusive Sherith Israel circle, and read, "Dress, fifty dollars, findings eight dollars and twenty cents," she announced to the family and to friends that Addie's new street suit would not be made by that highway robber, but by a dressmaker in the house. We would have Miss Lauber who, it was said, could turn out a finished costume between eight in the morning and sundown. A dressmaker who came to the house completed a dress in two days, working alone, or in one day with competent support from members of the family. Miss Lauber had been recommended as swift and stylish. Her price of four dollars a day was not so unreasonable as it sounded, for the extra dollar (other dressmakers received only three dollars) would be earned in time saved.

At seven-thirty on the morning of her coming the beds had been made and the breakfast table cleared; the household was trimmed for action. As the kitchen clock struck eight, the doorbell rang, and I ran downstairs to let in a tall, gaunt figure. Traveling up the long black coat, my eyes met a pallid, freckled face faintly lit by a gold-crowned tooth; singed wisps of yellow-red hair escaped from an unstable derby. She stopped a second, as if recovering a direction, then mounted the stairs with clipped buoyancy, a hand swinging a black satchel, an arm gripped upon an extra fashion book bought on the fly. Addie and Polly at the head of the stairs welcomed her with ardent eyes and, acting as escort to the back bedroom, delivered her to Mother and to the sewing machine, opened, oiled, dusted,

131

threaded, with extra filled bobbins in the drawer. The window was closed, the chair turned outward to receive her. Upon the bed lay folded yards of plum-colored broadcloth, gray sateen lining, whalebone, binding, a box of assorted pins. Nothing had been forgotten.

Miss Lauber fingered the cloth, and we waited upon her approbation.

"Nice material," she said. "For whom?"

Our eyes turned toward Addie.

"A becoming shade."

Her hat and coat were already on the bed and from the satchel she had drawn forth fashion books, a black sateen apron, and a long pair of scissors. "Now," she said, and she sat down and flattened a magazine upon the table. As she slowly turned the pages, pausing at each model to look at us for a sign, our eyes regarded the patterns avidly. When she stopped at one, which she declared to be appropriate to the material and, catching Mother's nod of agreement, arose scissors in hand, we stopped her and begged to be permitted to look into the other magazines. Mother opened them impatiently, one after another, thumbing the pages quickly, encouraging decision. How could they decide so quickly? We admired the basque of a cadet blue street dress, ornamented with horizontal rows of black silk braid and silver buttons; we marveled at the wavy circular skirt of a pink tulle evening dress; our eyes clung to the sleeve of a redingote that flared sharply at the waist. Irresistible details, we could not bear to relinquish one. We reasoned that a union in one model of the unique features of three must result in a production triply original and stylish. Could the dressmaker, could she possibly, achieve such a combination?

Miss Lauber gave a hurried glance at the designs arrested by our rigid fingers and did not see why she could not do so. Already she was cutting out the pattern on the table. We stood around, watching, eager to help, to contribute toward a creation that Addie, still holding the fashion book in her hand, was envisaging in its complicated completion.

"My children must always have something different, must have horns," Mother said.

Even as we examined the designs, the gray sateen lining was ready

132

to be tried on. Miss Lauber's tongue was spitting pins, her fingers running down Addie's side, pinching seams, her shears snipping away material from the shoulders. She complimented Mother upon the filled bobbins, and Mother smiled as we all sat down on the chairs and bed to witness the separate pieces of sateen spring into a unit. From the machine drawer hooks and eyes were nipped by fingers that, in fast-flying circles, attached them to the lining; it seemed but a minute before Addie was summoned to the second fitting. When we saw the smoothness, the absence of a single wrinkle, our eyes exchanged messages of satisfaction.

Mother nodded approval of such workmanship and told of other dressmakers, of the many fittings that had been required to achieve such flawlessness. Miss Lauber's small watery eyes glinted at the praise. When the whalebone casings had been stitched and the whale-bones inserted and sewed upon the seams, the cloth-covered lining was ready for the third fitting. We felt that the dress was practically made, and regretted that we had not purchased material for a blouse to fill the vacant hours ahead.

Addie hurried into town and returned in thirty minutes with sil-ver buttons and silk braid. By noon the skirt was cut, and Miss Lauber was running downstairs to the kitchen to press the seams. Work had been distributed among the family, and dressmaking was in full swing.

Olga Lessing, at her back window across the yard, framed with her lips, "How is she?" to which our lips answered, "A find."

Luncheon was like a party. The conversation was lively and tact-fully restricted to the subject of clothes and present fashions. Mother smiled benevolently upon the dressmaker, encouraging her to a sec-ond piece of apple pie and an extra cup of coffee, which Miss Lauber accepted, smiling her drizzled smile, warmed by the beckoning to sudden brotherhood. She declined a third cup of coffee and hurried upstairs, leaving us behind whispering our exaltation.

In the early afternoon the work became intensive; the overcast-ing of the seams, the facing and binding of the skirt, even the skirt hem might be entrusted to members of the family; but only the dressmaker could bind the basque, the sleeves, the collar and cuffs, place the three rows of braid at the proper intervals down each side of the front of the basque, and make the sixteen buttonholes to fit the sixteen buttons.

As Miss Lauber cut and sewed the skirt pocket and slid it into an open seam, Addie suddenly remembered the slit of a pocket in the bodice of Etta Kahn's blue serge dress from which a tiny handkerchief had sent out provocative points of coquetry. She looked appealingly at Miss Lauber. "I suppose that it would be too late to have a pocket like that in my dress."

"We will see," Miss Lauber answered, and she shaped the collar and cuffs, which later would be stiffened with buckram, and faced with the material of the dress, before being attached to the basque. When she gathered the skirt, spreading it with sensitive fingers within the cloth belt, Mother gave a sign that it was three o'clock, and I went downstairs for the glass of lemonade waiting on the kitchen table.

Miss Lauber lifted an eye as I placed the plate on the machine. She took a swallow, her fingers scarcely stopping, then stole another, until the glass was empty. The room had grown hot, and someone opened a window.

Now we made little excursions from the room, stopping long enough on our return to see how far the dress had advanced. How curious that she should be taking so long when it had been practically finished in the morning. By four o'clock the air was heavy, and Addie fidgeted under the long standing. The rolling collar, so attractive on the printed page, made her slender neck scrawny.

"That sleeve. What's wrong with the right sleeve?" Mother asked.

Miss Lauber pulled the sleeve into place, persuading it into smoothness but, her hand once removed, it sloped into a strange slant. She pulled out both sleeves and snipped out the tops, replacing them, only to see one maliciously twist into bias folds.

"It will fall into place with wear," she said, and Mother looked at her sharply. As a unit we turned upon her looks of suspicion under which her cheeks colored with excitement, the uncurled ends of her wiry hair pointing out like a drunken crown of thorns. When Addie tried on the dress for the final fitting, the waist also pulled to one side.

"Take it off," Miss Lauber said to Addie.

With a needle she began to pick out the stitches of the machine-sewed seam. It was growing dark, and Mother lit the gas jet over the machine; the kitchen clock struck six.

"This will have to be done over," Miss Lauber said, raising desperate eyes. Her freckled face was flaming. Mother's cheeks also were flaming. I turned to open the window, but it was already open. I saw the dressmaker through a haze.

"The skirt is done, anyway," she said, and placed it on the bed.

"Can you stay an extra hour?" Mother asked.

The dressmaker nodded. Her mouth was shifting pins when the dinner bell rang.

"Come down to dinner, and you can finish it later," Mother said, her irritation controlled by kindliness.

"No."

"Do come down. You'll feel better."

"No. I'd rather finish now."

We went to dinner, leaving Miss Lauber's long, bony fingers flexing feverishly.

"Why do they say they can make a dress in a day if they can't?" Mother wanted to know.

"She took too long over the pattern," Addie suggested.

"*She? You!* My children must always have horns."

At eight o'clock the dressmaker stood ready to be paid. Her face was shrunken, her derby tilted back from her forehead, her eyes scattered wildly above the long black coat that fell, as if weighted, to the carpet. She drew back from the extra money that Mother offered her before she accepted it and dropped it into her pocket.

"Good-by," she called back from the front stairs.

"Good-by, Miss Lauber," we replied in unison.

We lifted the dress that lay spread upon the bed and examined it. Addie put it on. After all, it wasn't bad. Even the sleeve fell into place if she held her arms close to her body. And it was not unbecoming. Still it did not look like a "Denny" dress.

"Why doesn't it?" we reproachfully asked of the fevered ghost of Miss Lauber at the sewing machine.

# 12

# *The Kitchen*

C oming into the kitchen from the shadow of dining room and
hall was like stepping into sunshine. A stripe of brown wood,
then a stripe of yellow, then a stripe of brown, then a stripe of
yellow, on and on, all the way to the wall. Glossy golden: that was
our kitchen floor, our inlaid floor. The steel top of the big range
shone; I could see my face in it. It was so clean that we fried pancakes on it. We lived in a wonderful house, cooking pancakes on
our stove instead of in a frying pan!

The kitchen was the temple in which Mother was priest and
Maggie Doyle, Levite. When Maggie first came to us to do general
housework, Mother explained to her the custom regarding diet and
the use of kitchen utensils. Not only was there a gulf between ani-
mal food, including all that had its origin in flesh, milk, and its
derivatives, but the distinction also applied to the utensils with which
they came in contact. No butter must touch meat of any kind nor
be served at table when meat was a course; no meat pot must know
the contact of milk. The distinction held to the least knife and tea-
spoon. So Moses had decreed, and so Mother explained to the tall,
gawky, bobbed-haired Irish girl come to take service.

Maggie Doyle smiled the amused, red-gummed smile that was
destined to elude us for more than a decade and said, "I know. I've
cooked Jews before."

In the tall dresser that stood between the two large closets were
two drawers and two small cupboards. Milk knives, forks, and

136

spoons were kept in the right-hand drawer; in the right cupboard below it were milk pots and pans. The meat cutlery and tins were arranged in the left compartments. Between them lay a gulf as deep as that between ancient Jew and Philistine. The distribution in the closet was more intricate. The lower shelf held the milk dishes, the second shelf the meat dishes. On the two upper shelves, undisturbed for fifty weeks of the year, the Passover dishes waited for the spring observance of the feast of the unleavened bread, in commemoration of the days when Israel, hastening from pursuit of Pharaoh, dared not wait for the dough to rise. As the Bavarian Jew and the Polish Jew became Jew under a common persecution, so the meat and milk dishes, individualized during the ordinary flow of circumstances, united as leaven under the taboo of the Passover, and were thrust into the shadow of the upper shelves during the week of holiday celebration. The lower shelves were dusted, washed, purged of dishes and of any leaven that they may have contained, even in memory, and they were as if they had never been.

All through the year, like a searchlight, the eye of Mother ranged over the kitchen. Woe to the lovelorn cook who stirred the mutton broth with a milk spoon, or to the brazen one who basted the turkey with a lump of butter. Woe, woe to the waitress who, breaking the plate, hoped to fill the gap with another purloined from the upper Passover shelf. Triple her guilt if she dared to return it after the contamination. A Passover vessel, once deflowered, though passed through flame could never recover its native purity.

Temptation to delinquency lay ambushed in cupboard drawer and closet bin. To possess one's self of a slice of bread and butter without committing a Mosaic offense was a feat. No movement was too slight to stir a sense of danger, as feet felt for safe ground between the taboos; and always present was the zest of an unpremeditated transgression undetected. If a sudden contraction of my heart gave warning that I had cut into the butter with a meat knife, I turned toward Mother, bent under the effort to cut stars into the cookie dough, and over her back I intercepted in Maggie Doyle's eyes the gleam of amused complicity. Nowhere was my fear of Mother so great as in the kitchen, where her native capacity for anger was reinforced by her priestly office. Awe of His agent, rather

137

than dread of the displeasure of the Lord, secured my faithful obedience. When I heard the tablets crack, I fled beneath her wrath.

As a little girl, and when I grew older, I loved the kitchen. So much had happened, was happening, and would happen again. There was this that you must always do, that which you must never do; here were punishments threatening if you did; there, retribution if you did not. Preparations were always going on for something new: cleanings, purifications, dishes that were personalities because they came into view for occasion from dark shadows into which they returned. There was exotic food that never appeared except upon holidays—beet soup, hard-boiled eggs eaten with salt water, home-brewed raisin wine, epicurean dishes made of Matzoth meal and the soaked Matzoth. So many people were about—God, Moses, Mother, tradespeople, and Maggie Doyle.

Maggie worked thirteen hours a day and ended the day with a dance. General housework included care of the sidewalk and outside steps, the back yard and garden, the alleyway between garden and fence, the floors of the basement and kitchen, windows, cooking and serving at table, washing and ironing of small pieces and flannel underwear—everything but the starched pieces, which were sent to the Chinese laundry. Before dinner Maggie went to her room to wash and put on a fresh dress. Sometimes she remained in her room half an hour or more. Mother never solved the riddle of how a maid could take so long to wash and to change her dress. If Mother complained, Maggie smiled but did not answer. Her reserve never yielded, and after ten years of service her private history, including the details of her approaching marriage, remained undivulged. To a question, she answered with an oblique glance or an open smile, and she told nothing.

"Did you have a good time at the party last night?" I asked.

"Why wouldn't I be having a good time?"

"What did you do?"

"A little of everything."

"Did you dance?"

"What would I be doing at a party if I wasn't dancing?"

That was all. I wondered what she talked about when she was out at night. I was always wondering what girls talked about when they were alone with their beaux.

"What did you talk about, Maggie, you and your beau?"

"Oh, we just talked."

"I know, but what did he say?" I persisted.

"Oh, he said nothing and I said the same," answered Maggie, adding, gratis, a side glance of amused insolence.

The kitchen offered the social potentialities of a ballroom, and Maggie missed none of them. Twice a day the tradesman or his emissary knocked at the kitchen door. In the morning he took the order, in the afternoon he delivered it. The grocer, the baker, the steam laundryman, the fish man, the chicken man, the butcher boy, came twice a day proffering a salty bit of conversation or a flashing glance of fire. Bent over the sink, Maggie Doyle aimed a shaft of repartee over her left shoulder in invitation, or she buried her scorn in a bowl of dough, or she leaned lightly against the jamb of the door in coquettish intimacy with the man who pleased her. His footsteps running down the back steps were gay as laughter. I wondered what she said to the men that made them linger at the open door. If I came near, she stopped talking and returned to her work.

Between us and the tradesmen who came to our door an equality existed. Not the butcher boy, perhaps, but that was different, for he brought meat wrapped in heavy brown paper through which blood trickled. It was a curious rule, I thought, that butcher boys had rosy cheeks and whistled as they drove their horses and wagons. I observed them as they clattered over the cobblestones and found no exception. Laundrymen, on the contrary, had long, serious faces and large families. You could ask a laundryman how his children were, and he would tell you that two were down with chicken pox or mumps. The men who came from the big markets were harder to classify. Our chicken man was on the Board of Education.

I liked the social life of the kitchen better than that of the parlor. The men brought the wind and the rain into the house on their faces and hair, and they bore the smell of fish and vegetable and meat. They were young and noisy and hurried. They were quick-tongued, with a joke upon their lips and a challenge in their eyes. They ran up the steps, burst into the room, scattered raindrops upon the floor, flung packages upon the table, joked with Maggie Doyle or Mother, and the door slammed behind their retreating footsteps. My fancy followed them into the street, and I could see the horse start with a run before they jumped into the seat and caught the reins.

When Christmas came, the tradesmen brought presents. Gifts, in kind, were expected of them, and we should have been shocked at the omission of the bottle of cream or the basket of fruit, which came with the holidays. The most welcome offering was that presented by the baker, a huge yellow cupcake hidden under a coat of heavy white icing with Merry Christmas outlined upon it in crinkly pink sugar letters.

Mother examined the gift with critical approval. "Shrunk!" she said, if the diameter showed the slightest diminution from the standard size.

The tradespeople were subject to constant toll. No glass protected their wares, and while we lingered in cordial conversation, unconscious fingers automatically dipped into box and barrel. Nothing was bought on trust; everything was sampled.

"How about the apples today, sour?"

"Try one," came the certain answer, and the fruit was proved before bought.

To market with Mother was a regaling experience, at each stall a tidbit was handed to me, and I returned home, my stomach filled with pickles and gingersnaps, tomatoes and picked shrimps, with perhaps a sliver of sausage. "Soup greens"—celery, turnips, parsley, and onions—were a straight tax on anything bought of the vegetable man.

"Do you call those soup greens?" Mother demanded if the donation were not generous, and the tradesman, abashed, added recklessly.

Many nations and races united to furnish us with our supplies. The baker was German; the fish man, Italian; the grocer, a Jew; the butcher, Irish; the steam laundryman, a New Englander. The vegetable vendor and the regular laundryman who came to the house were Chinese. The Chinamen were the high note of color and piquancy in the kitchen traffic of the day. Chung Lung was fruit and fishman. He carried the combined stock, suspended in two huge wicker baskets balanced upon a long pole, across his shoulders. He did not come to the kitchen door, but remained outside in the alley.

140

We heard the back doorbell and hurried down, Mother, Maggie, and I. The uncertainty of the contents of the baskets—today only apples and cauliflower; tomorrow, cherries and corn; today, shiny silver smelts; tomorrow, red shrimps with beards and black-beaded eyes—made a delight of his coming. Such laughter at the weighing: Mother adding a potato to the scale, Chung, his eyes screwed into slits, removing it; Mother scowling in indignation, Chung showing three black fangs in merry insistence upon his rights—all of us knowing all the while that we were playing a game. Such arguments and noisy disputes! Chung talked and talked a language, unintelligible to any of us but himself, his cadences rising high and falling again into murmurs.

"Yes, yes," cried Mother, red in the face with determination.

"No, no," cried Chung, grown suddenly solemn as if in defense of a religious conviction. Anger, indignation, resentment, an impasse; then the concession of a head of lettuce here, the withdrawal of an apple there, laughter, good humor, Maggie carrying the fruits of victory to the kitchen and I remaining outside so that Chung might teach me how to twist the tail of the shrimp to make the meat pop out, unbroken. I loved Chung Lung, and when, with a straining of muscle, he lifted the bent pole to his shoulders and trotted off, a little bowed under the heavy baskets, I called out to him, "Good-by, Chung, bring me a big peach tomorrow."

"All light, all light," he called back.

No bell announced the coming of Hi Lo. His name was Hi Lo, but we called him John, our generic name for all male Chinese. Hi Lo did not come. He was there. He moved about as one who had long enjoyed the freedom of the house. We would hear a noise upstairs and, to a questioning look, the answer came, "It's the Chinaman with the wash."

The wash left the house a huge soft white ball upon the high bony shoulder of Hi Lo; and resumed, starched to the breaking point, in a great heavy wicker basket. Hi Lo mounted the backstairs and deposited the wash neatly, in classified stacks, upon the bed of the back bedroom. Torn hems of sheets hung frankly between the piles. The wash gave out a strong human odor of a Chinese laundry and called forth a picture of a long cue and a shaven head bent over the ironing board, sprinkling the sheets and pillowcases with a mouthful of water, blown and vaporized by some delightful ingenuity.

We looked up from the pan of sugared cookies, which Mother was drawing out of the oven, and saw Hi Lo standing at the door.

"What you want?" Mother asked.

We talked pidgin English to Chinamen. Hi Lo grinned, revealing a yellow tooth perched high on a gum like a village on a cliff.

"Want money?"

Hi Lo nodded and grinned again. "Yep, want money, this time, last time." He held up two fingers.

"We no got money," said Father who had come downstairs. "All money gone." This was Father's weekly joke.

Hi Lo laughed loud. "You got heap money."

Mother grew serious. "There was a towel missing last week, John."

"No towel missing."

"I tell you there was. My list fifteen, and you bring fourteen."

"No, no."

"Did you ever hear such a thing?" This to us.

"My list fifteen, you understand?"

"No, no, eberyting right, fourteen."

"Your list"—Mother's voice was rising—"your list"—she hesitated for a word—"your list no good."

"My book velly good. I write it in book. Fourteen towel. You give me money."

"I give you money when you bring towel," said Mother. "You look in book."

"Book, book," shrieked Hi Lo. "I no come more," and, in a noisy fury of sound, he rushed from the house.

On the following week, while we were at dinner, he was in the doorway again.

"You give me money?" He grinned engagingly, as if the subject had never before been broached.

"You findee towel?" from Mother.

"Towel, towel! All time towel. No towel. I look book. You give me money."

It was useless to argue further. The lost towel, like the torn sheet, was the price we paid for cheap Chinese service.

"You pay him," said Mother to Father, saving her face by disengaging herself from the whole transaction.

Hi Lo was in the room now, standing over Father, laughing and pointing a long, bony finger at Father's trouser pocket.

"He got him," he confided to the table.

"How much?" asked Father.

"Four dollar-hap. I make him for four dollar quarter," he conceded grandly. And the contest ended with honors even.

The era was one of conviction in all things, and certainty ruled in the realm of household medicine. We were not afraid of disease; we knew that for each disease there was a cure, as there was the antidote for every poison. For sore throats there was an internal and external remedy. I received praise for my gargling. Polly let the vinegar moisten her throat and then ejected it with a grimace of distaste. I let it rest a little, swinging it from tonsil to tonsil, throwing my head back for lubrication. "She gargles fine," the doctor said, and I accepted the praise and developed the accomplishment. If the inflammation did not yield to the gargle, two external remedies were at hand. "Put on your stocking," Mother counseled, and when I undressed for the night I took a warm woolen stocking off my foot and wound it around my throat, close against the skin. A strip of salt pork, encasing the neck under a bandage of white flannel, was still better.

To wear so close to the body the flesh that must never enter it was strange excitement. I had faith in pork, for I reasoned that where there was so great a prohibition there must be power. If the cold descended into the chest, it was vanquished by goose grease rubbed into the pores with small circular movements and gentle pressure.

"Now," Mother said, as she locked the window, placed a square of flannel over the greased area, buttoned my woolen undershirt and my Canton-flannel nightgown, and drew the double blankets up to my chin with a quilt over all. "Now you'll be all right in the morning."

Spring cleaning included not only the house we lived in, but our bodies as well. The last rainfall was the signal for general purification, when each member of the household was given the daily dose of sulphur and molasses. A face covered with pimples was the result.

"Look," said Mother, triumphant as if a demon had been exorcised. "All that impurity out of your system. Aren't you glad?"

To every signal of distress a plaster was the answer. Every member of the house could turn one out in three minutes after the first call was in. When the flour and mustard were mixed and moistened, and placed between the folds of soft cloth, the plaster was rushed to the seat of the disorder and deposited with a "there you are" of conviction. A treacherous remedy, for it began with a clammy chill and ended with a burn. If I complained of the heat prematurely, Mother gave a look and slapped it back again. If I refrained from complaint and bore the sting heroically, it left a red mark and I was scolded for my carelessness while Mother covered the spot with sweet oil.

"Alcock's Porous Plaster cures every ill," announced the billboards, and everybody agreed that, for chronic discomfort, it was the remedy. The porous plaster, once clapped onto the body, withstood temperature and water and survived weeks of baths and dryings, eventually to be parted from the skin after savage resistance. The Spanish fly, hatched in hell, was a plaster as ominous to childhood as was an operation to maturity. Action was immediate: big blisters rose upon the spine. If distress continued after this extreme remedy had been applied, the doctor frowned and the patient accepted his suffering as delinquency.

Nobody we knew ever underwent an operation. Cousin Lenore was going to die because she had refused to have one. "I'll cheat them," she said, referring to the medical profession. Something awful was the matter with her; nobody named it; up to then it had always burst out, but someday it might burst in. I did not know what it was, but I was stimulated by her defiance.

"Suppose it should burst in," they would say. We understood that in that event Lenore would die. She continued to live for fifty years, however, and we all rejoiced because she had outwitted the doctors. Mrs. Spiro—that was a nightmare. The house was filled with whispers and I heard the words "pesthouse" and, later, when she came to see us, her face was full of holes which would be there until she died. We could not look at her, though we tried to, fearing we might hurt her feelings. We were all vaccinated and the doctor said, "Good," when Mother showed him my scabby arm. Almost as fearsome as "pesthouse" was the name associated with Mrs. Rosenthal: "insane asylum." Thin and pale, always dressed in black, she saw things which were not there and shook her head when Mother repeated and repeated that her brother did not hate her and did not want to steal her money.

And diphtheria! They looked in your throat and it was all white. Then it closed up and you were dead. I knew of these terrors, but they happened rarely and belonged to the category of earthquake and cyclone: events too catastrophic to be seriously taken as a menace to lives like ours, safeguarded by a burly doctor who roared with amusement at our symptoms and at Mother who cured them with teas and plasters.

When the dinner dishes had been washed and put into the closet at night, and the big tin basin and the dark washrag were housed in the cupboard under the sink; when the soap that must never touch a dish because of the interdicted lard in its content had removed every vestige of grease and crumb from the corrugated wooden sink board; when Maggie Doyle, her cheeks glowing with freshness after the thirteen hours of almost uninterrupted work, locked the kitchen door and disappeared in the darkness of the avenue where her beau awaited her coming; when the lights were out and the day was done, then the nightly procession began. As if at a preconcerted signal, down from the ceiling, up from the cellar, along spaceless cracks between range and wall, came the caravan of flat black bugs to the evening gathering. Their coming was enveloped in mystery as dark as their black surfaces. Where did they come from? How did they get here? What did they want? How did they know that the guard had been removed? Why did they come only at night like burglars? Why did they come when, after they were there, they did nothing but move about hither and thither? Mystery upon mystery, and no answer anywhere or at any time. I asked Mother. Her only answer was a kettle full of hot water, which she poured upon them. That was no answer; that only increased the wonder. At the first

145

touch of water they were gone as they had come, by the same invisible avenues, to the same unknown destination. An hour later, when the kitchen was dark again, they were back. How did they know the danger was passed? Who told them? Who gave the signal? I asked Father, but he said that he did not know. Curious, something that nobody knew, right on your kitchen sink. Why did Mother pour hot water on them when she did not even know why they came and what they wanted? They did not get into anything; they just moved about in black designs.

"Why mustn't I tell anybody that we have cockroaches?" I asked Mother.

"Do you think it is something to be proud of, to have cockroaches in your kitchen?" Mother asked.

I did. I liked them, but I was afraid to say so.

# 13

# *The Basement*

From the light and warmth of the kitchen I cautiously followed Mother down the cellar steps, my hand on the wall, my eyes upon the square of light coming from the frosted pane of the door leading to the street. The basement was dark and cold; the finished basement, distinguished from the unfinished part by white plastered walls and ceiling, gained by contrast a polished brightness. The hall, the washroom, the storeroom, and the icy cellar toilet, pariah among rooms because of the caste of its patronage, belonged to the finished half.

On Monday mornings cheer crept into the washroom. Then the cheeks of Maggie Doyle gleamed carmine through the thick steam as she wrung out the "light" family washing—woolen petticoats, union suits, wrappers, and Father's heavy red woolen shirts and drawers. She dropped them into the large straw basket, carried them out to the back garden and hung them on the line, stretched over the circle of beaten lawn in the center of which a slender palm dwindled under the weekly assault of waving flannel. On other days the shades were drawn and the windows and doors of the washroom bolted. Who could be sure that a burglar would not scale the high garden fence from the back alley, or hide in the garbage closet beneath the outside steps waiting for the night? Locked doors did not guarantee security.

As for the whisky-smelling, shifty-eyed night watchman, I suspected, although Mother said little, that the dollar she paid him each month was given less to secure than to divert his vigilance. My trust was in Mother. I knew that, if an unaccustomed sound penetrated to her bedroom in the early hours of the morning, she would leave Father asleep and, a tiny nightgowned figure, candle in hand, would descend the two flights of steps to search in the corners of the basement for the thief who dared trespass upon her property.

The door of the storeroom was locked and only in the company of Mother might I enter. Opulence without limit defined my dream of a storeroom. Mother had only to turn the key and I expected to see clean, ordered, rich-hued shelves combined with the gravity of a wine cellar. What was a storeroom if not a source of supply for a long winter, even for a famine, assurance against any household dilemma? An unexpected visitor from the country come to dinner? The storeroom. A kitchen catastrophe, a broken bottle, an empty jar? Another—a dozen others—in the storeroom. And surprise! Between visits what might not have been secreted there? A bunch of green bananas, a jovial jug of kümmel or, best of all, red apples polished in the sawdust of a huge barrel.

But each fresh visit to our storeroom disrupted a vision. Ours was a niggardly storeroom with gaps in the long shelves and more in the lower wine racks. I knew the glasses of currant jelly and each jar of strawberry and blackberry preserves. (There were not many of them.) In the kitchen I had watched Mother seal and cap them with white paper and tie them with a string. I knew the three crocks of spiced German plums and the two of pickled beets, the dried apples and the blue-and-white jar of preserved ginger, which nobody liked—annual Christmas gift from the Chinese laundryman. In one corner of the room cluttered rusting wire flower baskets and a garden hose; in another corner, in a small barrel, cucumbers bronzed in slimy liquid under floating tubes of kelp. Under the wine racks, in deep shadow, a mousetrap waited, unsprung. The room was dark but for the square of gray light patterned by bars of the garden window, outside of which the big gray house cat sat at his silent watch.

Mother and I moved about somberly. She stopped to finger a jar or bottle, lifted, examined it, and returned it to its place. From the top of the pickle barrel she raised the board and with a finger stirred

148

the green scum; then, without removing a pickle, replaced the board. I followed her, my eyes upon her hands. She passed a finger over the white shelf paper and examined it for dust. "*Naar* [fool]," she said to the cat, hopping behind glass and iron bar; then to me, "Come," and, selecting a glass of red currant jelly, she led the way out of the room and turned the key.

I felt my way up the dark staircase until my hand closed upon the knob of the kitchen door. The next time we went down together, weeks later, perhaps, I would again expect to behold ordered shelves high to the ceiling, packed with shining, labeled tins and shapely jars containing secrets of pleasure not yet tasted.

The long stretch of gloom beneath the double parlors, boxed in by rough unplastered walls and ceiling and splintery floor, was our unfinished basement. To enter it was to step down two steps carefully and stumble into darkness and wait until Maggie Doyle turned on the sputtering jet that revealed against the wall the two wooden bins from which she filled a black tin bucket with coal and her apron with kindling. But for the bins and the garden spade and rake leaning against the wall and the black blower and rusty bird cage, the room was empty. The blower, provided to heighten the cheer of the music room, had never found place upon that unlit hearth. The bird cage had housed no tenant since the day when the last pet canary, glassy-eyed, drooped and flickered to death against the warmth of Maggie Doyle's bosom. Where the wood and coal room reached its length (the end seemed a block away), it became John Chinaman's bedroom, defined by a single piece of furniture: the cot on which the family servant had slept in the distant days before the coming of Maggie Doyle. A feeble, dusty light entered the room between the bars of the small alley window.

On early mornings, while waiting for Maggie to fill her coal bucket, I sat on the edge of the cot and watched through the bars a rough-bearded tramp eating his breakfast on the alley steps. Every morning in winter some tramp would ring at the cellar door. The penciled signs up and down the jamb of the door spelt a code that revealed to tramps that our house was good for a meal. Father did not mind. No hungry man should leave his door unfed, he declared, and Mother agreed. If Maggie Doyle at times grumbled at the extra steps, I quoted Father in righteous rebuke and peeped through the crack to see if the tramp were really hungry, or just pretending. If he drank all the coffee and ate all the bread and butter, I knew that he was genuine and I reported the good news to the kitchen. Sometimes he just drank the coffee and put the bread in his pocket. That was all right, too. But there were mornings when a tramp left his breakfast uneaten. Why did he do that? Perhaps he was expecting an omelet, Maggie Doyle said. That was puzzling; I had thought that tramps wanted only food.

Beyond these winter mornings the basement continued to be an empty, lifeless cellar until the day when the seeing eye of Ludwig, the caterer, appraised it and pronounced it appropriate for a wedding dinner.

# 14

## *Suitors—Baiern*

E xcept on Sundays and on days at home, when callers were received in the parlor, Addie entertained friends in the music room. No luncheon or dinner was given to which a number of young people were invited; only evening parties and afternoons at home. All our friends had an afternoon at home. At first one afternoon in the week was given to visitors. Later, when people of acknowledged precedence received on two days of the month, we followed with alternate Thursdays. Addie's friends were partly drawn from the ranks of the Bavarians (the Baiern, we called them) and largely from the Poles. That the Baiern were superior to us, we knew. We took our position as the denominator takes its stand under the horizontal line. On the social counter the price tag "Polack" confessed second-class. Why Poles lacked the virtue of Bavarians I did not understand, though I observed that to others the inferiority was as obvious as it was to us that our ashman and butcher were of poorer grade than we, because they were ashman and butcher. (If the ashman had asked why he was not so good as we, I should have answered simply, "Because you're an ashman," and doubtless he would have agreed to the explanation.) In like manner I accepted the convention that our excellence was not that of the Baierns because we were Polish.

Upon this basis of discrimination everybody agreed and acted. The birthplace of parents determined the social rank of themselves and their offspring. Birth in the kingdom of Bavaria provided

151

entrance to the favored group, as a cradle in Poland denied it. Even ancient conjunction with Poland acted for disbarment. My parents were born in West Prussia, but the past political union of West Prussia with Poland counted against their birthplace and the blight descended unto the second and third generation.

Were I asked in the schoolroom the birthplace of my mother or father, in an agony of fear lest the truth be detected, I quickly answered, "Germany," and triumphantly circumvented the teacher, unaware that she was without suspicion of the social cleavage between desk and desk of her Jewish pupils. Had my parents come from a large city the reproach would have been somewhat mitigated, the prestige of birth in a metropolis being self-evident; but they grew up in villages so small that I could find them only upon a detailed map. Mother's village, Kulm, was not so reprehensible as Father's. If one said quickly, Kulm-near-the-Vistula, it acquired some of the dimensions of the stream. But Fordon, Father's birthplace, remained only an undecipherable little point on the map of Prussia and all I could do, when questioned, was to repress the pain of disgrace. Thus we grew up under the shadow of a territorial bar sinister, our sense of inferiority deepened by the acquiescence of our parents and the facts of the social life about us.

Many of Addie's friends were of the superior caste; Evelyn Taussig was Polish, but Proudy Dinkenspiel, her aunt, who lived next door to her, had married a Bavarian in a mining camp in those early fifties when girls were few and a dance was divided among five partners. We knew that the Taussigs had aspirations to break through the walls of their set and we feared their success. The number of the boys in the rich family offered opportunity for excellent connections. When Elias, Jonah, Nathan, Benjamin, and Morris had acquired Bavarian wives, the family would be intrenched in social security forever. Though Evelyn was not comely, but large and bouncing with blue eyes leaping from a florid face, her social potentialities commanded respect. Leopold Stone, tall, handsome, erect (a tree, Mother said), man of the world, was known to have visited the Taussig home twice in two weeks. Anything might happen. The possibility of a marriage was often discussed in our family.

"If he needs the money badly enough, he might," Mother said, and then followed the blighting dictum that condemned us within the pale forever: "No Baiern marries a Pole unless he is *krumm* or *lahm* or *stumm* [crooked or lame or dumb]."

"But if one fell in love with a girl?" Polly protested.

"If he fell in love, he'd fall out again," came the answer.

Norma Samuels lifted her thin nose high, as though she detected curious odors by right of the uncle who was both Bavarian and physician—a profession that almost, but not quite, compensated for territorial inferiority. We, alas, had no relative on whose social standing we might hope to erect a claim, and our position remained a precarious one. We lived on the verge, without the aggressiveness to force our way across and establish ourselves within the zone of privilege, an achievement which would have been possible had Mother been less frugal or Father more adaptable.

In the midst of the Bavarians, I was sensitive and uncomfortable. In the home of the Kahns, I shrank before the double grandeur of their ancestry, which was not only Bavarian but Parisian. At the Lowenthals, if I suspected inquiry in the cold regard of the four stalwart older sisters, I responded with nervous fluency and, when the visit was returned, a higher polish to my entertainment deflected from the attention of the distinguished guest the presence of inferior company. My social uneasiness, being constant, stimulated the development of a strong conversational offensive. Pleasure was rarely simple or unmixed with fear. I never completely belonged, never felt that I might stretch myself comfortably and doze in the circle in which I lived, but must keep alert, protecting weak places.

We responded to the inequality according to our temperaments. Polly stormed at the pride of caste and released her resentment in abuse. Addie, always noncombative, did nothing to better her position. She accepted pleasure as it came naturally, realizing that she had none of the fight that forces obstacles. For me romance waited in the unknown and I was destined to beat against any closed door, certain that behind it waited that delight that would be the answer to the searchings of an acute curiosity.

Not only were we disquieted by the possibility of new Bavarian affiliations among the members of our group, but any advantageous betrothal was greeted by Mother with resentment and with reproach of Father for his social shortcomings. No sooner had an engagement been announced, a younger brother or sister bringing the glad tidings, than a shadow fell upon the house for the day. Often the prospective groom would be a stranger, perhaps the old bachelor brother of a friend of the family who, after years of seclusion, had been persuaded that the last bell had rung for marriage; or he might be a rising merchant from Nevada. In either case conjecture was in the air and the blow softened by thought of the suitor's age, or of the separation from the family and city, entailed by an out-of-town marriage. On the other hand, he might be a young city merchant already enjoying good credit; or, worse, the son and heir of a member of an old firm; or, worst of all, an attorney with high degrees at the Odd Fellows, equipped at any moment with an eloquent speech for a wedding dinner, or a B'nai B'rith banquet. Beneath the blow of such a betrothal Mother sat still, her hands folded.

Addie's friends came to the house with their fancywork carried in bags of shellacked macramé lace. Some made insertions or edgings of tatting, a cluster of little white wheels worked by a shiny hand shuttle that struck and retreated like a hummingbird. Addie embroidered scallops on flannel petticoats. The praise of a girl was "her hands are never idle." Her fancywork was exhibited to mothers of marriageable men, or left casually upon the marble-topped parlor table when a caller was expected, just as the achievement of her baking was served for his refreshment.

One afternoon Addie's friends had gathered in the music room, their fingers crocheting, embroidering, and pointing shuttles as they talked. I was lying on the red leather couch in the dining room reading *Molly Bawn,* a sunlit romance by the Duchess. Molly was beautiful, though unadorned. Her possessions were greater than wealth: golden hair, dimples, a daring saucy tongue instant with repartee. She washed and ironed her one simple muslin dress and it outshone velvet and satin. I read and floated into circumstances of beauty and conquest. The front doorbell rang and I answered it; anybody answered the bell for, when company was expected, a member of the family was more dependable than gawky Maggie Doyle' swinging a sudsy apron over her arm. At the door stood Benjie, the little Taussig boy.

"Evelyn is wanted at home," he said. A strange message. No-body had ever been wanted at home. I went into the music room. "Evelyn is wanted at home," I said. "Benjie came to let her know."

Everyone stopped working to regard Evelyn, who awkwardly gathered up the cloth which she was embroidering and dropped it into her basket unfolded. She looked at no one. Self-conscious, happy, helpless, she left the room.

An hour later, while we sat at dinner, the front doorbell rang.

Mother answered it. She came back alone. "Evelyn Taussig is engaged to Leopold Stone."

So must an ancestor have announced the destruction of the Temple of Jerusalem.

"No!" cried Father, bringing a fist down upon the table.

"Yes," retorted Mother, mocking him. A silence followed. A run-ning fire of self-condemnation encircled the table. We felt ourselves weaklings in the struggle. Father tapped three times upon the table with one finger, his signal of concern. Mother's face veered away from him slowly and rested at her angle of accusation.

Polly flirted and had innumerable beaux; Addie had only suitors. Polly made eyes across the table, or curved a glance like a lariat and brought a victim to her side. She bridged formal introduction. Her eyes called, the object answered, and they were acquainted. Her long, green-blue eyes could see a man directly behind her. I would watch, hoping to detect the mysterious technique with its unfailing result, but it eluded me.

"Can't you see from the corners of your eyes?" she asked.

No, I couldn't, and was saddened, accepting the limitation as a lack of feminine potency.

Addie was a sensitive girl without aggressiveness or combat, shrinking before argument or opposition into dark corners, until the sight of some unhappiness stimulated her activity, filled her ves-sels with blood, dislodged her from her retreat, and shot her out on compulsive missions of charity. She could hear a sigh across the border of another state. At the first impact of distress she was dressed, hatted and gloved, hurrying to the rescue, creating little oases of artificial harmony in troubled territory.

155

To the seamstress went the imported hat bought at Coughlin's; to the piano tuner's wife, the soft padded coat reserved for convalescence. She never met a member of the family with any other greeting than: "If you'll give fifty cents, I'll give fifty. Poor soul!" The "poor soul" was her quarry, whether the cause or victim of her present misfortune.

If there was no visible distress upon her horizon, Addie created it to fill the vacuum until, haunted by the image she had made, she had excuse for succor. She gave away all she had and anything that a visiting relative may have left hanging in her closet. She loved the unfortunate. To the hungry she sent meat and vegetables, veiling the charity with autumn leaves. She obliterated the injustice of the world with currant jelly.

"She's lonely because she's too selfish to make a friend," Polly expostulated when Addie threatened to leave her sickroom to visit an acquaintance.

"She's unhappy," Addie cried triumphantly, and leaped from her bed.

Her own good fortune inspired in her a gentle melancholy. "I ought to be a very happy girl," she said, and sighed deeply, recalling her squirrel-lined coat and the devotion of her family. When she smiled it was as one already passed away, acquiescing in another's recital of her own happiness. She loved sorrow for the opportunity it gave her to exercise her gift for charity but, even more, she loved sorrow for itself.

Addie would have liked to be saucy and challenging like Polly, endowed with Polly's priceless gift of repartee. But she remained a perfect lady. Benish Levy's oldest daughter? A perfect lady—and accomplished—was the invariable judgment.

Among Addie's many suitors were some whom she never saw, who were submitted and rejected without reaching the stage when they came to spend the evening. Others, brought by acquaintances of my parents, added sparkle to the evening's entertainment with "lively remarks." They accented Addie's accomplishments. "She baked these cookies?" "She embroidered those napkins?" Before such praise Addie withdrew more deeply into her reserve, while Mother, not to be diverted by cheap strategy, continued to examine

156

the aspirant with proud, critical eye. Open discussion waited upon the departure of the company. If Father and Mother agreed upon the desirability of the suitor, Addie had but to say, "I couldn't bear to have him touch me" for Father to exclaim, "That settles it! Never marry a man you don't care for, my child," and the field was free for the next suitor.

My parents set the highest value upon health and the outward signs of vigor. If Mother murmured, *"Blaas* [pale]*"* under her breath as she guided through the hall the white-faced young man come a-wooing, he was practically done for before he entered into conversation. Father valued stability, solid qualities that insured future security. He esteemed capacity more than capital. Next to stability came health. "Sturdy young man," Mother, too, would comment in approval.

Sunday callers were entertained by Addie in the parlor. Baum was a Sunday afternoon visitor. He burst into the house as if projected from a cannon. Polly and I stood at the bedroom window and looked through the shutters, waiting for the moment when he might be expected to run up the steps. Every Sunday-afternoon caller wore a high hat, but Baum's fluffy golden whiskers distinguished him from the other men, who wore mustaches or beards, and his canary-colored gloves marked him for our sport. Four Sundays ended the suit of Baum, who retired in excellent form.

*"Matzoth warum blast du? Kein Butter, kein Salz* [Matzoth, why blow? No butter, no salt—why all those airs]?" Mother said of him.

Abraham Hirshman, oldest member of the rising dry-goods firm of Hirshman Brothers of San Jose (only a short distance from the city and therefore not really of the country), presented his claim more aggressively. On his last visit Polly and I listened as he heavily walked up and down the floor of the music room. Later, we had a vision of red cheeks and a black beard shooting through the hall into the street, while Addie tearfully stood at the door of the dining room, tearing the fringe of her polonaise and murmuring between sobs, "He said that I encouraged him. He called me a coquette."

Three weeks were needed for Abraham to achieve consolation in the home of Conrad Weil, the wealthy lace importer who lived in the big white house with the two bronze dogs on the lawn.

157

"Don't you think you could have grown to like him?" Father asked, reluctant to see so promising a prospect leave the field.

"I couldn't bear to have him touch me," Addie replied.

"That finishes that," said Father, his right hand coming down heavily on his knee.

I did not know why Addie did not marry Samuel Loeb. He was quiet and good-natured, had high color, and a perfect set of teeth. Seeing him stand at the piano, turning pages, while Addie tossed her head in vocal coquetry, justified the printing of betrothal cards. Polly and I sat on the bed upstairs, counting the number of engagement stands of flowers that might reasonably be expected; but nothing came of it. Later, he married a social favorite and Mother declared anew that she had particular daughters.

Everybody agreed that August Friedlander was a fitting alliance for Addie. Although still a young man (he was twenty-six), he had a good business in a growing town across the bay. Father made inquiries of the merchants from whom August bought his goods, and they all agreed upon his integrity and good credit. His pallor was disturbing, but questions delicately put by Father, such as, "Pretty tired at the end of the day, I suppose?" elicited the laughing assurance that he had never been sick a day in his life. Uneasiness might not have been quieted had he been clean-shaven, but he wore a mustache and goatee (we were delighted by his close resemblance to Hermann, the prestidigitator), so the area of pallor exposed was not extensive. Father objected also to his thin hands and prominent veins.

"I don't like those hands. Did you notice, Yetta?"

"Veins," Mother said.

August's younger brother, David, who accompanied him on his visits, was short and broad and plump. August sat on the sofa, his brother on the piano stool. He smiled broadly, showing white teeth, rarely entered into conversation, but circled around on the piano stool, occasionally filling a pause by chanting:

"Tiddle de wink, tiddle de wink, tiddle de wink . . ."

He smiled so engagingly when he repeated the refrain that no one questioned its relevancy. Father wished that August were not so serious, that he had some of the humor of his brother, that he were not all business. August had never heard *Il Trovatore*, he admitted to

Father's chagrin; but, on the other hand, while his brother was bald, August had a heavy growth of hair, and Levi Strauss, the millionaire manufacturer of I X L Overalls, told Father that he was the brains of the business.

Both Father and Mother agreed that he was better qualified than any other suitor who had yet appeared, and they encouraged him to come often. At later visits the family retired, the brother was omitted, and August and Addie conversed behind the closed folding doors.

"Well?" Father asked after a month. "What do you say?"

"I like him," Addie said, and within twenty-four hours I was hurrying to the neighbors, announcing the betrothal and spreading consternation in the homes of marriageable daughters down the two blocks.

# 15

# Wedding

As the day of Addie's wedding approached, our unfinished basement quickened to life and began to take on an unimaginable
grace. Wood and coal bins, garden implements, bird cage and blower,
John Chinaman's bedroom cot were whisked away like stage property. The unplastered walls disappeared behind unbleached sheet-
ing that August himself had brought from his department store and
stretched from ceiling to floor. All the decorations had been entrusted to him, as to skill entitled to confidence by long experience
in window dressing. It was he who draped the ropes of smilax that
drooped so accurately in garlands from the ceiling; he who drew
the remaining strands in two parallel lines along the length of the
long, long tables and relieved the monotony of the white walls with
pairs of crinkled fans of colored paper tilted toward each other in
unpremeditated salutation, a third fan hovering above them, here
and there, like a belated bird ready to alight.

When the candelabra were lit, when the glasses sent out sparkles,
and the silver shone between the streams of verdure on the white
cloth, the whole room radiated festival. The wood and coal room
had vanished, become a distant memory.

Not less magical than the elevation of the basement to a banquet
hall was the metamorphosis of the bride. At four o'clock Strozynsky,
the fashionable hairdresser, came to the house. Addie sat before the
long mirror in Mother's bedroom waiting for him, anxiously, hopefully. Never before had he dressed her hair, the price of his service

being prohibitive for any occasion less ceremonial. He was an artist, and no hoped-for loveliness was too extravagant to be expected from his hands.

We took our positions against the wall and the bed from which we might observe the transmutation of Addie's simple plainness into allurement and beauty. Had she emerged from his ministrations a golden Helen, we should not have been surprised; the price, the man—nothing was impossible. His appearance was baffling; I could not relate his corseted figure, enameled cheeks, artificially waved hair, and rouged lips to anything but a hairdresser's manikin; but when he darted forward and twisted a strand of hair, and Addie's face lengthened, and when he retreated to appraise her between narrowed lids and returned to give another twist and Addie's forehead rose to amplitude, his eccentricities became the natural fantastic accouterment of a sorcerer. Slender, agile, he danced around her, an invisible pallet in his hand. "What shall it be?" he asked himself aloud, "I have it, Mary Stuart!" he answered himself.

My spirit clapped hands. His sensitive fingers loosened her brown hair, nipping hairpins here and there. Then his eye fell upon Polly.

"That beautiful girl, who is she?" he asked Addie.

"My sister."

After that, he scarcely saw Addie; his eyes turned to Polly again and again while his fingers worked strange disruptive changes in the aspect of the bride. When the veil had been adjusted (two sharp twists, emphasizing the Stuart hood), he stood at a distance regarding his work.

"There!" he cried.

The transformation was alarming but wonderful. Addie did look like Mary Stuart; the draping of the veil established the resemblance.

"Wonderful, wonderful," we exclaimed in excited admiration as he gathered up his tools and, after one last twist to a horn of the hood, prepared to leave.

"Wait a little and see what I will do for *you*," he whispered into Polly's ear loudly as he departed. "Cleopatra!"

Addie arose and looked at herself in the glass. She was terrified. In the heavy, inflexible, long-trained, white brocaded satin gown, weighted with crinoline throughout rows of box pleats, she felt herself unfamiliar and unreal—a strangeness now intensified and complicated by this added obligation to assume the role of a Scottish queen, whom she recalled only as a beautiful lady of sorrow slowly walking to the block. She sought our faces in appeal. Then, strengthened by the admiration in our eyes, she again turned to the royal reflection in the mirror.

"Is it all right, truly?" she faltered.

"It's extraordinary," we cried, and it was.

We were having not only the fashionable hairdresser, but the fashionable caterer as well. We had never had one before. Ludwig catered not only to the Gerstles and the Slosses, but to the Mackays on the next block. He was to supply everything except the fowl. "What could a caterer know about fowl?" Mother asked. A German woman cook had come to prepare them but, after she left, the night before the wedding, Mother went down to the washroom, where the chickens were laid out upon the ironing table in rows and seasoned them all over again, convinced that no anemic Gentile palate could be trusted to season poultry. Ludwig had dictated the quantity to be ordered, agreeing to Mother's direction that all food and wine in excess would be left and not carried away. I knew about the dessert, though the secret was kept from the other members of the family. Pyramids of nougat and macaroon! I had listened when Ludwig described them to Mother, following his hand as he drew them on the air. They grew in height with the hours before the wedding until their tops menaced the low ceiling. The lighted candles at their summit were contributions of my own fancy.

Father sat at the head of the bride's table, looking over the guests. He was at peace, secure in the knowledge that his Addie had married a good man who would treat her tenderly and be competent to provide for her. He was proud, too, that the assembly included so many of the substantial downtown merchants, heads of large wholesale houses with whom August did business. That their presence was an obligation of business courtesy in no way diminished his pleasure. After all, here they were adding prestige to the wedding as their costly gifts gave distinction to the display of wedding presents upstairs. They had come alone, but their wives were not expected to accompany them. The oldest son of Kalisher, the wealthy shoe merchant, had come with his father—an expression of friendship and good will for August. He was seated beside Polly. Father looked upon them happily; Polly was beautiful. Father's hand rested upon the folded cardboard, beside his plate, enclosing the printed verses that I had composed to honor the day. A copy lay beside the plate of each guest.

> *As streams from ancient sources flow*
> *From summits near the sun,*
> *So stranger hearts with love aglow*
> *Uniting flow as one.*

Father turned to smile at me; his cup was full. He lifted a finger and signaled to the waiter. "Don't save the champagne."

The waiter nodded solemnly.

As if upon the raising of a curtain, the dinner opened and unfolded in interest and suspense to the very end. The length of it filled me with pride. So this was what it meant to have a dinner served by a famous caterer! And all the while I knew what was yet to come.

At last waiters stood at the door, three abreast, bearing high pyramids. The guests exclaimed, "Ah!" The pyramids were struck and broken. "No, no," the guests cried in protest. But the waiters, unheeding, broke the glory into irregular brittle fragments of nougat and macaroon and deposited them beside the ice cream on each plate. A sharp rap descended upon the noise. It was repeated until the raised voice of the toastmaster had carried over the clamor.

"Ladies and gentlemen. Gentlemen, I beg you. I beg you."

"Ssh!" from the tables. "Be quiet. Speeches. Who is it?"

A louder voice commanded roughly, "Be quiet there! Please be quiet. Newman is talking."

Then a long "Sssh!"

"Who is it? Who is talking?"

"It's Newman."

"Who?"

"Eph Newman."

"Sit down. I can't see him."

Then a silence.

"Ladies and gentlemen," Newman began. "It is with great surprise that I find myself called upon to make a speech. I am no orator like other worthy gentlemen whom I behold at this festive board. Still"—his body stiffened and the smile fled from his lips—"there are just a few words that I would like to say."

Everybody settled deep into his seat, knowing from earlier experience that, once on his feet, only insistent manipulation of Newman's coattails by his wife would induce him to relinquish the floor.

"I've known Benish Levy since 1852, or was it '53?" He stopped and looked across at Father.

"Long enough," Father answered dryly, and everybody laughed.

Newman laughed loudest before he stiffened into gravity again. "We've done business together for over thirty years, and I'll say that never in all those years have I known him to be guilty of a dishonorable act. Benish Levy is a man of his word. I'd take his note any day."

"For how much, Newman?"

"For any amount," answered Newman in the flush of wine and enthusiasm.

"Put it on paper, Eph."

Again the muscles of Newman's wine-reddened face contracted. "Like father, like daughter. I've known the blushing bride (Mary Stuart's face blanched with embarrassment) since she was so high," indicating the exact altitude of Addie's juvenile head by an extended right arm, "and I can say without hesitation that she has always been a perfect lady. Yes, gentlemen and ladies, a perfect lady. So say I, happy is the bridegroom, August M. Friedlander of Oakland, California, who claims her for his joyful bride. And now, friends . . ."

Everybody sighed in relief, feeling that the end was in sight.

Newman lifted the champagne-filled glass into the air on a level with his ruddy nose. "And now, friends, I wish to propose a toast. But one moment more. Holding the glass of bubbling wine in my hand, I am forcibly reminded of another occasion," and Newman meandered into memories of business and social experiences until successive tuggings of his coattails at length brought him reluctantly to the toast.

"Health and happiness to the happy couple and to the father and mother, without whom we could not be enjoying the presence of the bride this evening."

Cheers and loud stamping discouraged any renewal of the speech.

"Did you see what I gave?" Wilzynski, sitting opposite me, said to his neighbor. He took a heavy pinch of snuff and looked around the table in radiant enthusiasm. "Did you see? A silver-plated bucket *and* a cup *and* a bowl, all lined with gold." His head rocked gently upon the rolls of his three red chins.

"That's what I gave." His eyes, narrowed to slits by pleats of flesh, sent out sparkles of joy. "A silver bucket. There were two. I selected the largest one. I spared no expense." He pounded the floor with his gold-knobbed cane.

"It is you who should be giving a speech. You would give a fine one," my table companion, the young partner of Stein and Stein, commission merchants, said to me.

"Oh no. I couldn't."

"You could do anything after this," he said, fingering the verses. "You are a second George Eliot."

"Not yet," I said in gentle rebuke.

The rabbi was on his feet. He hoped for a large, happy family as the result of this auspicious union. The older people smiled benignly, but Addie trembled under the shock.

The toastmaster was speaking. "I will now call upon a gentleman who, coming to us from the land of gold mines, is specially qualified to speak to you upon this golden occasion. I will ask Mr. Jacob Meyer of Virginia City, Nevada, to favor us with a few words."

Meyer arose, quick and straight on his long, agile legs, all his large, strong teeth shining, the devil flashing in his black eyes. He looked like a gambler from Poker Flat. Father looked down, prepared for Meyer's mocking shafts that always had power to prick him.

"No doubt you have heard many things said about me, some of them not to my credit."

"Never, never, Jake!"

"Still, I'll wager that nobody here ever accused Jake Meyer of

165

being a speechmaker, eh?" Meyer raised his head, throwing back ripples of glossy black hyacinthine locks, and pointed his long, narrow beard at Father. "Why so serious tonight, Benish? Always serious, even when he marries his daughter to a fine young man. Here, Benish, jolly up! Why let everybody else drink your champagne? Have some yourself! You pay for it."

"Talking too much, *wie immer* [as usual]," Mother commented.

"Ladies and gentlemen, you have enjoyed a magnificent dinner; I might say a banquet. But you can never know what it might have been if Benish had listened when I begged him to buy Consolidated Virginia. Eh, Benish? With the whole Comstock Lode to choose from, he must buy Crown Point. Always different. Everybody buys Consolidated, he buys Crown Point. Where is Crown Point today? Where is Crown Point, Benish?"

Father disdained to answer.

"*Naar* [Fool]!" muttered Mother to whom the ten thousand dollars sunk in Father's sole excursion into speculation was still a tormenting memory.

"Never mind," continued Meyer. "Let bygones be bygones. A daring speculator, Benish will make up for it at the next wedding. And observing the bride's beautiful sister, I feel safe to prophesy that we won't have long to wait, eh, Polly?"

Polly arose as if she were going to answer; then, at a sharp look from Mother, she sat down again. Mother motioned to her low-cut dress, her cheeks flushing, and Polly came to her. Mother stooped and tore a crêpeline ruffle from the hem of Polly's skirt. "*Scham dich lieber* [You should be ashamed of yourself]," she whispered fiercely, and Polly quickly stuffed the pleated tulle into the bosom of her corsage.

The fire had left Meyer's eye. His teeth disappeared under a severe line of his lips, constrained to soberness; and in a low voice, charged as if with threat against any unforeseen opposition to his toast, he said slowly, "Ladies and gentlemen, Addie is a fine girl and I love her as I do my own daughter, and Benish Levy is my oldest friend. I ask you one and all to drink to the health of the bride and groom and to the long life of my dear friends, Mr. and Mrs. Benjamin Levy."

Formal addresses followed from the downtown merchants who testified to the excellent position which August held in the world of affairs.

"A rising young man with a future." "Where you see a fine tree, you expect good fruit." "Like mother, like daughter."

By this time the lack of ventilation in the low-ceilinged room made itself felt, and an adventuresome young man removed one of the fans which decorated the wall. He looked at the reverse side of the fan, laughed aloud, and showed it to his neighbor. Soon everybody was tearing fans from the walls and shouting with merriment as they read, "Buy your goods at Friedlander's. Prices are right."

"Gentlemen, let me command your attention," the toastmaster entreated. "The musicians are already playing upstairs, and the young folks desire to dance. But before we arise, it will be my pleasure to read the telegrams sent by the numerous friends of the family so unfortunate as not to be able to partake of this splendid collation."

As the young people reluctantly resigned themselves to attention, he slowly opened his spectacle case, removed the glasses, drew a white silk handkerchief from his pocket, polished the lenses, and adjusted them to his nose to read impressively: "Grass Valley. Mr. and Mrs. August Friedlander, San Francisco, California. Congratulations to the happy couple. Mrs. Herman joins me. B. Herman."

The toastmaster dropped the message into a basket and picked up the next telegram. "Mr. and Mrs. August Friedlander, San Francisco, California. *Mazel und Bruche uber de ganze Mespocha* [Good luck to the entire family]. Signed, Samuel Samuels." This provoked laughter from the older people to whom a return to the familiar Yiddish formula deepened their well-being; but the younger guests knitted their brows in inquiry, denying knowledge of a tongue so compromising to their pretensions.

Then, "Downieville, Sierra County. Heartiest congratulations to the whole family, especially to darling Addie. Signed, Cousin Bella."

"A soup ladle," Mother commented.

On and on the toastmaster read with undiminished relish, sharing the pride of the family that no friend had failed them from *der rothe Kauffman* (the redheaded Kauffman) at Mokelumne Hill to *Tobriner der Lahme* (lame Tobriner) in Sonora.

167

From the mines in northern California good wishes poured like gold-laden streams. "Sophie and I are drinking a toast to the bride and groom. Wish it was real champagne," wired Rosenbloom from Murphy's Camp. "May all your troubles be little ones," came as a blessing from Kauffman Brothers of Calaveras, at which knowing glances were directed upon the bride's table and Mother muttered, "*Kauffman ein Witz geworden* [Kauffman becomes a wit]."

After the last telegram had been relentlessly delivered, the guests ascended the back-garden steps and trooped through the dining room into the parlors, marveling at the suitability of the house for celebration with its parlors opening into the music room and the music room opening into the large dining room. An orchestra—piano, flute, and violin—was already playing "The Blue Danube" waltz and the feet of the young people glided upon the canvas-covered floors. Every bachelor sought a dance with the bride. The freer movements of the schottische and polka loosened the foundation of Strozynsky's handiwork and the Stuart hood rocked in accelerating nonchalance.

Polly, her head high and cool, waltzed three times in the arms of Emanuel Kalisher. It was a perfect wedding.

Mother did not sanction indecorous flight, and Addie waited for the good wishes of the last guest to abdicate bridal robes for tailored suit and turban, and to mingle kisses and tears with those of the family. Then August, grasping the handle of the smartly strapped telescope wicker basket, with Addie beside him, ran down the steps to the waiting carriage.

When everybody had gone, Father locked the storm and street doors and turned out the lights one by one in the great chandeliers. We all went upstairs to the front bedroom to have another look at the presents.

"Pottawatomie," Mother said of the plush album, offering from August's brother in Kansas, but we concluded that for the most part the obligations of the occasion had been met appropriately.

After a last look we reluctantly went to bed; all but Mother who removed her diamond brooch, retaining of her luster only the pendent earrings. She exchanged her long, black velvet gown for her purple wrapper, and descended into the basement to examine the

168

salvage of the feast. I fell asleep to her voice, raised in abuse of the caterer. Ludwig, in defiance of his promise, had carried off every-thing; all the poultry, the unopened bottles of wine—everything but the wreckage of a nougat pyramid.

"Robber!"

# 16

# *Rosh Hashona*

T he excitement began at eight in the morning, although my parents did not leave for the synagogue until nine-thirty. The preparations were the same year after year. One event followed upon another as if after careful rehearsal.

"Where are my cuff buttons, Yetta?" Every year the same question.

"They are in the buttonholes." Every year the same answer.

"There is only one."

"There are two."

"I can find only one."

"I put them both in myself."

"Where is it, then?"

Father clumsily lowered himself to his knees, but Mother ran to him, pushed him aside, stretched an arm under the bed, and arose with the white pearl button between her fingers. *"Lahme Hände* [Lame hands]," she said, presenting it to him.

The white piqué vest with the small blue and yellow flowers had returned after a year of retirement. Like the *primavera,* it reappeared over the threshold of the bedroom, sprinkled with forget-me-nots and daisies. As long back as I could remember there had been no predecessor; it had always been the piqué vest. The starch of annual laundering had stiffened and shrunk it, the buttonholes had become slits, so that inserting the flat pearl buttons made a demand on Father beyond his dexterity. He had grown stout with the years; each New Year's Day found him heavier than the year before, while the area of the vest contracted; each year called for increased ingenuity. As he labored, his eye roamed the ceiling, leaving the operation wholly to his thumbs and fingers. His face grew a pink that was pallor beside the magenta that spread to the top of his head when he tried to button the vest across the arch of his abdomen. That he might have bought a new vest suggested itself to no one. New Year's, Father, the piqué vest, composed a normal trinity.

Watching Father, as he sought by deep breathing to induce a retreat of his abdomen into the constricted enclosure, awoke sensations piquant and varied. As I followed his struggle, I, too, inhaled heavily, held my breath to the point of dizziness, fumbled with clumsy fingers over moist button surfaces, suffered the dismay of threatened failure until, suddenly, the button penetrated the slit. Then I rejoiced with Father in the triumph of his praiseworthy accomplishment. The result justified the labor. The waistcoat gave to Father a stamp of worldly smartness. But it was not always on a note of triumph that the struggle ended. There were other times when the slash of linen rooted Father to the rug on which he stood; moments when he turned his head to Mother helplessly, his fingers blindly fumbling with the fastenings.

Without a word, her eyes shooting reproaches, Mother seized the vest and hurried to the kitchen so that Maggie Doyle might make repairs. Here was double catastrophe. Had not the Law decreed that upon the sacred days neither manservant nor maidservant might labor, and did not Father know the Law? He did, but though his eyes betrayed concern, fear of offense to Mother must have triumphed over guilt in the sight of the Lord, for he raised no staying hand.

Mother returned, the bandaged vest was buttoned a second time, and Father, fortified by its snug support, entered into the armor of his black broadcloth Sabbath coat [so heavily padded that it looked as if it could stand by itself], and peacefully continued his dressing. Taking from the commode drawer the narrow, red-backed brush which had been there as far back as memory carried, he caressed the perfect polish of his stovepipe hat and stood before the mirror to adjust it upon his head accurately. He was ready.

171

"Ready, Yetta?" he asked.

"Don't bother me." Mother had hardly begun.

The morning was not without importance to her, for Rosh Hashona was as Easter Sunday to the Gentiles in its opportunity for handsome raiment, and to Mother raiment meant a new winter bonnet. Wearing it she exercised, with one gesture, her full aesthetic impulse. Her bonnets were extravagant in price and elegantly spectacular. There would not be a more beautiful or higher-priced one in the synagogue. They were always of the same pattern, crushed folds of black velvet, framing the head tightly and broadly, with a "fantasie" on one side of finely threaded feather and jet, high and trembling, which to an ear sufficiently sensitive might have been heard to tinkle. Broad ribbons of satin-backed velvet met in a loose bow under the chin, the ends spreading to expose a rose-point collar and round diamond brooch. Mother looked in the glass with smileless approval.

"Ready?" Father asked again.

"Mind your own business," Mother remarked tranquilly, without removing her eyes from the mirror.

Directed by the heavy odor of gasoline, her hand reached toward the pair of white kid gloves upon the bureau.

"Why can't you put on your gloves on the way?" Father protested, his impatience mounting to anger. Mother's lips pursed and her eyes assumed a detached vagueness as she seated herself and slowly drew them on, finger by finger. Like the piqué vest they had suffered shrinkage under repeated purifications. We stood about fearful of a split; if it came, a neighboring finger would close swiftly over the break, denying its verity.

"Button it," Mother commanded; a cramped, reddened palm in its smelly casing reached out to us, and after delicate smoothings and pullings the glove was buttoned.

Father was already in the hall when Mother arose to receive the black all-over beaded cape, long tabs in the front, short in the back, which we dropped upon her shoulders.

"The books. Have you got the books?" Father called back sharply.

"Why should I have the books? I never keep them."

Father hurried to his closet and possessed himself of the two black gilt-tooled leather books of the service. At last they started, Father leading until he turned and discovered that Mother was not following him.

"Where are you? Are you ever coming?" he demanded. Mother reappeared from her closet, two spots of red upon her cheeks. She carried a long-handled parasol of heavy black lace. Silently she stepped into the hall.

"Good-by, good-by," we called after them, encouraging them down the steps. "We'll be coming later."

"My stylish daughters," Mother said from the base of the stairs before she disappeared again, this time into the kitchen to warn Maggie Doyle not to forget to baste the chicken. Then she started toward the street door, but stopped to enter the parlor and pull down the shade that was letting in a beam of sunshine.

"For God's sake, come!" Father shouted from the street.

"Devil," observed Mother, slowly descending the steps to join him.

We crowded at the window to see whether they had really gone and to watch them down the street: Father, tall, short-necked, broad-backed, his feet shoving a path before him; Mother, short, erect, her bonnet firmly set upon her small head, above the double roll of pompadour, her back narrow and straight, the black gros-grain silk skirt flaring stiffly from a tiny waist. Each carried a book of the service under an arm. When they reached the corner, the large parasol opened and Mother disappeared under a canopy of lace.

# 17

# *The Synagogue*

On the morning of Yom Kippur, the sacred day of days, Father, Mother, and I went to the synagogue at an early hour. We owned two seats in the second row on the center aisle. As the pews were not ordinarily filled, except on holidays, the ownership of two seats might be largely interpreted, might be made to include a third member of the family, slender or submissive to compression, the understanding being that any strain beyond two would be held excessive on the Sabbath and inadmissible on holidays.

This morning, as we stopped at our pew, we saw that our neighbors, the Goldsmiths, were already established there—father, mother, daughter, and the redheaded *bar mizvah* son spread out like a cultivated vineyard. At our approach they contracted as a unit, whispering to one another without moving their lips, their eyes glued to their books in an excess of devotion. No shrinkage, however, could reduce the amplitude of four bodies to the measure of two. Well enough did Mr. Goldsmith see Mother standing erect, the jet of her bonnet tinkling, making no movement to enter the pew. He looked up, as if discovering us, his shrewd eyes calling an invitation to a humorous interpretation of his dilemma. But Mother turned away and looked toward the entrance door of the synagogue until the sexton approached and trained an eye upon the occupants of the pew. He pointed an index finger, jerking it upward in admonition, as if to say, "Arise," and the redheaded son of Mr. Goldsmith arose, fingering his new gold watch chain, his freckled face flushing as he disappeared into an empty pew close against the wall. Only then did we take our places, three of us occupying two seats in unquestioned privilege.

With deliberation Mother opened her stiff, black, leather gold-tooled prayerbook and, having found the place in the service, retreated into her devotion. She read the text in Hebrew, and I, leaning against her, read the translated page:

> "From everlasting to everlasting is the existence of the one true God. Thou rulest the whole universe with kindness and fillest thy creatures with love, O Eternal Being, unto whom alone our praises are due."

Into the text percolated an alien note: "Chutzpa [cheek]," Mother was muttering, and again, "Chutzpa." Through her lowered lids, I intercepted the fierce, oblique glance directed at our neighbor.

The old sexton shuffled down the aisle looking to the right and to the left, seeking; now he touched the shoulder of a man sitting close to the end of the pew, bending to whisper; now he nodded to another beyond the reach of his finger, his lips moving, naming a name. I hoped that he would pass by our pew, that he would not touch Father, whispering to him. But no, he stopped and communicated the word which would be the signal for father to go up to the altar and say a prayer before the reading from the Scroll of the Law, or at the close of the reading to fit the Scroll into the white satin cover, crested with tinkling bells, and return it to the Ark behind the white velvet curtain, a participation for which Father would have to wear his prayer shawl. To bend, to abstract the prayer shawl from the little wooden box beneath his seat, to drop it over the shoulders and ascend to the altar was but a succession of simple movements to any other man. Father alone made of it an occasion for struggle and confusion. Repeated failure should have hinted the futility of the strain, but still hoping to pierce the keyhole of his box without rising from his seat, he bent far forward, his hand frantically jabbing in the direction of his box. Only when his top hat suffered displacement by collision with a neck in the front pew did he yield, turn about, and drop upon his knees. To the sensitive ear of the family, each fresh effort to penetrate the slot magnified the tinkle of his keys until it grew to a volume that reached to the choir.

175

"*Wilst du noch aufstehen* [Are you ever going to get up]?" Mother demanded of the strained breadth of broadcloth arched beneath her, and when Father finally raised a moist roll of neck and arose, it was as if he were returning from a long journey. Hardly had he seated himself and adjusted his white silk shawl when the reader called, "Yaamode Laivy," and Father arose, walked up the side steps to the altar, and approached the reading desk. He raised the fringe of his shawl to his lips, offered a prayer, and listened to a reading from a portion of the Law selected for the day. Again he prayed, received a blessing for himself, another for his family, whispered a donation for the synagogue, and returned to our pew, crowding us against our neighbors as he relaxed. Later, when the reading was over, he returned to the altar to assist in the fitting of the scroll into its tinkling mantle.

"*Immer verdreht* [Always topsy-turvy]," Mother communicated to her prayerbook, defining her estimate of Father's skill. "*Immer links verkehrt* [Always backside front]."

In front of us sat the Friedenthals, a basketful of them, and the Meyerfelds. Across the aisle were more of them, the overflow that could not find accommodation in the first row. As president of the congregation, Mr. Friedenthal sat on the pulpit in the high-backed chair on one side of the Ark, balanced on the other side by the vice-president, Mr. Meyerfeld.

Father did not like Mr. Friedenthal, whom he called a proud man. He was tall and spare, thin-nosed and tightlipped. I admired his aristocratic bearing. Father resented his reserve, though he was glad to trust his money to him on interest. Father wished he would accept even more. He would have given him all he would take. Father said that he was a man of honor, above reproach, but proud.

There were three daughters, Rachel, Lena, and Norma. When Rachel refined her name to Rae and Lena to Lillian, Mother scoffed, resenting the denatured names as a further straining away from their birth toward social altitudes beyond ours. "Christian Endeavorers," she called them. Mrs. Friedenthal, a gentle, compassionate woman, was affable but retreating. Mother said that she was stuck up, that they were all stuck up. She never relinquished the memory of her visit to Mrs. Friedenthal when she had suggested a marriage between her own nephew—a fine-looking young man in a good position—and one of Mrs. Friedenthal's daughters, and Mrs. Friedenthal had retreated behind a change of subject. "She'll yet be sorry," Mother prophesied hopefully.

The Meyerfelds, the Friedenthals, and the Greens were the crest from which social grades radiated to the back pews and gallery. Among the flutter of Friedenthals, Ella Green Meyerfeld sat in splendor beside her husband, Mrs. Friedenthal's brother. She was of the stem of the M. Greens, who occupied the front row of the side seats on the right of the altar. Mr. Green possessed great wealth and well-favored daughters who gave balls and fancy-dress parties to which Bavarians came and mixed freely with the Poles. The second daughter, a tall, beautiful blond, bore so unmistakably the stamp of high lineage that the judgment of the congregation differed only on a question of degree. "A queen," said some. Others said, "An empress."

Ella Green Meyerfeld wore conspicuous gowns of rich texture and carried a handkerchief of exquisite fineness which she touched to her nose frequently, to the extreme pleasure of Father to whom the gesture represented the very excess of exotic elegance. During the service there was constant communication between the daughter in the side pew and the daughter in the pew in front of us— precious communications by smile and brow which I longed to share. The Friedenthal and Meyerfeld women came in late and took their seats and made a flutter, their advanced modes drawing back to earth many a mood charged for spiritual flight.

Mother, without raising her eyes from her book, could sense their approach, and when she injected into the verses of adoration of the Lord, "Another new one, look," I turned quickly in time to witness the coming of the oldest Friedenthal daughter, sidling self-consciously down the aisle, her eyes fixed upon the family pew, as if fearful that countercurrents might swerve her from safe anchorage. From the smiles and whispered explanations of the lateness of her arrival, I understood that her dress had been delayed, that it had only just arrived, and if I caught the name of Miss Denny, I visualized the impoverished, ancient witch of a dressmaker—feverish, driven, bedraggled, a liar, a thief—but a designer lit by genius.

From our seat we could look across to the Schumans, who sat in the side seats to the left of the altar. Nothing, not even a racial contour of feature, integrated as family or tribe the four isolated figures who, as if by accident, always came and left together. The high cheekbones of Mrs. Schuman caught the light and deepened to purple the hue of congested cheeks, thinning the grayness of her watery eyes. They united with the crest of a high jetted bonnet into a belligerency which modified pouting lips into sullenness. Of the cast of Mr. Schuman's face—flabby, blown, impassive—many impressions could be found in the synagogue.

The tall, lithe son, lolling in the aisle seat, dissociated himself from his family and his race by outward glances which returned to his book from time to time, after long excursions over the field of the congregation, the Gentile glance of a visitor to whom the ritual, though curious, was not devoid of interest. Like many another young blade, who never appeared in the synagogue except upon this autumn holiday, he would have explained away, as a gesture of respect to his parents, his presence, which more truthfully witnessed his surrender to the authority and stern menace of this thrice-sanctified day.

Between mother and son, detached like an arrogance of spirit, the deformed daughter sat in scorn, a long face with pale skin stretched tight from high cheekbone to high cheekbone to pointed chin, and gray, insolent eyes challenging definition. For me to look upon the Schumans, however, was not to behold the present picture, but to recall the bitter memory of their terrifying entrance into the synagogue upon their return from Europe, the remembrance of which was to accelerate my pulse even months after the happening.

That they should have come back to the city was distressing enough, because nobody had anticipated their return. But that they should have reappeared in the synagogue! It was silks that Mrs. Schuman had stolen at a shop in London. Some said silks; some said gloves, also, but of the silks there was a certainty. There had been the theft, the apprehension, and the terrible scandal. The Schuman pew had been empty a year; the gap had become an architectural detail, the family almost forgotten, lost in the vagueness that was Europe, when on a Saturday morning, just as the cantor raised the Torah to proclaim the unity of the Lord, a "Sssh" came from the rear of the building. It ran down the aisles until, like a wind spreading over a field, the whisper of "Sssh, sssh, Schuman" hissed over the congregation.

Many turned to look, but I kept my eyes on my book, ashamed to look squarely; and out of the tail of them, I saw, first, Mr. Schuman, his face wooden as ever; then, Mrs. Schuman, her bonneted head high, her congested cheeks a shade more blue than in former years. At a distance, as if alone, followed their daughter, walking slowly, with the familiar, slightly twisted gait, her eyes holding the same old challenge, the same contemptuous appraisal. Seated, they withstood the concentrated gaze of the whole congregation whose eyes, riveted upon the altar, lost no shade of flush or pallor. Over and over I protested their coming. I could not bear their humiliation.

Absorbed in the memory of that day, I did not observe that the organist was already weaving transitions of mood, leading to the choir solo. The congregation relaxed opulently, as if to receive the full enjoyment of a concert program. So elaborate in ornament was the solo that Father turned his head to discover whether the singer was not an artist engaged, in the Gentile mode of the reformed synagogue, to magnify the musical service of the day. Mother had to pluck his sleeve to persuade his head back into line. So challenging a finale, such bravura, demanded acknowledgment, and the long pause following upon it was resonant with silent acclamation.

The rabbi had left his seat and slowly mounted to the reading desk. Olive-skinned, tall, and slender, he looked like a prince of Egypt. A coldly intellectual man, he was curiously misplaced in the orthodox pulpit of a congregation of merchants and shopkeepers. His mental endowment was beyond their need, and when he graciously trained upon them the full strength of his eloquence, it was less for their edification than to give exercise to his own accomplishment. His congregation loved him, reaching with satisfaction toward an erudition beyond their understanding.

In the heart of the congregation—erect, and smilingly negligent— sat the woman who was the sole recipient of his tenderness. Second only to the re-entry of the Schumans in dramatic interest had been the arrival from London of the rabbi's wife shortly after his investiture. A rousing vitality emanating from high-colored cheeks, snapping black eyes, and red lips, hit between the eyes a congregation keyed to the expectation of the delicacy and super-refinement of an English gentlewoman. A tight bodice of black velvet proclaimed the bosom beneath it, and a close green turban fed to carmine a face singularly handsome and lustrous in good humor and friendliness. Expectation might have recovered from its surprise and made its adjustment but for the short strands of black hair rounded into circles and plastered beside the ears. Never before had "spit curls" invaded the synagogue or been seen upon the cheeks of any other than a "fancy lady."

Nevertheless, because the rabbi regarded her with tenderness, projecting upon her coarse features some image of grace, the members of the synagogue grew to accept her, not as a separate entity but rather as a weakness of their beloved rabbi, like a flashy waistcoat. And so she pursued her happy way, trailing velvet skirts over the dusty streets, a white poodle barking to her robust laughter. Nor was her way a solitary one. She liked people, confided in them like a child, and gathered into her intimate life a few women who found her generous humor engaging.

The rabbi stood at the higher reading desk, his white satin gown a shroud against the white velvet curtains. He waited until the last tardy member was seated, the last muscle commanded, until every recreant eye had converged toward his own. Then he began in a low voice which presently rose and later swelled to a volume of accusation, darkened to prophetic gloom, and finally emerged again into hope and promise. My interest lived in the manipulation of the text which would be lost and recovered and lost again like a trail, until at the very end of the hour, after we had traveled far, far away on foreign highways, it reappeared with comforting familiarity recovered by some unpredictable ingenuity. The thunder against moral laxity exposed and vilified was welcome to my ear which received enjoyment from the inundation of the volume of sound, and from experience I knew of the ointment that would be applied to the bruises of flagellation.

We found pleasure in rebuke as well as in solace; we wore our rabbi like an ornament and thrilled in our ownership of his eloquence.

Under denunciation of our shortcomings the sense of sin voluptuously melted into appreciation of the art that had awakened it, and when the rabbi, paled by the vehemence of accusation and appeal, regained his seat, the congregation regarded with tender approval how he wiped the perspiration from his forehead with his soft white silk handkerchief.

After the tumult of the sermon was over, I welcomed the empty spaces of the pulpit, the vertical fall of the white velvet curtains, the president and vice-president motionless in the high-backed chairs, the rabbi spent, slanted in his flowing white robe, his white velvet cap touchingly awry. Except for the flickering lights of the seven-branched candlesticks and the everlasting red light above the Ark, the altar rested in quiet. The picture dispensed repose and comfort under which tense muscles relaxed and a neighbor whispered the question, *"Eine schoene drosche* [A fine sermon]?" to which another answered, *"Und wie* [And how]!"

After interest in the sermon ebbed, the younger members sought relaxation in the foyer where the strain of enforced silence was released into sudden excited chatter. Boys and girls met by appointment to trip gaily away for a promenade up and down the block, or a visit to a distant synagogue. Some stopped to dive into a candy shop furtively and secure provision for the hour of sundown when the fast would be over, hastening back to their synagogue for the vesper when all the members of the family regathered so as to return home in unbroken formation.

The lull that followed the morning sermon ushered in the memorial service for the dead—the long, long hour devoted to remembrance and offering. A few mourners sat dry-eyed, more wiped away a tear, and occasionally a sob, exposing fresh grief, broke from behind a heavy crepe veil. At that sound the heart contracted and the congregation turned toward the mourner. Faces sobered at the reminder of death, twisting into quick sympathy and common fear. Following one another in a long train, a father or son took his place on the altar between cantor and president, read a chapter from the Bible, and whispered a donation in memory of someone, perhaps long dead. The officers of the synagogue incorporated into the service the amount in uninterrupted chant. An old forgotten name

popped from the past like a ghost from a midnight grave. Sometimes whole families reappeared, crowding the altar with familiar
shapes which came and vanished like figures upon a screen.

We had no dead and I experienced regret, quickly smothered, at
my exclusion from the full measure of the excitement of an intimate resurrection. I regretted, too, that my lack of understanding
of Hebrew denied me knowledge of the amount of the whispered
donation. I should have liked to have been able to measure the grief
by its offering, instead of being obliged to make my deduction from
the grunt of a neighbor. I envied Father, who greeted Greenberg's
impressive donation (Greenberg whose recent failure had been so
disastrous to Father) with *"Fur mein Geld* [For my money]." How
soothing to an anxious ghost to be valued generously, I reflected.
How surprising and humiliating the revelation of a niggardly appraisal! I anticipated my own death and the lavish benefaction that
would divulge to the congregation an incurable anguish.

It was difficult to fill the long hours of the afternoon, given to
confession and repentance. As the unbroken presence of my family
excluded me from entering into the memorial service, so poverty in
sin denied me purification. Among the long list of transgressors I
sought a place; I should have liked to have joined the congregation
in a private trespass, but any sin that I was able to muster was too
frail to mingle with the flood of lamentation rolling to the throne of
God. I had not scoffed nor been stiff-necked, rather erring toward
weak conciliations and shyness. I had not committed iniquity nor
wrought unrighteousness; nor, lacking the robustness of opposition, had I manifested a rebellious spirit. A questioning mind edged
with intolerable curiosity gave me no opportunity to counsel evil,
nor should I have found an audience to such an inclination; and so
I was obliged to leave contrition to my parents and to the other
older people who had lived long enough to have known what it
was to scoff and be proud, to corrupt themselves and "commit
abominations." Without reluctance, therefore, when the memorial
service was over, I yielded my place to Addie, who arrived with
heavy wraps and a lemon pierced with cloves for my parents to
smell, and revive their strength diminished by the rigors of the fast.
I would return for N'illah, the closing service of the day.

The N'illah service passed before my eyes like a dream. Senses blurred by the heat and rhythmic, spatial repetition of a verse lowered me into deep lassitude. Behind a curtain of trembling light and heat on the higher platform the white figure of the rabbi stood elongated, his face paled to the whiteness of his robe, his dusky hair and beard blackened against the white velvet of the Ark. "Open unto us, O God, the gates of mercy, before the closing of the gates, ere the day is done." The voice came down from a height above the altar which floated before me like a vision. Upon the mists before it, high white gates, widespread, slowly approached each other. "The day vanishes, the sun is setting; let us enter Thy gates."

A wave of sound came from the congregation. It rose and washed over me on its way to the altar, ebbing again into a broken murmur. Then another and another, bending me beneath the undulating weight of rich sensation. I looked up and saw the stained glass of the western windows stir and glow under the rays of the sinking sun. The sun *was* sinking, the day *was* departing, just as it was being said. Then it was true. Suddenly it was all true. In a moment what had been a dream became actuality and the service of the day—sin, confession, forgiveness—was charged with meaning, concerned me. I was frightened; I who had confessed no sin, who *had* hardened my heart, who *had* been stiff-necked and scoffing. About me the congregation sat as one unit, heads bowed, lips moving under a common feeling. I sat without, a stranger, alone. In a panic I sought a sin, a remorse, even the smallest one indicative of a contrite heart, but before I could seize upon one the gates had closed and the N'illah service was over.

After N'illah, the Day of Atonement unfurled to its end in grandeur. "Hear, O Israel: The Lord our God, the Lord is One," burst forth from rabbi and congregation like a national anthem. Then three times the rabbi and congregation chanted together, "Praised be His name whose glorious kingdom is for ever and ever," and seven times in sonorous accents, "The Lord, He is God." Full-throated I joined in the chorus of affirmation.

With the blowing of the ram's horn and the benediction the fast was over, and the congregation, dazed by the heavy air and the long fast, slowly moved toward the door, stopping to make inquiry for the well-being of one another. Father and Eph Newman remained seated, chanting aloud. Mother protested, *"Chapt Gott bei den füssen* [Grabs God by His feet],*"* and she tapped Father on the shoulder until he returned his prayer shawl to the box and came out with us. Polly and Addie were at the door to greet us. We labored to the street, step by step. Three closed carriages, hired from Michelson's stables, drove up to the sidewalk and groups of Friedenthals and Greens and Meyerfelds disappeared within them. The drivers slammed the doors behind them, jumped into their seats, and drove away on a double curve.

Better than us!

The cold air cut between our shoulder blades. We drew our coats and capes closer about our necks and followed the crowd down the street to the cable car that would take us to our home.

# 18

# *Saturday Night*

On Saturday night the city joined in the promenade on Market Street, the broad thoroughfare that begins at the water front and cuts its straight path of miles to Twin Peaks. The sidewalks were wide and the crowd walking toward the bay met the crowd walking toward the ocean. The outpouring of the population was spontaneous as if in response to an urge for instant celebration.

Every quarter of the city discharged its residents into the broad procession. Ladies and gentlemen of imposing social repute; their German and Irish servant girls, arms held fast in the arms of their sweethearts; French, Spaniards, gaunt, hard-working Portuguese; Mexicans, the Indian showing in reddened skin and high cheekbone— everybody, anybody, left home and shop, hotel, restaurant, and beer garden to empty into Market Street in a river of color. Sailors of every nation deserted their ships at the water front and, hurrying up Market Street in groups, joined the vibrating mass excited by the lights and stir and the gaiety of the throng. "This is San Francisco," their faces said. It was carnival; no confetti, but the air a criss-cross of a thousand messages; no masks, but eyes frankly charged with challenge. Down Market from Powell to Kearny, three long blocks, up Kearny to Bush, three short ones, then back again, over and over for hours, until a glance of curiosity deepened to one of interest; interest expanded into a smile, and a smile into anything.

Father and I went downtown every Saturday night. We walked through avenues of light in a world hardly solid. Something was

185

happening everywhere, every minute, something to be happy about. Vendors shouted solicitation to their wares; we nodded to people we knew, as if in confirmation of a bit of knowledge freshly learned. We waved to friends too far away to reach the news that we, too, were there, and their faces lit when they saw us and they waved back. We walked and walked and still something kept happening afresh.

"Look," I said to Father. The sailors were no longer alone; girls were hanging on their arms and they were laughing together. A police whistle shrilled through the murmur and we stood still.

"What's the trouble?" Father asked a man.

"A masher," he said. "She gave him a whack on the head."

There was a line of mashers before the big cigar stores. In front of the Baldwin Hotel on Market Street and of Mose Gunst's on Kearny Street they stood three deep from the cigar counter to the sidewalk. They were dressy men, dandies young and old who stood facing the street, smoking long cigars, or picking their teeth with quill toothpicks. The smarter ones wore pale-colored spats. When we passed them I turned my head away; some women crossed the street rather than pass Mose Gunst's.

Mashers talked to women without being introduced. Sometimes a woman said, "How dare you, sir" to one, or just "Sir," and left him standing in the middle of the sidewalk looking sheepish. Everybody applauded her, but I felt that she had lowered herself. I practiced my behavior should a masher ever talk to me. I was divided between "How dare you, sir" and "You are mistaken, sir, I am a lady."

We did not always walk up Kearny Street. Some Saturday nights, and these were the ones I liked best, we turned north into Dupont Street which ran parallel to Kearny. Close to Market, Dupont was a dingy street beyond the border of light and traffic, lined with dull shops and old houses; farther north it transformed itself into the core of the most romantic quarter of the city. Only two blocks of hill to climb and we could be ankle deep in a foreign soil. But it was something more supersensible than joss house or opium den that made of the street a tingling experience.

Off Dupont Street, to the right, a narrow alley ran like a slit through a wall. One side was completely occupied by one-storied

186

cottages, as if the street were made of a piece, each with a short flight of steps and a shallow bay window. In each embrasure back of the center pane a woman sat, her glossy dark hair piled high. Her cheeks were painted, her eyes glazed; she wore a bright-colored Mother Hubbard gown. One sat at every window as far as eye could see down the alley toward Kearny Street. They sat motionless, looking straight ahead.

When we went by and I looked down the alley my heart stopped and then beat fast. The women and the whole alley were still as if under enchantment. On neighboring streets life was pressing forward and backward; here it was arrested as if it suddenly had stopped at a word, a spell. From my dreams at night I knew the feeling of strangeness in a thick forest, but in a forest I feared things that were like other things. Once at a fair I saw a woman's head served on a glass tray and was told that it was an optical illusion. That had been strange, too, but not like this. This was like nothing else. Except for the one time it never changed, but remained an enchanted street of silence. I should have liked to remain at the opening of the alley for hours, looking; but we always walked by as if it were not there. Father did not seem to know that it was there or, if he did, it did not interest him, for he never looked at it.

One night a political procession was marching on Kearny Street. We were on Dupont Street when we heard the band. "Hurry, hurry," I begged, and Father rushed me through the alley. We ran so quickly that I saw nothing. "You old fool, take that child away from this," I heard behind me and trembled. Father did not hear. When we returned home I did not speak of what I had heard.

From the opposite side of Dupont Street another lane ran through into Stockton Street, a narrow street bordered with ordinary two-storied houses, their blinds lowered. One afternoon on Market Street I saw walking ahead of me a young girl whose family we knew. I used to enjoy the stories of unusual adventure that she claimed befell her, even though my parents discredited them. My parents often spoke of how her people were having a hard time with her. She roamed the city with an older woman who had a bad reputation—a tall, swarthy woman with a loping walk and a heavy bosom. Nobody could keep them apart. Because of the exaggerated

187

difference in height, Mother called them the palm leaf and the lemon, symbols carried down the aisle of the synagogue on the Feast of Tabernacles.

The girl was slender and beautiful. The exquisite line of her nose, I felt, singled her out for romantic experience. Her hair was of a pale gold, and incredibly large blue eyes sent out exploring glances as she walked down the street. She was dressed in pale gray that never changed to a warmer color. I thought her refined looking, quite Gentile. She walked fast and I tried to overtake her, but before I succeeded she turned into Dupont Street and quickly disappeared into the narrow street. Why I was so shaken I could not have told.

If we lengthened our walk to upper Kearny Street I kept watch for the saloons with swinging doors in the hope that they might open wide enough for me to look into them deeper. My expectation was for a stagger or a brawl, but the men I saw stood upright in friendly conversation, not even leaning against the bar. After midnight, I told myself, the decorum would break and I would hear the roaring of a drunk or the scuffle of a man dragged home by a wife or child. (Oh, Father, oh, Father, come home with me now!) But Father gave me no opportunity to test my confidence, and instead led *me* away against my protests.

When swinging doors disclosed couples dancing, saloons were no longer saloons but dives. There were many on upper Kearny Street, some on a level with the street, others below. Sailors shoved one another down into the basement. One night a girl stood on the steps talking to a sailor. He wanted to leave, but her hand was on his shoulder as if she were persuading him to stay. Her hair was soft and dark, parted in the middle and drawn over her ears, and her face was gentle and pale. I wanted to stay looking at her, but Father turned back and we walked down Kearny until our steps quickened again to the heightened beat of Market Street. The double stream moved unchecked. Unseen flags were still flying. The call of a vendor of hot tamales steaming over a broad oil burner cut through the noises of the crowd. We bought a tamale to take home. A seller of the latest popular songs waved sheets of music before our eyes and entreated attention with samples of his stock.

*"Down went McGinty to the bottom of the say,*
*And he must be very wet . . .*
*For they haven't found him yet . . .*
*Dressed in his best suit of clothes."*

He persuaded so engagingly that we bought a copy for Polly.

In front of the Baldwin Theater the Salvation Army, looking friendly and at home out in the street, sang, "Onward, Christian Soldiers." My feet changed to a resolute beat and I echoed the words low, omitting the name of Jesus.

"Now we go home," Father said, and out of the brilliance of the lamp-lit street we walked through increasing darkness to O'Farrell and reached home filled to the brim with new melodies and the story of friends glimpsed and spoken to. But when I went to bed sadness kept rising in me. I could not fall asleep for thinking of the pale girl with smoothly parted hair standing with her hand upon the arm of the young sailor.

# 19

# *The Earthquake*

After a funeral Father and Mother would walk about the cemetery of the Hills of Eternity visiting the shades of old friends and relatives. Mother always stopped before the marble mausoleum of the Friedenthals. How she wanted a marble vault! Not a large one like this, but still a vault of marble.

"It would be nice to have a marble vault, no, Levy?" Mother asked. "You would like a vault, wouldn't you?"

*"Todt ist todt* [Dead is dead]," Father said.

Later, when Father entered upon his last illness, Mother did not return to the subject.

After Father died Mother and I went out to the cemetery to select a plot. Mr. Brownstone, the sexton, accompanied us. We sought a plot in the cemetery of the congregation Sherith Israel, next to The Home of Peace, which housed the more aristocratic dust of the members of the Temple Emanuel. I felt as ill at ease among the bones of the people buried there as I had felt among their living bodies.

The sexton showed Mother five lots. "This is a fine one," he said, pointing to a large corner.

"It is big," Mother conceded.

"And inexpensive," Brownstone urged. "Less expensive than some of the smaller ones."

"A bargain, I suppose?" Mother distrusted Brownstone. "Who owns the one next to it?"

Brownstone put on his spectacles and sought the name on his chart. "The Peisers," he read, "Jacob Peiser."

Mother waved a hand in quick rejection.

"I never associated with the Peisers in my life. Why should I begin when I am dead?"

She finally bought a corner lot on a side avenue with space for a garden and built upon it a vault with six crypts. She paid $5000 for it. Later, though she regarded it with satisfaction, she continued to suspect that Brownstone had outwitted her in the deal.

On the first day of every month Mother and I took the streetcar and jogged an hour's distance along the coast, following the shore line past one cemetery after another—Catholic, Protestant, Italian—past junk shops, blacksmiths, and makers of monuments. At the gate of The Home of Peace the car stopped with a jerk. Black-robed, heavily veiled women shuffled down the steps bearing their high-toned grief with them. We descended at the Hills of Eternity, and Mother hastened to the office of the florist at the entrance to buy a bouquet of purple asters.

We walked up the broad avenue and turned toward our vault. Mother unlocked the bronze doors and entered. Reluctantly, I followed her. She looked about critically for dust, squeezed the stems of the flowers into the tall bronze vase which stood on the window ledge and placed it on the floor below Father's crypt. I did not know what to do with myself; I was without feeling. Those shelves were not a grave to me. I could not identify Father with the long, thin, gilded lettering: B.H. LEVY. How Father must hate being there, I thought, if people could hate where he was.

Mother stood still, facing Father's crypt. Her lips moved in a silent Hebrew prayer. Suddenly her cheeks flushed. "Thieves!" she muttered. "And they told me the upkeep of the garden would be included in the price." She was addressing the board of the synagogue. Again her eyes closed and her lips moved in prayer.

"Come," she called sharply, and led the way into the sunshine. She locked the door and examined the strip of garden, murmuring protests as she flicked a dead leaf from the hedge of myrtle.

As we walked down the avenue to the entrance we stopped to look at other plots, appraising the care they were receiving. Waiting

191

for the streetcar, Mother's eyes returned to the cemetery. She nodded approval. "A nice vault," she said. I told myself that nobody would ever put me into it; I would have my ashes scattered.

The look on Addie's face when, upon an anniversary of Father's death she accompanied Mother and me to the cemetery, told me that she felt as I did about the vault. However, I knew that, dislike it as she might, she would ask to be buried with Father and Mother so that they might not feel lonely and might continue to receive care from their children. Even after death she could not resist the urge to improve upon the hazards of life and make good any comfort that God had failed to provide for His children.

Shortly after Father's death Polly married the handsome, smartly dressed traveling salesman whom she chose among her suitors. "*Stutzer* [dandy]," Mother called him, because his airs were unsupported by the solidity of a business. Polly moved to an apartment and Mother and I were left alone in the big house.

Breakfast was over. Mother lifted her emptied cup and replaced it upon its saucer.

"I am going to rent the house," she said.

"What house?"

"How many houses have I got? This house. It's too big for two people."

"Rent it? To whom?"

"How do I know to whom? The agent said it would be easy to rent."

"Not the furniture?"

"Everything."

I could not believe what I was hearing. She had trained me to regard the dislodgment of a chair as a violation of a law of God. And here she was, ready at one stroke to commit our home to an unknown tenant.

I thought of the house in terms of rooms and of the rooms in terms of objects: walnut bedroom set, brocaded satin curtains, Japanese lacquered temple. Could Mother be willing to abandon them to a stranger insensitive to their elegance?

Had they been worn or shabby, it would have been different. But to my eyes not one object had changed since the day we had moved in, not one had lost its earliest freshness. The pile of the flowered velvet carpet, unflattened by the feet of children or of guests, the scarlet satin-embossed draperies undimmed by rays of sunlight, the flesh of the musical cupids—everything had remained without blemish or deterioration. Stepped upon ever so lightly, the miraculous spittoons still threw back their upholstered lids, startling the stranger to amazed ejaculation. Who but the Benish Levys had satin-topped spittoons?

I identified myself with the old house. I knew how it must feel after having shared the drama of the life of a family over long years to find itself nobody's home, no home at all, just a house, a white house.

"What am I now?" I could hear it entreat, demanding identity.

By the heat of her defense, Mother betrayed her discomfort. But I was gradually forced to admit that two people could not live with propriety in a two-story and finished basement residence. Finally I agreed to the renting.

However, for months after we had left it, I could not face 920 without a pang of self-reproach. If I walked down the shady side of the street, my head turning aside in denial of it, the white house advanced from its background, the better to pursue my hurrying feet with accusation. Once, inadvertently, I regarded it full-faced; a lace curtain swung out from an open parlor window and my back crinkled. Discomfort eased only with the return of Signora X and Signor Y to San Francisco as stars of the Tivoli Opera House.

One day our real estate agent called upon Mother.

"Signora X and Signor Y want to rent 920 O'Farrell," he said.

"Which one?" Mother asked.

"Both."

"Not together?"

"Yes, together."

"But they aren't married!" Mother cried.

Rent our home to a man and woman living together? We would not consider such an offer.

They asked a second time. We tried to refuse. We could not. We felt honored. Mother smiled indulgently. She was dazzled.

193

"Those actors!" she said.

"How Father would have loved to have them in his house!" I thought.

And so they came to live in 920 O'Farrell, in our house, in our kitchen where, for years, Saturday upon Saturday, Passover upon Passover, closets and dishes—to the last knife and fork—had been guarded from impurity to the point of agony.

To my mind the whole house was now steeped in an atmosphere of immorality. We peeked through the window curtains of the upper back bedroom of the Louis Lessings and strained our eyes to watch Aïda toss the lettuce and beat the yolks and oil for her salad dressing (I added the garlic which I could not see). In our delight we crowded each other for space at the window; I waited eagerly for the slow, burning kiss which should climax an illicit love, but had to content myself with bursts of song.

"*La mort, la mort!*" Signora X boomed, and she swung a plump arm and shook our big kitchen salt shaker over her salad.

Over the months I brought home colored tourist guides from offices of steamship companies. During meals I read aloud from them. Mother listened, glazed-eyed and deaf, silent except for an order to Maggie Doyle, who winked at me as she left the room.

"Why do you sit around here doing nothing?" Mother demanded one day in the early spring. "Why don't you go somewhere? Why don't you go to Europe?" That was Mother. Habitually penurious, fighting at every step the extraction of a dollar, Mother yielded her resistance as the demand upon her rose from five to a hundred dollars and melted before the demand for a thousand. My campaign was won.

An hour later I was on my way to the office of the Cunard Line. The agent smiled to see me, so often had I been there, so many questions had I asked.

"I am going!" I cried, and I believed that he, too, was happy.

As I became absorbed in preparation for travel, in the purchase of a fur-lined steamer coat and a huge canvas-covered trunk roomy enough to hold clothes for any climate and every occasion ("You *can* buy hairpins in London," Addie's husband protested), the finger of reproach of the old home lowered; and when, after threatened failure, I secured seats a year in advance for the full Wagnerian Opera Festival in Bayreuth, 920 O'Farrell Street had almost settled back into its place among its neighbors.

In my travels I walked about the ruins of ancient cities, tourist-wise, speculating upon evidence of destruction too vast, too remote, to be actual. I returned home to behold a devastation as great as any I had witnessed, created not by the earthquake alone, but by the fire which had followed upon it. I had left closely packed city streets; I returned to a barren waste of hills and to isolated buildings in unconvincing locations. Nothing was in its right place; nothing was where it used to be.

I sought reassurance in some remembered landmark which would restore to me my lost identity. Tenderly I recalled our shopping district. Much of the imported elegance of our apparel could be traced to the shelves of The White House, the trustworthy department store of Raphael Weill, aristocratic Frenchman, link between San Francisco and Paris.

"The White House?" I demanded of the bleary-eyed news vendor on Market Street. "I can't find it. It was always on the corner of Kearny and Post."

"It's on Grant Avenue and Sutter," he said; and I beheld the reliable old shop of which we had been so proud rise into the air, cross the line of the horizon, and descend upon an alien site, intact.

"Grant Avenue?" I cried. "I never heard of it."

"It's the new name for Dupont Street," the man said. He looked at me obliquely, questioning my awareness of the unsavory associations of Dupont Street.

The White House—Raphael Weill—Dupont Street—I could not tolerate the dislocation. I burst into tears.

Upon the outside of the little cable car, on the dummy, I rode up the hills of California Street, seeking indestructibility in the mansions of "railroad kings" and "mining magnates." I found a steel frame, a broken flight of steps, and the twisted fragment of a gilded iron fence.

As we swung around Pine Street and down Jones, I called to the motorman to stop at O'Farrell. The car stopped and I descended upon a waste of land which reiterated the story of the unimpeded progress of the fire all the way up to Van Ness Avenue where dynamite had halted its advance. Not one building remained to confirm my memory.

What had been the home of the Martin Davises and the home of the John Boases and the home of the S.S. Lessings, from Polk Street to the avenue, a whole block—substantial, solid as a cube, guaranteed to wear for generations—had disappeared.

The home of the Benish Levys, the only house with storm doors, the only garden with a gravel walk, the only house with brocaded spittoons, the house so white it looked like marble, had disappeared as if it had never been, along with a city behind it.

Once again O'Farrell Street had become a stretch of land, 920 a lot, a building site, between Polk and Van Ness, thirty feet wide and one hundred and twenty feet deep. Father had predicted in pride of its acreage, "Five feet wider than the lot of the Levisons, only seventy-five feet from the corner of the avenue. Someday in the future it will be valuable to a purchaser with money who will need the extra depth for his mansion on Van Ness and will be willing to pay for it." As Father had prophesied, so the years brought it to pass. But it was not for mansions that the lots on Van Ness were destined. One automobile company after another bought ground along the length of the avenue and erected their showrooms upon it. And today motorcars drive into the repair department of the Cadillac Motor Company over the invisible, spotless, velvet parlor carpet of my 920 O'Farrell Street.

# Other California Legacy Books

UNDER THE FIFTH SUN: LATINO LITERATURE FROM CALIFORNIA
*Edited by Rick Heide, foreword by Juan Velasco*
This unique anthology covers more than two centuries of Latino presence in California, combining vibrant works of poetry, fiction, commentary, and memoir.

THE JOURNEY OF THE FLAME
*By Walter Nordhoff, foreword by Rebecca Solnit*
Considered a masterpiece of California literature, *The Journey of the Flame* is the tale of a young boy's adventures from Baja California to Monterey in the early nineteenth century.

ONE DAY ON BEETLE ROCK
*By Sally Carrighar, foreword by David Rains Wallace,*
*illustrations by Carl Dennis Buell*
Written with exquisite detail, Carrighar brings readers to an exhilarating consciousness of the skills, intelligence, and adaptations of Sierra wildlife.

DEATH VALLEY IN '49
*By William Lewis Manly, edited by LeRoy and Jean Johnson,*
*introduction by Patricia Nelson Limerick*
This California classic provides a rare and personal glimpse into westward migration and the struggle to survive the desert crossing.

ELDORADO: ADVENTURES IN THE PATH OF EMPIRE
*By Bayard Taylor, introduction by James D. Houston, afterword by Roger Kahn*
A quintessential recounting of the California gold rush, as seen through the eyes of a New York reporter.

FOOL'S PARADISE: A CAREY MCWILLIAMS READER
*Foreword by Wilson Carey McWilliams, introduction by Gray Brechin*
Examines some of historian/journalist Carey McWilliams' most incisive writing on California and Los Angeles.

NOVEMBER GRASS
*By Judy Van der Veer, foreword by Ursula K. Le Guin*
This novel transports readers to the coastal hills of San Diego County
and brings clarity to questions of birth, death, and love.

LANDS OF PROMISE AND DESPAIR:
CHRONICLES OF EARLY CALIFORNIA, 1535–1846
*Edited by Rose Marie Beebe and Robert M. Senkewicz*
This groundbreaking collection presents an insider's view of Spanish and
Mexican California from the writings of early explorers and residents.

THE SHIRLEY LETTERS: FROM THE CALIFORNIA MINES, 1851–1852
*By Louise Amelia Knapp Smith Clappe,*
*introduction by Marlene Smith-Baranzini*
With the grandeur of the Sierra Nevada as background, this collection
presents an engaging, humorous, and empathetic picture of the gold rush.

UNFINISHED MESSAGE: SELECTED WORKS OF TOSHIO MORI
*Introduction by Lawson Fusao Inada*
This collection features short stories, a never-before-published novella,
and letters from a pioneer Japanese American author.

UNFOLDING BEAUTY: CELEBRATING CALIFORNIA'S LANDSCAPES
*Edited by Terry Beers*
The beauty of California is reflected in this collection of pieces by
John Muir, John Steinbeck, Wallace Stegner, Jack Kerouac, Joan Didion,
and sixty-four other writers.

———

If you would like to be added to the California Legacy mailing list,
please send your name, address, phone number, and email address to:

California Legacy Project
English Department
Santa Clara University
Santa Clara, CA 95053

For more on California Legacy titles, events, or other information,
please visit www.californialegacy.org.